The Trouble Between Us

The Trouble Between Us

An Uneasy History of White and Black Women

in the Feminist Movement

Winifred Breines

OXFORD
UNIVERSITY PRESS

OXFORD
UNIVERSITY PRESS

Oxford University Press, Inc., publishes works that further
Oxford University's objective of excellence
in research, scholarship, and education.

Oxford   New York
Auckland   Cape Town   Dar es Salaam   Hong Kong   Karachi
Kuala Lumpur   Madrid   Melbourne   Mexico City   Nairobi
New Delhi   Shanghai   Taipei   Toronto

With offices in
Argentina   Austria   Brazil   Chile   Czech Republic   France   Greece
Guatemala   Hungary   Italy   Japan   Poland   Portugal   Singapore
South Korea   Switzerland   Thailand   Turkey   Ukraine   Vietnam

Published by Oxford University Press, Inc.
198 Madison Avenue, New York, New York 10016

First issued as an Oxford University Press paperback 2007

www.oup.com

Oxford is a registered trademark of Oxford University Press

Library of Congress Cataloging-in-Publication Data
Breines, Wini.
The trouble between us : an uneasy history of white and Black women in the feminist
movement / Winifred Breines.
p. cm.
Includes bibliographical references and index.
ISBN 978-0-19-517904-0; 978-0-19-533459-3 (pbk.)
1. Feminism—United States—History—20th century. 2. African American
feminists—History—20th century. 3. Women radicals—United States—History—
20th century. 4. African American radicals—History—20th century. 5. Women and
socialism—United States—History—20th century. 6. Racism—United States—History—
20th century. 7. Radicalism—United States—History—20th century. 8. United States—Social
conditions—1960–1980. I. Title.
HV1421.B734   2006
305.42'0973—dc22   2005050877

Printed in the United States of America
on acid-free paper

To Benjamin, Maxwell, Ilan, Allison, and Tamar

and their parents, my children,

Natasha, Scott, Raphael, and Rinat

Acknowledgments

I want to thank the many people who have helped me with this book. I relied on Alice Echols, Robin D. G. Kelley, and Paul Breines for reading and suggestions throughout the years. People who read parts of the manuscript or had extended conversations with me include Kay Trimberger, Alice Wexler, Ros Baxandall, Judy Stacey, Nancy Cott, Louise Rice, Tess Ewing, Alex Bloom, Jim Smethurst, and Jenny Mansbridge. My wonderful year at the National Humanities Center included important feedback from John Dittmer, Frank Mort, Gunther Peck, and Orin Starn. The fellowship I held there was endowed by the Rockefeller Foundation. I thank the Center for providing me with a year to write and new colleagues and friends. In the course of the work, I corresponded and conversed with many women whose thoughts and experiences were invaluable for the book. Boston activists include Marcia Folsom, Barbara Smith, Tia Cross, Laurie Crumpacker, Margo Okazawa-Rey, Kattie Portis, Sondra Stein, Demita Frazier, Diane Balser, Libby Bouvier, Linda Gordon, Evelynn Hammonds, Rochelle Ruthchild, Nancy Falk, Carole Neville, and Fran Ansley. Suzanne McCormack's work on Boston women's liberation activist Carole McEldowney led me to important documents. People in other places and other movements include Connie Curry, Elaine Baker, Dorothy Burlage, Vicki Gabriner, Nan Bauer Maglin, Maureen Reddy, Vivian Rothstein, Chude Pam Allen, and Julian Bond. Photographers Tia Cross, Ellen Shub, and Susan Fleischmann generously gave of their time as did Libby Bouvier and Rochelle Ruthchild in my search for photographs. Patricia Arend and Jaronda Miller helped with research and preparation of the manuscript. I thank you all.

Sara Hutcheon, reference librarian at the Schlesinger Library, and Joan D. Krizack, university archivist and head of the Special Collections Department at Northeastern University, both guided me through pertinent archives. Nancy Richard, formerly of the Northeastern archives, conducted invaluable interviews and collected materials about the Boston women's movement. Aaron Schmidt aided my search for photographs at the Boston Public Library. The faculty seminar in which I presented my work at the Center for the Study of Social Transformation at the University of Michigan was tremendously helpful as I thought through issues in the book. Literary agent Lisa Adams supplied invaluable advice. I am grateful to Northeastern University for supporting my research over the years and for contributing wonderful long-term colleagues to my life and work, especially Debby Kaufman and Maureen Kelleher.

At Oxford, my excellent editor, Susan Ferber, dragged me kicking and screaming through many revisions, but I know that it is a much better book because of her. Many, many thanks to Susan and to Niko Pfund for his editorial help and encouragement.

Marcia Folsom, Ruth Perry, and Susan Suleiman supported me throughout this process with good advice, delicious food, and many laughs. I am grateful to my brother and sister, Russell Jacoby and Lauren Jacoby, for being there. Ron Hill's love, patience, and encouragement kept me sane and happy. Thanks and love to you all.

Contents

The Trouble Between Us

Introduction

There is no way . . . to avoid the messiness that writing
about the sixties currently seems to generate.
—James C. Hall, *Mercy, Mercy Me: African American
Culture and the American Sixties* (2001)

[S]o long as individuals are vying for how they as well as the
Story (or stories) of the Movement will be remembered, this
history remains alive.
—Margo V. Perkins, *Autobiography as Activism: Three Black
Women of the Sixties* (2000)

I cannot accept the notion that the racial privilege of my
whiteness should enforce my silence about race and
ethnicity. . . . The land mines are everywhere—my own
ignorances based on racial privilege and the rush of others to
dismiss, censor, not hear, condemn, withdraw. Yet I ask you
to hear me out. I offer these reflections in the spirit of
dialogue—a precondition . . . for growth and change
in the academy and feminist movement.
—Susan Stanford Friedman, *Mappings: Feminism and
the Cultural Geographies of Encounter* (1998)

In a different time, not so long ago, one that seems almost unfathomable today, black and white movement activists came together to create a free and racially integrated society in the United States. They were motivated by deeply felt ideals and hopes for an integrated society. It did not take female civil rights movement participants long, however, to realize that race and gender problems existed not only in the larger society but also among themselves. Working together taught them about the possibilities of interracial connection as well as about their deep dissimilarities. They carried their dashed hopes in the government and disturbing discoveries of difference into subsequent movements, struggling to hold on to their optimistic beliefs. From the civil rights movement into the Black Power movement, the New Left, and the student movement, young women went forward to create the socialist feminist movements, white and black. The central trajectory of those years saw them first working together politically in solidarity in the civil rights movement and then dramatically shifting toward separation based on new definitions of distinct identities, eventually moving into a provisional reconciliation very different from their earlier bonds. White feminists believed that there could be a universal sisterhood, that black women would join the movement. But that didn't happen. The 1970s were filled with efforts at reconciliation and failures, work at understanding how race operates in the United States and recriminations—far from the earlier, easier times of idealism and high expectations. White and black feminism developed on parallel tracks, distant from earlier notions of solidarity and integration. But socialist feminists persevered, in part because of their deep desire for an inclusive women's movement. That desire had its sources in the residual ideals and hope with which they had begun and which never completely disappeared.

This is a story of female social movement activists, feminists whose commitment led them to develop new ways of thinking about race, class, and gender and of reconnecting across race. They learned that in order to be inclusive, they had to lose some of their ideals, to construct relationships based on who they were and not who they wanted to be or wanted others to be. White women worked hard to understand their own racism and how a women's movement could become inclusive. Black women worked hard to make white women understand how race, class, and gender intersected in black women's lives. Only by the end of the 1970s did white and black feminists move back toward one another, testing whether ground existed for trust and coalitions. They never reconnected on the basis of idealism. The basis of social movements is more realistic and less inspiring today. While we cannot return to those times of hope and inspiration, the example of feminists doggedly working through issues of race and slowly reaching out to one another provides us with chastening lessons that it can be done.

Feminists were not the only ones in political motion during those years. They were part of a youth movement that crossed national boundaries. The 1960s and 1970s were the most socially explosive years of the second half of the twentieth century in the United States, years in which the major struggle against legal racial segregation was completed, race and sex discrimination were put on the agenda, sexual norms were transformed, the war in Vietnam was opposed by millions of Americans, and large sectors of the population began to distrust their government and major corporations. With the civil rights movement as a model, young people took the lead in opposing the existing society. They questioned authority. Upheaval and division pervaded the society as supporters of the war and the government mobilized against the social movements. African Americans and other people of color, youth, women, homosexuals, environmentalists—all those who joined the movements—broke with the past and often took to the streets. Activists in the civil rights and Black Power movements, the antiwar movement, the counterculture, and the feminist and gay and lesbian movements believed that their actions would transform society, and they were themselves transformed in the process. Accomplishments for which the movements of the 1960s can take credit include the end of apartheid in the South and the increasing space for racial dialogue, the antiwar movement that contributed to ending the fighting in Vietnam, the recognition of the contributions of African Americans and other people of color to the life of the nation, tolerance for difference in how people look and live their lives, the growth of gender equity and opportunities for those who had been excluded, and expanded sexual knowledge and openness. So many of these changes are taken for granted now that it is important to recall how dramatic those years were and how significant the movements were in making American society more democratic.

The United States had been on the winning side in World War II and prospered after the war. Optimism infused the postwar mood. Millions of babies were born, the suburbs grew, consumerism exploded. Growing numbers of white people joined the middle class—opportunities for more education and white-collar jobs increased. They owned more houses, consumer goods, and cars. There was little concern about racism or sexism or class inequality. White Americans congratulated themselves and celebrated their way of life. At the same time, African Americans, for the most part left out of the postwar abundance and opportunities available to whites, particularly in the South, were building the civil rights movement. Throughout the 1950s, legal and political events unfolded that eventually led four young black men in 1960 in Greensboro, North Carolina, to sit down at a lunch counter reserved for whites and demand to be served. The sit-ins by black students spread all over the South, signaling the debut of the youthful civil rights movement.

In that same year, the Student Non-Violent Coordinating Committee (SNCC), the most important youthful, radical organization in the southern civil rights movement, was organized. The early years of the 1960s also found leftist and radical students involved in politics on campuses around the country. New Left and peace groups, including the white radical student organization Students for a Democratic Society (SDS), grew to become national political actors. The escalating war in Vietnam fanned the flames of youthful opposition to the government. Radical African Americans developed a third world consciousness that linked them to people of color internationally and heightened their antipathy to the Vietnam War. Feminism developed toward the end of the decade, as did gay liberation. Ironically, out of the apparently placid 1950s, when teenagers and students appeared to be uninterested in politics, radical youth movements were taking shape. In the case of middle-class white youth, the political, economic, and cultural system they challenged had been, in fact, kind to them. But young white people were inspired by the civil rights movement, and black and white youth's sense of morality led them to question domestic and international inequality and the suffering created by American capitalism and militarism. Democracy and freedom were on their minds.

In the following pages, I look at the women's liberation movement, or feminism, of the 1960s and 1970s, the movement that began by questioning women's secondary status and ranged far and wide as it examined all aspects of female experience, including gender, race, class, sexuality, work, family, religion, law, and culture. This book seeks to answer a highly sensitive question among former participants, a question that may seem odd or surprising to many readers and seemed odd and disturbing to many white feminists at the time: why didn't a racially integrated women's liberation movement develop in the United States? It examines race in the second wave of the radical women's movement, with a focus on black and white socialist feminism, which grew out of the civil rights, Black Power, New Left, and antiwar movements. Socialist feminism was the feminist current most closely linked to the anticapitalist New Left and black movement, especially the Black Panther party. Its goal was to create a society in which resources were shared equally, not simply to provide more opportunities for women. Undoubtedly, the issue of feminist racism is unfamiliar to most people who identify the women's movement as being about gender, not race. Yet one of the central struggles of young white socialist feminists was to create a racially inclusive movement. And for most of those years, black women rejected and attacked the feminist movement as racist.

The interest of the story of race in the women's movement lies precisely in the profound racial distance and tentative reconciliation between women, which is a microcosm of the racial project of American society during the past half century. Racism remains one of the country's enduring problems. Youthful feminists were a vanguard in the ongoing historical process of whites and blacks directly facing one another and interacting on an equal basis. This is a continuing national experience: after the Second World War, African Americans demanded their rightful place in American society, and since that time everyone in this country, particularly whites, has had to engage with race. The specific, local, seemingly marginal story of a relatively small group of black and white politically leftist women who grappled with the issues of feminism and race is in no way marginal. They were a particularly self-conscious group, with a well-developed language for interpreting oppression, hierarchy, and privilege, a particularly self-conscious group in the long process of black-white racial integration initiated by the civil rights movement. These black and white women were thrown together and forced to learn many difficult lessons about race, class, and gender. One of these was that they had to separate in order to find one another years later. This is an ongoing experiment. Their engagement in the process was an American experience, one that nonfeminists, nonveteran activists, men, young people, and anyone with a concern about race can study with interest because so many white Americans and Americans of color are now experiencing their own versions of crossing racial lines and because this is a significant part of America's future. Interracial relationships are on the country's agenda. Thus while this is a story of radical social movement activists, it reverberates far beyond them. Young feminists bravely confronted racism in American society, among themselves, and within themselves. Their story provides a vantage point from which to examine an important, troubled struggle pioneered by radical women. It is one of many committed cross-racial political experiments that have taken place in the more than fifty years since the 1954 Supreme Court decision to outlaw school segregation.

I became interested in this topic because I was disturbed by the charge, found repeatedly in writing on second wave feminism, that the white women's movement was racist. As a white woman and a former activist from this period, I wondered why African-American women consistently accused white feminists of racism when many were self-consciously opposed to racism and attempted to build an interracial feminist movement. I was mystified and irritated about this dramatic disjunction which, I recognize, is not uncommon between dominant progressive whites and people of other races. The interest in the story of race in the women's movement also lies in the place of hope and ideals during this time. The movements of the early 1960s that so deeply influenced youthful feminism were shaped by a postwar idealism in which racial difference was almost expressly denied. Goals included a color-blind democracy and, for white women who became feminists, a universal sisterhood. But it didn't happen that way between white and black women. White feminists discovered that their idealism was flawed, that there was trouble between us.

The accepted historical narrative of youthful second wave feminism has been that it was a white movement due to its racism. Black women were not welcome or were repelled by white women's racism. Feminist racist attitudes and racial bias had led to such a narrow conception of women's discrimination and liberation, of gender, that African-American women could not see themselves in the movement. This narrative, however, is too simple. I had been an early women's liberation activist, engaged in the Boston socialist feminist group Bread and Roses, and I knew that we took antiracist positions and were conscious of race and class differences. Over time, though, I noticed something unanticipated: beginning in the SNCC years, interpretations of the troubles between white and black women usually diverged along racial lines. Perspectives, at that time and since, divided racially. Why this was surprising to me in a society built on racial difference had something to do with my assumption that people who participated in the social movements of the 1960s were on the same side politically. For me, a middle-class, liberal white, this meant that they would see things in nonracial terms, that racial differences between activists were relatively unimportant. I was wrong. The existence of sexism and the role of women in SNCC, for example, have been contested for more than forty years, with race central to the debate. The SNCC story is critical for understanding subsequent developments in gender consciousness among white and black women. Their experiences in civil rights and other 1960s movements accompanied them into feminism, shaping their gender politics. After the SNCC years, white and black women's explanations for the relationships between them continue to be contested along racial lines. Some white women are convinced that interracial romantic relationships between black men and white women in the civil rights and Black Power movements damaged relationships between the women, leaving heterosexual black women hurt and resentful. Others recall that whites were no longer welcome in the black freedom movement, that they were summarily expelled. As feminists, they recall making overtures to African Americans and being rejected.

Some believe that black women "race-baited" the white women's movement—used the small number of women of color in it to discredit feminism. White feminists recall, too, that there were African-American women in the early women's movement, which there were, although not many.[1] Black feminists tell of racism in the women's movement. They recount experiences of being rejected or ignored or objectified by white women. They felt that feminism was not relevant to their lives as black and primarily working-class women and that white women were insensitive, often insulting and obtuse, about their interests. They suggest that privileged white feminists could focus only on issues of personal concern and were unable to comprehend that, for black feminists, race and class discrimination were as important as sex discrimination. They argue that black feminists existed early in women's liberation history and that their presence has been erased. Can these contradictory histories and memories, in which gender, race, and class are central themes, be reconciled? Do they need to be?

Part of the story of this work has been my own slowness to recognize the assumptions inherent in my questions. Nostalgia is prominent among them. The promise of the early 1960s shaped me and others of my generation. I have not easily let go of a humanistic, universal, racially integrated sisterhood and brotherhood ideal where, hand in hand, we would work to create a just world, a vision I took from the civil rights movement. "I think when we look back on the civil rights movement, what we see driving people spiritually is exactly the desire for a transcendent connection—a form of universalism. . . . people were able to link their particularity to a deeper universality that was always in the making, but never fixed and always aspirational," wrote African-American philosopher and political progressive Cornel West.[2] And for many 1960s activists, the New Left, socialism, and Marxism reinforced a universalism that the early civil rights movement embodied. Feminist philosopher Marilyn Frye wrote of the early women's liberation movement that Marxism and liberalism "supported the idea that commonalities [sic], likenesses, and equality among the participating women would be the key to their political identity and unity."[3] Other feminists remarked, "We imagined, naively, that our 'I' was 'we' ";[4] "we thought all women were us, and we were all women. Of course we knew better even then."[5]

The 1950s, too, contributed to my cohort's ideals. The postwar liberalism I imbibed in my northern, white, middle-class, suburban family and in the larger society abstractly embraced the value of American tolerance and acceptance of one another regardless of race. This was ironic because in the South a life-and-death struggle against racism was under way. But young whites in the North had not confronted Jim Crow and were not yet aware of how racism functioned. Most knew no black people. In fact, color-blindness, our supposed sameness, moved us; it certainly did me. I remember reading and rereading the book version of "The Family of Man" photograph exhibit. Edward Steichen curated the 1955 Museum of Modern Art exhibit, which became a book that found its way to "most middle-class American living rooms in the 1950s and 1960s."[6] In Steichen's words, the exhibit "was conceived as a mirror of the universal elements and emotions in the everydayness of life—as a mirror of the essential oneness of mankind throughout the world"; it stressed the "universal brotherhood of man."[7] As an adolescent, I identified with the nine brave black teenagers who, accompanied by the National Guard for months, integrated the all-white Central High School in Little Rock, Arkansas, in 1957. I was horrified at southern white racists and wanted to befriend the students. John Lewis, former head of SNCC and now a U.S. congressman from Georgia, was inspired too. Years later, he remarked that it is ironic that his integrationist views would be considered moderate: "It is a radical idea. It's revolutionary to talk about the creation of the beloved community, the creation of a truly interracial democracy, a truly integrated society." He continued that he has a vision of a society that transcends race, "where you can lay down the burden of race—I'm talking about just *lay it down*—and treat people as human beings, regardless of the color of their skin."[8]

My research questions have been shaped by these ideas, one of which I began to realize was white nostalgia. I was able to be nostalgic for integration and the insignificance of race because of my whiteness. I did not yet seriously recognize the abuses of racism; I did not know how deeply race matters, which enabled me to participate in a reverie of harmony and togetherness. It was beyond my comprehension that whites who were opposed to racism could be unconsciously racist. The idea had not yet crossed my mind that white people, members of the dominant, privileged group, including even those who want to reject their privilege, inevitably absorb their group's attitudes—which means they are arrogant and ignorant despite themselves. Because black people called it to their attention, white people learned that they live as white people—that simply by being white we are granted privileges not granted to African Americans or people of other races and ethnic backgrounds. The heart of the issue, what white radical feminists had to deal with, was that racism, or its absence, is not only a matter of personal intention. It is also a social structural system that works subconsciously in individuals. Black feminists consistently confronted their white sisters, saying, "Look at this, you have to do something about the stereotypes and prejudice at work in you whether or not you are aware of them." Although they tried mightily, movement activists in the second half of the twentieth century could not evade the history of whites' enslavement of blacks and the dreadful story of racial oppression in which white women have colluded since. Inevitably, in the process, nostalgia and idealism were compromised.

Precisely because feminism seemed to be a moment of possibility for cross-racial bonds on a mass scale, I began revisiting the 1960s and women who were engaged in social movements for social change. Activists carried the civil rights–inspired image of an interracial community with them into the student, antiwar, and feminist movements. The antiracist values I brought to feminism made me slow in revising the questions. For young whites, the early, idealistic, "family of man" phase seems to have contained the assumption that upholding universalist ideals, like integration, made the one who upholds them into a newer sort of white person than most white people. It made us different, we thought. The stunning question raised by black people challenged that assumption, brought it to light. Having to contend with that could be said to be the phase in which we still find ourselves. Revising deeply held racial ideas and relationships is not easy, and the story I tell here is exactly that: it was not easily accomplished by the movements. Young women labored intensively to build a diverse feminist movement, and despite their expectations of achieving their goals quickly, it took time. In the late 1960s, white feminists embraced gender identity politics—a politics based on identifying and organizing separately on the basis of group characteristics—but they simultaneously harbored a political image of universal community that made little sense to women who were not like them, women who found a simple gender politics to be inadequate.

It is significant that many white civil rights movement activists remember the interracial connections of the early 1960s as the high point of their lives. For those who write about it, crossing the black/white racial divide in political work, interracial friendships, cooperation, hope, and devotion to racial justice transformed everything. Their lives became meaningful in an American culture rigid with repressive racial and gender rules; it moved them and moves them still. The way they tell it, the experiences have never been surpassed. They are emotional and eloquent about the beauty of their time in Mississippi or elsewhere in the South. Listen to SNCC activist Casey Hayden, who after the civil rights movement, longed for it profoundly: "The movement today is commonly known as the civil rights movement, but it was considerably more than that. To me, it was everything: home and family, food and work, love and a reason to live. When I was no longer welcome there, and then when it was no longer there at all, it was hard to go on." She continued, "And we did love each other so much. We were living in a community so true to itself that all we wanted was to organize everyone into it, make the whole world beloved with us, make the whole world our beloved."[9] Another participant, Pat Watters, described listening to the civil rights anthem "We Shall Overcome," "when its words come pouring forth, 'The truth will make us free . . . ,' 'We'll walk hand in hand . . . ,' and most of all, 'Black and white together,' I feel the old, choked, aching joy and, for a second, the old leap of hope, boundless hope. We *shall* overcome."[10] Lise Vogel, a civil rights movement volunteer, new leftist, antiwar activist, and socialist feminist, put it this way in 1995: "[I]n Mississippi I knew the transcendent moments in which Blacks and whites seemed truly to come together in struggle." She continued, "In subsequent years the gap between the permanence of racism and the movement's vision of justice, community and love produced in me a kind of enraged mourning—a grief to which it is difficult to see an end."[11] Another northern volunteer who became a socialist feminist, Vivian Rothstein, wrote, "Freedom Summer took us all past the segregation that defines American life—the divisions of Black and White, rich and poor, northern and southern. Connecting us in pursuit of a larger moral purpose, it made us bigger than ourselves."[12] She recalled, "When I thought of my experience in the early civil rights movement—the excitement, laughter, the music, the enervating fear—I thought of accounts unsettled, mysteries unresolved, friendships severed, and feelings of serenity, even momentary ecstasy, now lost beyond recovery."[13] A northern SNCC volunteer, Elaine DeLott Baker, said, "The feeling of being one mind and one body is so profound that its memory is palpable. I think of Mississippi as a sacrament. It was in that communion that I experienced a grace whose memory has sustained me as I have moved along in my life and work."[14] Such idealism was common among young activists in the 1960s. Years later, African-American feminist Barbara Smith stated, "I like idealism. Even though it doesn't always pan out. I think it's the most positive and potentially most revolutionary way to proceed because you're reaching for all of it. And even if you don't get half of it, you're doing alright."[15]

But the romanticization of interracial harmony in the civil rights movement was less palpable among African Americans. How could they see it in the same light after the violence against civil rights workers and black people and their disappointment in the federal government's equivocal enforcement of their rights and protection? They wanted to be free; they wanted equal opportunity, justice, and peace, to be able to live any life they chose. Integration was not necessarily the goal although, po-

Clasped hands belong to a SNCC volunteer and a student
in the Freedom School, Valley View, Mississippi, 1964.
© 1978 Matt Herron/Take Stock.

litically, it was the means to ending segregation and unequal citizenship. Neither was building community with whites. Equality was. For African Americans, the word *loss* would be more accurately employed to refer to the demise of the promise of racial justice than to the ideal of integration. Or, perhaps, *ambivalence* is more accurate. African Americans were not immune to the dream of integration. But by the late 1960s and early 1970s, African Americans, Chicanos, Puerto Ricans, Asian Americans, women, and gays and lesbians, among other groups, recognized their marginalization and subordination. Identity politics made sense. Integration was not on their minds. With the decade's assassinations of President John F. Kennedy, Malcolm X, Dr. Martin Luther King, Jr., and liberal candidate for president in 1968 Senator Robert Kennedy; with state repression and the continuing brutality of the war in Vietnam, it was difficult to maintain integration hopes. "The assassin's bullet not only killed a period of history. It killed a hope, and it killed a dream," wrote Eldridge Cleaver, a leader of the Black Panther party, about the murder of Dr. King.[16] Faith in the government dissipated for radical activists. Politics became a great deal more frightening. Idealism had lost its place.

In more recent years, I began to wonder if I were perhaps asking the wrong questions. Instead of grieving for lost interracial connections among women, which in fact were problematic even in SNCC, a more promising strategy consisted of examining white and black feminists' political histories as a way to understand why they were unsuccessful in crossing the color line—and how by the late 1970s they were able to devise ways of working together based not on idealism and universalism but on difference. Perhaps even conceiving of the political effort as unsuccessful was inaccurate, although it appeared that way to me initially. But, I realized, this was a complicated process. Crossing the color line is messy, not just theoretical; it is snail-like in its pace; it is infinitely difficult; it requires personal interaction and risk. Understanding race and racism and one's personal place in those structures and changing the racial status quo entail major work. The image of community that I "missed" could not have lasted precisely for the reasons that radical political activists understood by the late 1960s: the American political and economic system does not foster equality, justice, freedom, or community. We often forgot to apply that insight to our own fledgling organizations and relationships, blaming each other and mourning instead.

Among participants, there are few topics that raise more trepidation than racism in the radical women's movement. It is a raw subject replete with silence, resentment, and uncertainty.[17] Academic Margo Perkins wrote, "That the 1960s are still, for those who were intimately involved in the political events of that era, a living history makes it both an exciting and a difficult period to write about." One way of understanding this is as "activists challenging *each other's* individual recollections of the Movement and the people involved. . . . the effort to seize control over how this history will be remembered is no small matter."[18] Scores of years later, how the story is told still matters to those who were there. There are numerous reasons for this. In the case of feminism, one explanation is that many years of activists' lives were devoted to it. They invested time, energy, and hope into transforming American society and still are invested. Another is that feminists had high hopes for the profound and permanent changes the movement would bring to their lives, including the end of sexism and racism. The horizons of young people raised in the 1950s and early 1960s were wide indeed. Yet despite feminism's achievements, many activists are disappointed. And they are often angry at each other for not living up to their ideals, for interpretations and behavior then that they haven't forgiven even now. American society is still capitalist, racist, and sexist. Because so many women continue to face difficult living and working conditions, because so much has not changed, a sense of disappointment or loss is sometimes palpable among the earliest cohort of radical activists in second wave feminism.[19] Race in the women's movement brings up anger, sadness, frustration, confusion, guilt, regret, dismay, and even rage, as it does when it is addressed in the larger society.

This book synthesizes original documents (in public archives, my own collection, and published books), memoirs, secondary accounts, interviews, fiction, and conversations to construct a story of white and black feminist racial politics in the late 1960s and 1970s. Accounts and interviews written years later are utilized, even as I recognize the complicated baggage that memories carry. In researching the material, I came to see that memories and positions taken by women about what happened, and about what they remember happened, tell us a great deal about what was and still is at stake for them about race, class, gender, and sex. I realized that I was in no position to actually decipher what transpired but was able to perceive patterns and interests in interpretations that revealed much about tensions and commonalties at the time. Texts and speeches written by movement participants have taken on lives of their own as they have been debated over years. Individuals' memories and commitments color how the stories are represented and are frequently fiercely contested. I eventually concluded about SNCC, for example, that interpretations and memories of women's experiences were, or had become, as important as, or were indistinguishable from, the lived experience. Historical contestation is often as critical as what actually occurred. My research has made me aware that participants' memories of what happened often seemed to supplant what actually happened, if the latter could be ascertained. And retrospective written accounts have become part of the story. Whites have written more about gender in the civil rights movement and feminism than have African Americans, and their attention has often focused on whites. African Americans criticize movement scholarship for precisely this reason. Representations of 1960s experiences even now are in a permanent state of transition. They change over time. In addition, young scholars are revisiting the movements with fresh eyes. They all sift through the data, shaping the movements according to what happened, what participants did and said then and how they later interpreted their actions and statements, secondary accounts over the years, and, not least, how today's political and social climates shape questions and responses.

I examine the following: the Mississippi Freedom Summer project of 1964; women in the Black Power movement; the Boston-based Bread and Roses organization and white socialist feminism; the Boston-based Combahee River Collective and black socialist feminism; and late 1970s and early 1980s cross-racial feminist political work. In the development of the feminist movement, one of the most dramatic political shifts was from a desire to overcome difference to its promotion. Integration or interracialism as a goal migrated toward difference and an embrace of identity that precluded togetherness. This was a disturbing process but, in retrospect, probably inevitable. Postwar young people, especially whites, knew very little about racism and sexism. They had to separate to learn who they were in the race, class, and gender terms constructed by American society. It was a stage in a long process. I suggest later in the book that the movements did not invent identity politics. Black Power and other identity movements developed because of their participants' exclusion from the American dream of equality and justice and the American government's failure to respond to minorities' demands and needs. Just as identity politics divided the society that created such politics in the first place, they divided the movements. People who had been activists together, or who

imagined they could be, were no longer. The movements were sites of political and cultural struggle not only against the dominant society but
among activists themselves as well. This is one way of thinking about the
story this book tells. As they segregated themselves in order to struggle for
their rights, the movements became more isolated from each other, blacks
from whites, women from men, gays and lesbians from heterosexuals. In
the process, their idealism was shaken.

White and black socialist feminists, then, worked against enormous
odds in order to recover each other and devise a politics in which they
could work together. They had to invent new racial, gendered, and sexual
selves in the effort to develop collective political work. They were forced
to acknowledge differences they did not know they had, did not want to
have, and that nevertheless deeply divided them. Idealistic notions of
racial togetherness and community became casualties. White nostalgia
had to be discarded. Eventually the problem they faced was to find their
way back to each other, to discover and devise political connections. It
was a challenging task for this generation of young people, who knew
each other so little across race. In retrospect, it was a process that had only
just begun, although they were impatient for it to conclude with success.
Their histories and memories can be reconciled only through recognizing
that the legacies of racism that kept them apart and unequal and so uneasy with one another have taken, and are continuing to take, a lifetime to
undo. It's a peculiar and fascinating trajectory: separation was a vital in-
gredient in feminist political work and yet eventually feminists had to im-
provise political links to one another. One way of looking at the movement is to recognize that blacks and whites rarely had a positive history or
connection in the United States and that only through organizing on their
own were blacks able to achieve some pride and attention for their griev-
ances, a process that women replicated with men.[20] During the 1970s,
socialist feminists divided themselves into racial, ethnic, and sexual categories the better to deal with difference, which became the defining feature of feminism in this period. By the end of the decade, they came together not in simple sisterhood but in interactions that acknowledged
their differences. The radical women's movement came full circle, from a
goal of integration to a politics of separation to tentative efforts to reconnect. With tenacity, feminists confronted social institutions and one other,
across race, often with hope and frequently in pain and frustration, and
by the late 1970s they were soberly moving toward one another in a self-

conscious effort to construct an antiracist feminist movement together, a movement that had the potential of being home to them all. Far from irrelevant, the political and personal efforts to deal with race and racism by radical women, a marginal sector of the American political scene for almost forty years, provides us, decades later, with a tentative map to the detours, bumps, and occasional smooth byways that all Americans need as we negotiate race in the years to come.

B y 1964, the Student Non-Violent Coordinating Committee had been working in the South for more than four years. It had been founded on the momentum of the lunch counter sit-in movement and become the most important nonviolent radical civil rights organization, composed almost entirely of youth, many of them students. The organization had shouldered national responsibilities in the massive struggle for civil rights, confronting a system of racial apartheid based on terror and violence while simultaneously attempting to build a new society, the "beloved community." Members organized in rural communities, across generations, in an attempt to achieve equality for poor, mainly rural, African Americans. Their central project was organizing the disenfranchised to be able to vote and participate in American life. Organizers worked tirelessly and bravely to desegregate the South and achieve African Americans' rights through civil disobedience, voter registration, organizing, and education. Hundreds of individuals had been threatened and beaten, many more had risked their lives and livelihoods, and some had died in the struggle.[1] Organizers and staff were emotionally drained in the face of years of white racist terror and government inertia. In a controversial decision stemming from this situation, SNCC or COFO (the Council of Federated Organizations, a coalition of civil rights groups primarily staffed by SNCC members) organized Freedom Summer in 1964. They invited white northern students into the South as civil rights workers in order to challenge the government and the country to pay attention to what was happening in Mississippi—to support the movement's demands for voting rights and justice and to protect civil rights workers, volunteers, organizers, and those who registered or tried to vote. It was a pragmatic decision that many opposed. SNCC activists recognized that white middle-class volunteers would draw attention and galvanize government action in a way that black people's suffering and struggles simply had not.

Freedom Summer was the first time that large numbers of black and white young people had spent so much time together.[2] It was especially eye opening for the whites who had had almost no contact with black people before, had never been in the South, and were used to being in charge. They entered a situation that was controlled by black people, including some powerful female leaders, among them Ella Baker, Fannie Lou Hamer, Diane Nash, Ruby Doris Smith Robinson, Prathia Hall, Jean Wheeler Smith, Bernice Reagon, Dorie Ladner, and Joyce Ladner. With little preparation or experience of one another, large numbers of primarily northern whites and southern blacks worked together in the movement. The cultural and political experiences of black organizers and white volunteers, many of whom came from elite and safe northern college campuses to which they would return, contrasted dramatically. Middle- and upper-middle-class summer volunteers were often more skilled, confident, organizationally experienced, and, certainly, socially connected, than black southern SNCC organizers. Making the decision to sponsor Freedom Summer had been difficult in part because organizers understood this would be true—the volunteers' whiteness and connections were the reason for the entire plan. Over the course of the summer, the volunteers' privilege generated resentment. Most of the whites were well-meaning, hard working, committed, and courageous. But some were insensitive, arrogant, overbearing, and guilty, and their privilege often made them unaware of these traits.[3] Inevitably, some black SNCC workers felt invaded, inadequate, resentful, and angry. Leader Bob Moses explained, "Negro students, you know, actually feel this is their own movement. This is the strongest feeling among Negro students—that this is the one thing that belongs to them in the whole country; and I think this causes the emotional reaction toward white people coming and participating."[4]

SNCC's nonviolent, integrationist, and utopian elements inspired idealistic young people in their vision and practice of nonhierarchical democracy and interracial community. Even at their most pragmatic, hope and courage defined the young activists. Within several years, however, African-American activists were forced to temper their optimism: they were losing faith in the government and in whites. Hope and doubt intermingled so that at times they trusted whites and could imagine an integrated society and, more often, by the summer of 1964 and later, that dream was compromised. While harboring an inspiring, lifelong interracial image from those years, white activists also recognized the political difficulties they all faced. Furthermore, gender and sex issues generated tensions which, in the case of women, foreshadowed problems they would encounter in feminism. Freedom Summer, then, represents a historical moment of despair—which was why black SNCC organizers invited

Mississippi Summer Project volunteers at Oxford, Ohio, prior to their departure for Mississippi, 1964. © Steve Schapiro

whites to participate—and of inspiration. The inspiration is a baseline against which to measure the distance that developed between white and black women in the movements. These years in SNCC represent a connection between blacks and whites that was often interpreted differently by them but was, nevertheless, a time of heartfelt interracial solidarity. Freedom Summer was both a beginning and an end of togetherness across race. Most important for this story, women learned that gender did not necessarily ensure interracial solidarity.

The young activists were divided by race, class, sex, regional culture, and time of entry into and time spent in the civil rights movement. But they were not always divided along the most obvious lines. For example, in some cases, northerners across race shared more, especially in culture and style, than did blacks or whites. Older black Mississippians embraced young whites more enthusiastically than younger black activists did. Activists who had been in the movement for years had more in common with each other, across race, than they did with new volunteers. The divisions, then, depended on context and issue. Sometimes the young people were able to bridge those differences, creating a community or at least enormous affection and support for one another. Despite divisions, one of the important stories of the early civil rights movement, and particularly of SNCC, is of love and respect and friendship across the races.[5] "The fact that some of us had deep friendships that crossed all racial lines is simply a miracle," wrote a white SNCC organizer.[6]

Subsequent movement developments have tended to overshadow the interracial friendships that remain one of the hidden legacies of the civil rights movement. This was particularly true for the mostly southern white and black young people who worked together in the early years of SNCC before Freedom Summer, when the group was smaller and participants knew each other well. But it was also true for volunteers who came in 1964 and 1965, many of whom developed close relationships with the families who housed them. Civil rights historian Charles Payne wrote that most of the literature on the movement stresses racial friction, particularly the hostility white volunteers encountered from SNCC-COFO workers, but he emphasized that "the volunteers were so warmly received by so many of the local residents across the state, especially the older ones and the children." Volunteers were adopted by families, resulting in relation-

Edie Black, summer volunteer, teaching at the Freedom School in Mileston, Mississippi, Mississippi Summer Project, 1964. © 1978 Matt Herron/Take Stock.

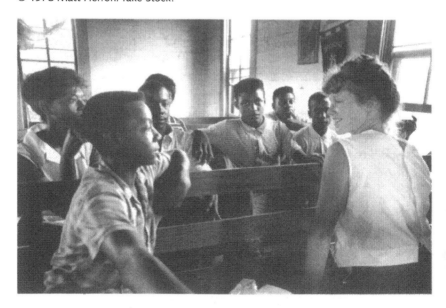

ships that lasted for years.[7] Older local residents tended to be more welcoming to the young whites than were SNCC organizers. Payne explained
that this is part of the Christian tradition of southern black humanism—
the belief in the essential oneness of humankind. In addition, older blacks
had a depth of experience with white people and recognized a complexity
to interracial relationships in ways that younger organizers could not. He
also suggested that some of the willingness to accept the white volunteers
can be attributed to a kind of "worshipful servility" among the older people, which some COFO workers found offensive.[8] That older community
people were welcoming to white volunteers compounded some young
blacks' feelings of resentment, especially as they interpreted that welcome
as ingrained obsequiousness to whites.[9]

After Freedom Summer, a retreat was held in the fall of 1964 in Waveland, Mississippi, in order to confront organizational and political dilemmas that SNCC faced. The organization had come to a turning point in
terms of its size, organizational direction, and racial politics. Among
many position papers, one was presented about problems that women experienced in the civil rights group. Mary King and Casey Hayden, two
long-time white, female staff members, authored the paper but would not
sign their names because they were afraid of ridicule.[10] The memo listed a
pattern in SNCC in which men were more powerful than women and
made up the leadership while women, despite their importance, often
were expected to fulfill traditional female roles and defer to men in final
decision making. King and Hayden made an analogy between an assumption by whites that they are superior to blacks and men's assumption that
they are superior to women, pointing out that both assumptions undermined subordinates: "Consider why it is in SNCC that women who are
competent, qualified, and experienced, are automatically assigned to the
'female' kinds of jobs such as typing, desk work, telephone work, filing, library work, cooking, and the assistant kind of administrative work but
rarely 'executive' kind." SNCC women keep the organization running on a
daily basis and are discontented with their status, they suggested. They
pleaded for serious consideration of the issues even though most of the
men were threatened by discussion of the subject.[11]

In order to more fully understand King and Hayden's perspective,
some background on the crisis in SNCC is required. Two events of that
summer of 1964 created the turning point. Freedom Summer was one.
The second was the rejection of the Mississippi Freedom Democratic

party (MFDP) at the Democratic Party National Convention in Atlantic City in August. Throughout the spring and summer, SNCC had undertaken to build an alternative to the whites-only Democratic party in Mississippi. This strategy allowed blacks to register in an alternate political system and to present themselves as the legitimate party in Atlantic City. Convinced that their organization and case were persuasive, everyone involved was profoundly disenchanted in Atlantic City when the challenge failed. These two events, in conjunction with the murder of three civil rights workers that summer, created disillusionment about the possibility of attaining racial justice through an interracial movement. Critical for understanding the racial politics that ensued, they help to situate the debates about gender and sex as well.

"The summer project [Freedom Summer] was one of the last major interracial civil rights efforts of the 1960s," wrote historian Clayborne Carson, author of the foundational history of SNCC.[12] By the time Stokely Carmichael became chair in 1966 on a militant, racial separatist platform, the early nonviolent, "beloved community" years were over.[13] In that year, SNCC became a black organization. Bob Moses, perhaps the most important SNCC leader, said years later, "I always think of Mississippi and the Freedom Summer as it was 'damned if you do and damned if you don't.' . . . The Movement never really recovered from that summer, and the price of sort of freeing Mississippi was the destabilization of SNCC."[14] Within SNCC, differences in northern and southern perspectives were critical, as were those between blacks and whites and between veterans and newcomers. A divisive debate was taking place about whether the organizational structure of SNCC should be open and nonhierarchical, its original form, or needed to be more strategic, centralized, and formal to be effective.[15]

The racial climate in SNCC is critical for comprehending the organizational and gender tensions. Young black activists repeatedly refer to their disillusionment after years of nonviolent struggle, voter registration work, and commitment to American liberalism. They began to doubt whites' capacity to change and whether the civil rights movement should or could depend on whites—friends or government officials. The long history of the African-American struggle for integration as the way to achieve equality began to make less strategic sense for numerous disillusioned young people moving toward black nationalism. Notions of self-defense and black self-determination merged with Malcolm X's influence as his ideas moved into the South. Black Power was on the agenda. After the summer of 1964, discussion intensified about the role of whites in SNCC. Black SNCC workers had had mixed experiences with whites and resented the newcomers, which led to the expulsion of whites in 1966. Thus whites, women and men, who had committed themselves to SNCC, some of whom had been involved from the beginning, discovered themselves in an unhappy position in 1964 and 1965.

SNCC organizers argued about whether or not the original participatory democratic structure of SNCC was still viable given the size and scope of the group after the summer of 1964. Those who opposed loose structure advocated a tighter, more hierarchical organization as more efficient. They saw centralization as a way to regain their purpose and path, to recreate the solidarity of the early years. SNCC staffers were sharply divided over these positions and fought bitterly among themselves as they felt the future of the organization was at stake. Sociologist Francesca Polletta suggested that conflicts, for example, between old and new staff, northerners and southerners, field staff and Atlanta-based personnel, and blacks and whites, were all framed and channeled into the structure debate and that debate was racially inflected. Loose structure was associated with whites: "Whites often invoked the requirement of democracy when faced with the prospect of their own exclusion." Centralized structure was associated with a black orientation. "By the spring of 1965 'tight structure' had come to be seen as a bulwark against the dominance of whites," wrote Polletta.[16]

The 1964 and 1965 volunteers had created an organization that was too large in which to maintain the trust and familiarity of the original group. Growth from a small, intimate, mainly black, beloved community to a large interracial organization filled with newcomers from different backgrounds, who hadn't experienced the early years, burdened SNCC. Numbers provide some sense of the changes. In April 1962, there were 20 staff members. A year later, there were 12 office workers, 60 field secretaries, and 121 full-time volunteers.[17] After the summer of 1964, SNCC had close to 200 staff members, and many of the new members were white.[18] Before 1964, there were not many whites: in 1961, there was only 1 white field organizer, Bob Zellner, and in late 1963, of 41 field staff, there were 6 whites. After 1964, the proportion of whites went up to 20 percent, although not for long. By the summer of 1965, there were 200 staff and 250 volunteers from a range of backgrounds.[19] This expansion, in conjunction with exhaustion, frustration, loss, and problems with participatory democracy, led to factions that engaged in long, bitter discussions about organizational form, leadership, goals, race, and program.[20] When King and Hayden raised the issue of women, they did so in the spirit of early SNCC, hoping that enough of the early idealism and decentralized democratic inclinations survived so that their concerns could be addressed.

In 1965, King and Hayden wrote another statement, which they signed, called "A Kind of Memo: Sex and Caste," about the exclusion and subordination of women in society and in the movement, hoping that they might recreate a shared sense of themselves, as blacks and whites and women and men, in SNCC. They also sent it to women in the New Left and peace and freedom movements, where it had an enormous impact. They again argued that there were analogies between the "treatment of Negroes and treatment of women in our society as a whole." In the movements, women seemed to be excluded from power, which they identified as a caste system. But, they noted, people who can readily see a racial caste system are blind to a sex caste system. They discussed women and work, personal relationships, institutions such as marriage and child rearing, and men's defensive reactions to such topics. They hoped to open a dialogue about women's equality in order to create a community of support for themselves as women and as committed activists for two principal reasons: so that SNCC's original interracial and democratic vision would guide the organization and so that they would be able to continue to work in the movement. King and Hayden pointed out that the goal of social movements for social change, such as civil rights, peace, and the New Left, was to build a better society, and women's equality was crucial to that effort.[21] Both memos were hopeful about SNCC's and the movements' potential for taking women seriously.

The second memo's greatest impact was on white northern New Left women, who enthusiastically responded by challenging movement men and developing women's liberation groups.[22] The white women had been involved in civil rights, Students for a Democratic Society (SDS), and early anti–Vietnam War marches. They were activists on their campuses, and some had organized in poor northern communities. By 1965 and 1966, they were explicitly critical of their second-class status in the New Left. They wrote their own papers and distributed King and Hayden's second paper, "A Kind of Memo," as part of New Left radical women's early articulation of feminism. They were more than receptive to the SNCC paper as they themselves had begun to object to male domination in the movements and in society.

In SNCC, the memos generated angry, impassioned debates that have lasted for more than forty years, as did SNCC organizer—and later chair—Stokely Carmichael's famous pronouncement at the Waveland conference: "The position of women in SNCC is prone!"[23] One night during the retreat, according to King, a group of people were relaxing after days of traumatic meetings about the future of SNCC when Stokely Carmichael, joking and playful, uttered his now iconic line. King continued the story: "Stokely threw back his head and roared outrageously with laughter. We all collapsed with hilarity. His ribald comment was uproarious and wild. It drew us all closer together, because, even in that moment, he was poking fun at his own attitudes."[24] King and most SNCC insiders understood the comment as a joke, not as the sexist statement it was subsequently interpreted to be.

From the outset, it appears that most of the SNCC staff, including black women, were unresponsive to the gender issues that King and Hayden raised. Years later, King stated that her fears of mockery were well founded since, with some exceptions, the paper was greeted with derision. White feminist historian Sarah Evans argued that black women were in the forefront of the struggle for female equality, and there are indications that some young black women were aware of and disturbed by sexism. Yet hostility was generated by the memos at the time and subsequently by texts that linked white feminism to sexism in SNCC. White women were the ones who publicly raised gender issues in SNCC, and the issues were embraced by white women elsewhere in the movement—which may have confirmed for black women that these were white women's concerns, or at least the narrow focus on gender was. Carmichael's statement, in response to their 1964 memo, was taken literally and cited repeatedly in the story of the development of white radical second wave feminism and in the divisions between white and black women, not as a friendly joke but as a sexist statement that indicated the gender problems that women faced in SNCC. White feminist commentators have taken it as a clear statement of male chauvinism.

SNCC activists and historians and white feminists have devoted a good deal of attention to Carmichael's declaration. "Endlessly repeated, Stokely Carmichael's joke about the desirable position of movement women resonated in ways he never intended or imagined," wrote feminist historian Ruth Rosen.[25] The statement has taken on iconic proportions in the history of gender in SNCC and the women's liberation movement. It is a touchstone for a variety of interpretations of the situation of women in the organization and for what transpired between black and white women (interestingly, less so about women and men). The discussion reveals the divergence of their trajectories from a moment in SNCC in the early 1960s when integration, inspired by hope and faith, seemed possible and inspired more hope. If SNCC "did a great deal to invent the sixties," in Charles Payne's words, SNCC gender disputes and the controversies they provoked helped to invent the women's liberation movement and provoked some black women's alienation from that movement.[26]

Black SNCC women, with some early female white civil rights activists in agreement, have taken exception to the attention Carmichael's remark has received. They understood it as a joke and not as a seriously sexist statement. Recent writing by black women on SNCC reinforces the point that too much attention has been paid to the issues of sexism and interracial sex in SNCC, that whites have chosen these topics for reasons having more to do with their own agendas than with what actually was important and what happened during the SNCC years.[27] They argue that SNCC was not plagued by such issues nor do they explain much about SNCC.

Until recently, what has been written about gender in SNCC is the story of the memos and their significance, of Carmichael's comment and white feminists' use of it. Not a black woman–centered story, it is one in which white women took the initiative and black women did or did not respond. From the start, then, it has been more a story of the development of white feminism and less a story of SNCC women. Or, perhaps, it is both. But what we learn is that they are not easily contained in the same narrative. Civil rights movement writing by whites has generated the criticism that they have been most interested in the authors' white selves and their white history and that white women "carried on" then and (and now) about gender issues that at the time, in the face of the Ku Klux Klan and racist lawlessness, were practically irrelevant to the organizing work at hand. In other words, the experiences of white activists are not the most important stories of the civil rights movement but, in the words of Charles Payne, many historians have recounted the civil rights movement as if "history is something that happens when the White Folks show up and stops when they leave."[28] From this perspective, concentrating on 1964's Freedom Summer downplays the previous years of local black organizing and distorts what is most important about SNCC and its accomplishments. This is being redressed as more historians study the civil rights movement. It is being redressed, too, by more studies of women in the social movements of the 1960s and 1970s, a number of which are considered below. In the case of this book, however, whose topic is precisely how activist women's experiences in earlier movements, sometimes with one another, generated gender and feminist consciousness, Freedom Summer is an important interracial place to begin.

One of the difficulties in constructing a new story is that black SNCC women have spoken less than white women. From the outset, then, there are racial divisions in the accounts of gender difficulties, indeed about the existence of difficulties at all. Although white women wrote the 1964 memo, it was occasionally attributed—by white feminists—to Ruby Doris Smith Robinson, one of the most respected and powerful black women in SNCC. Historian Evans suggests that the myth of her authorship indicated "an important truth: that black women occupied positions of growing strength and power which challenged sexual discrimination."[29] The rumor of Robinson's authorship suggests the possibility that some black women directly confronted gender issues in SNCC, which white feminists ardently wanted to be true. Mary King, however, found it a complete mystery that her memo could be attributed to Robinson.[30] Perhaps the early acceptance and repetition by white women of the possibility of Robinson's authorship of the first anonymous sexism memo and Evans's portrayal of black women in the forefront of gender issues were efforts by white women to create a narrative of cross-racial sisterhood. That subtext reveals whites' hope and, perhaps, expectation, that white and black women shared concerns that could bring them together.

In recognition of how race created different experiences for movement women, black SNCC member Jean Wheeler Smith speculated that SNCC history

keeps getting rewritten and revised to the convenience of the people who are rewriting it. Maybe also there were some differences between the way the black women in the organization experienced their situation and the way white women experienced it. Casey [Hayden] and I seem to have had about the same experience, but it may be that that changed in later times and that after about 1965 people did not feel as much a part of the organization.[31]

Wheeler Smith pointed to the variations in the SNCC gender stories and acknowledged that their content often reflects the race of the author, especially in 1964 and after. So did SNCC activist Bernice Reagon, who noted of her experiences: "I think there might be White women who could tell you a very different story than I am telling you."[32] Both African-American women observe that black and white women's experiences, which appear to have been similar, were not. Or, if they had been, things had changed enough by 1964 and 1965 so that race became a more prevalent and more divisive lens through which to interpret events.

Paradoxically, despite the fact that the memos were about gender, King and Hayden have always been at pains to distance themselves from the gender meaning of what they wrote. They have unequivocally stated that they were never victims of sexism in SNCC. "I didn't feel exploited," Hayden said firmly. "None of this stuff that's written about sexual exploitation applied to my experience. None of it."[33] Actually, almost every female SNCC veteran has disavowed experiencing sexism. "Female activists, black and white, including those who had written the original position paper on women, flatly rejected the notion that SNCC was in any way sexist," wrote Cheryl Greenberg, the editor of the published transcripts from a 1988 SNCC reunion conference.[34] Thus, despite the fact that they wrote the memos, King and Hayden later dissociated themselves from their gender meaning. Black women did not respond to their memos, which suggests one reason for King and Hayden's disavowal—a reluctance to distance themselves from black women. They understood themselves to be calling on the original democratic ethos of SNCC as a way to solve problems and move forward, not as making fundamental gender criticisms of the organization. One of the more striking characteristics of former SNCC organizers is their protectiveness toward the organization. Even many years later, they are still ardently loyal to SNCC. "In the years after I left, I [felt] . . . enormous grief and a certain amount of bitterness, yet there was loyalty and I know I never opened my mouth to the press. The loyalty is very strongly there," wrote Penny Patch, a white SNCC activist, about the growing rift between whites and blacks in SNCC.[35] In her recent interviews of Jewish women who worked in the South, Debra L. Schultz remarked on

the care with which some women . . . talk about interracial
tensions in the movement. Proud of their ability to cross bound-

aries in personal and political relationships, they seek to protect
the historical legacy of the movement by remaining focused on
its main objectives. They also wish to preserve the cross-racial,
cross-class relationships forged in the midst of struggle.[36]

Her observation is relevant here: remaining focused on SNCC's racial objectives is a way of remaining loyal. King and Hayden and the other early
white women members who helped to write the memo felt closer to
SNCC than they did to white women in other movements, including the
white feminist movement.[37]

Because it was an early, critical, and significant book in the study of
the origins of the second wave women's movement, white historian Sara
Evans's *Personal Politics: The Roots of Women's Liberation in the Civil
Rights Movement and the New Left*, published in 1979, is a central text here.
It, too, is iconic, like Carmichael's "prone" statement. The book presented
an interpretation of the relationship of youthful white feminism to the
New Left and the civil rights movement that has become "one of those
rare scholarly arguments that has persisted virtually unchallenged for
more than two decades."[38] Evans argued that the women's liberation
movement had its sources in the civil rights movement and the New Left.
Based on the gender experiences of white southern women who became
civil rights activists and who were early members of SNCC and of the
white summer volunteers who came to the South, young white women's
experiences of sexism, especially in the New Left, led them to feminism,
Evans contended.[39] Her central argument was that strong black women
were the models for feminism that young white women took back with
them into the other movements of the 1960s and that became the basis of
the youthful, radical women's movement. In this multigenerational movement, older black women, usually based in the community, inspired
younger women. Through movement experiences and the example of
older black women, young black women also became more self-confident,
took on increasing responsibility, and were unwilling to put up with unse-
rious behavior. Evans argued, "Black women struck the first blow for female equality in SNCC."[40] She also suggested that for some black women
who worked out in the field alongside the men, a personal life was nonex-
istent. They resented black men's interest in white women and felt conflicted about conventional feminine upbringing and new possibilities.
Evans maintained that interracial sex was inevitably controversial, that

some white women were promiscuous, that some black men thought of white women as conquests, and that it happened and created tensions. She wrote that black women were angry about white women and black men's liaisons and that some white women were afraid of that anger.

In Evans's view, while the 1964 memo was about sexism, its subtext was really a lament about committed whites, especially long-time civil rights workers, no longer having a place in SNCC as it shifted from an integrated nonviolent community to nationalism and Black Power: "It expressed Hayden and King's pain and isolation as white women in the movement. The black women were on a different historical trajectory. They would fight some of the same battles as women, but in a different context and in their own way."[41] White women sensed their own growing precariousness in SNCC as the organization changed and as hostility toward whites grew; they were still part of the inner circle but increasingly marginalized. By 1965, and even as early as 1964, the memo authors saw the handwriting on the wall and were fearful that there was no place for them in the civil rights movement. King has acknowledged this; the personal relationships she and Hayden had with black women in the movement "began to tear," and in their second document they were in part responding to this "estrangement," wanting to heal rifts with female black leaders, many of whom had been their friends.[42] King and Hayden, then, were worried not only about whether there was going to be room for a variety of political and social perspectives, including women's, but whether or not there would be room for whites at all. White SNCC organizer Penny Patch wrote that "in the aftermath of the Summer Project, the racial climate within SNCC was changing markedly." The pain she was feeling

> reflected the fact that the antiwhite feelings I had become aware of the previous spring were increasing. I was beginning to feel a growing distance between my black SNCC comrades and me, and I no longer felt as welcome as before in my beloved SNCC community. Unlike some of the newer white staff or summer volunteers, I experienced little overt hostility. People simply withdrew from me.[43]

The King/Hayden memo was as much about race as it was about gender, and the organizational debates were laden with race and gender meaning that were not obvious at the time.

Personal Politics raised the ire of SNCC activists, white and black. Years later, King argued that the interpretation of their memos in Evans's widely read and influential book is wrong. Women's status in the movement was never the issue, King countered, and the interpretation of women as subordinate and relegated to typing and making coffee is simply incorrect. This, however, was not Evans's main argument about women in SNCC; rather it was about how black and white women became strong through their experiences. But, more important, it *is* how Evans's work has been interpreted. King pointed out that women in SNCC had profoundly significant roles, and SNCC's encouragement and support of and responsiveness to women leaders is well known: "In preparing to raise the question of women, we believed we were also broadening the debate in favor of a decentralized and manifestly democratic SNCC."[44] She and Hayden supported the egalitarian, less bureaucratic organizational position that they believed was the most democratic and true to the early SNCC vision. The 1964 memo, according to King, was as much about worry about the loss of the original spirit of the movement as it was about women. And they worried about the shift away from participatory democracy in part because embedded in those early politics was an interracial vision. A decentralized and democratic SNCC was an integrated SNCC. Subsequently, Hayden wrote that the Waveland memo was not about gender in the movement but about "maintaining the radical nonviolent core of SNCC, our old womanist, integrationist way, in which leaders and power politics were disarmed."[45]

Despite Evans's argument that black women led the way in the fight against sexism, black SNCC women were affronted by what they felt were her tone and points they interpreted as inaccuracies in the text. SNCC leader Joyce Ladner referred to Evans's book as "totally rubbish."[46] She was not alone in construing it as an insult to black women's integrity and dedication. To identify SNCC women as second-class citizens, to emphasize male leadership and female subordination, to discuss sexual discrimination and interracial sex in SNCC was to diminish their work, dedication, and accomplishments. To have a young white woman who had not been in the movement write a book, a celebrated book at that, about what they defined as a diminishment of SNCC and themselves infuriated them. Male privilege was so much less significant than race in the life-and-death struggle for freedom in which they were engaged. Yet Evans and other white feminist interpretations of Carmichael's comment about the position of women in SNCC appeared to suggest otherwise.[47]

In 1977, former SNCC activist Cynthia Washington, a black woman, wrote:

> During the fall of 1964, I had a conversation with Casey Hayden about the role of women in SNCC. She complained that all the women got to do was type, that their role was limited to office work no matter where they were. What she said didn't make any particular sense to me because, at the time, I had my own project in Bolivar County, Miss. A number of the other black women also directed their own projects. What Casey and other white women seemed to want was an opportunity to prove they could do something other than office work. I assumed that if they could do something else, they'd probably be doing that. I remember driving back to Mississippi in my truck, thinking how crazy they were. I couldn't understand what they wanted. As far as I could see, being a project director wasn't much fun.[48]

According to Washington, her own relative autonomy as a project director in SNCC undercut the charge of sexism against black movement men; she herself was proof that women were regarded as equal to men. The common response, then and more recently, by black women to the 1964 and 1965 memos by Hayden and King, Carmichael's remark, and feminist accounts of sexism in SNCC suggested that feminism was a white women's issue. In these accounts, black women were out in the field, organizing and working as equals with men, while white women were confined to the offices and less dangerous and more traditionally feminine work. In 1988, after the conference at Trinity College that marked the first large SNCC reunion since the end of the movement and the first organized panel on the role of women in SNCC, Joyce Ladner suggested that the King/Hayden sexism memo articulated privileged white women's concerns, which were irrelevant to black women. According to Ladner, despite widespread publicity, the position paper went almost unnoticed and had little impact on black women in the movement. Like Evans, she argued that the larger impact was felt among white middle-class movement women outside the South to whom King and Hayden had sent the second memo. A profound dissonance existed in the perceptions of those women in the civil rights movement (mainly white) who felt they were oppressed by male-dominated leadership and those who (mainly black) have maintained to the present day that they were rarely victims of sex discrimination.[49] At the 1988 conference panel entitled "SNCC Women and the Stirrings of Feminism"—at which Evans's book was an invisible presence—black female activist Jean Wheeler Smith stated that there is this "common notion that women were oppressed in SNCC. I just was not oppressed in SNCC. I wasn't subordinate, I was high functioning. I did anything I was big enough to do and I got help from everybody around me for any project that I wanted to pursue." Wheeler continued that she never felt any limitations in SNCC, which she believed to be an egalitarian organization. Prathia Hall, another black organizer, expressed "outrage at the notion that any of us could have been oppressed because of gender in SNCC."[50] In 1998, historian Cynthia Griggs Fleming summarized their views in 1964: "very few women in SNCC were interested in exploring gender issues at that time, and a number of black women went so far as to repudiate the paper."[51]

Southern black women came from a culture in which they had been raised to assume a great deal of responsibility.[52] They were vital to the civil rights movement, tireless grassroots organizers and office workers. The female activist tradition was long-standing for African Americans. As Joyce Ladner stated, "We came from a long line of people, of women, who were doers, strong black women, who had historically never allowed anyone to place any limitations on them." According to Ladner, a generation of young black SNCC women from the South had inherited a black women's tradition, a Sojourner Truth or Harriet Tubman tradition: "Our mothers and fathers taught us that we are 'as good as anyone.' Never allow anyone to call you out of your name. Never allow anyone to abuse you or misuse you. Always defend yourself." She continued about SNCC:

> None of these women I began to meet knew they were oppressed because of their gender; no one had ever told them that. They were like my mother—they had grown up in a culture where they had had the opportunity to use all of their skills and all of their talents to fight racial and class oppression, more racial than anything else. They took their sexuality for granted, for it was not as problematic to them as their race and their poverty.

In the civil rights movement, "We assumed we were equal. When we got to SNCC I would have been ready to fight some guy if he said, 'You can't do this because you're a woman.' I would have said, 'What the hell are you talking about?' A lot of the women in SNCC were very very tough and independent minded." Furthermore, Ladner claimed, "Sure there were no women who ever chaired SNCC, but I bet you ten to one Ruby Doris [Smith Robinson] dominated SNCC."[53]

Ladner argued that white women volunteers were different: they came from the North—and here she does not refer to the original white SNCC women, most of whom were southern, but to the wave of women who arrived with Freedom Summer—and were not encouraged to develop their full potential in their own cultures or in the civil rights movement and were thus discontented. The feminist movement would find its strongest supporters among white women from primarily urban, educated, elite backgrounds in the North. Ladner's argument about the irrelevance for black women of the charge of sexism in SNCC highlights many black women's critique of the women's liberation movement as a white women's movement inapplicable to the concerns of black women.[54]

In the published proceedings of the 1988 SNCC conference, it is notable that only one woman, a white woman, Kathie Sarachild, publicly discussed sexism in SNCC during the panel on the role of women in the organization. She had been a 1964 Mississippi summer volunteer and became a radical feminist leader—exactly the prototype of the white woman Sara Evans featured. Through her conference intervention, she reproduced both the tensions of 1964 and the reactions to Evans's book. Indicating that the stakes were still high, Jean Wheeler Smith responded by criticizing Sarachild for bringing up negative aspects of SNCC in light of her opening remarks about the positive significance of the organization in generating the second wave women's movement. "[A]nd then you focused on the opposite," she charged. African-American SNCC activist Michael Thelwell recited some of the names of female SNCC leaders and remarked, "look at these women and tell me which man will oppress them," and Casey Hayden also dismissed Sarachild's remarks with a joke that housework in the Freedom Houses wasn't really a problem because no one cleaned them.[55]

Ten years after the 1988 SNCC conference, two books by black women, Belinda Robnett's *How Long? How Long? African American Women in the Struggle for Civil Rights* (1997) and Cynthia Griggs Fleming's *Soon We Will Not Cry: The Liberation of Ruby Doris Smith Robinson* (1998), addressed gender issues in SNCC with the goal of rebalancing the story. The new books used the framework of earlier literature, the gender canon of SNCC. What separates theirs from other secondary accounts revolves around the issue of whether women were subordinate in SNCC and whether interracial heterosexual relationships were significant enough to warrant the attention they have received. In dramatic, even inflammatory, accusations, Robnett suggested that white authors "have taken up the thesis that Black men seduced, raped and exploited White women" and that "White women were sexually exploited in SNCC." According to Robnett, Evans blamed black women for the problems between them and white women, suggesting that black women felt inferior to white women and that "most Black men in SNCC sought the company of White women."[56] The misconceptions reached by these previous commentaries are in part based on the fact that, in Robnett's words, they "focus on White women's experiences in SNCC." She stated:

> [T]he actual daily actions of Blacks and Whites in the movement
> defied the classic stereotypes of the Black man as rapist, the
> White woman as fragile victim, and the Black woman as angry
> and ugly Amazon, which later researchers would unwittingly
> resurrect. Instead, what becomes clear is that Blacks and
> Whites, men and women, mainly shared positive, life-altering
> experiences.[57]

These were drastic and misleading pronouncements about the earlier work; none of the authors she discussed suggested that white women were sexually exploited victims nor that black men were their rapists.

Both Robnett and Fleming confirmed black female SNCC activists' positions that they were treated as equals, SNCC changed their lives and empowered them, their history and culture considered them to be strong and capable, sexism was not an issue for them, and interracial sex was just not that important. After the Freedom Rides in 1961, Joyce Ladner began to meet women like Diane Nash and Ruby Doris Smith Robinson. She knew people in Mississippi "who had grown up feeling as stifled as I, who had grown up feeling that they had ideas they wanted to express and couldn't. To have things they wanted to do with their lives and to feel totally constrained is a horrible feeling." When she met like-minded people, "it was like I'd died and gone to heaven." Ladner noted, "[F]or many of us, SNCC gave us the first structured opportunity to really use our potential, to use our abilities, and to express our views on the world."[58] Most white women worked in offices or schools and not organizing in the field because it was dangerous for everyone if they were out in the field; it was a pragmatic decision. If men were in formal leadership positions, it did not mean that women were not leaders. The women did not resent their lack of formal leadership positions. Long-time SNCC women understood the constraints on their participation and, according to Robnett, "did not attribute their experiences to sexism in the movement."[59] Robnett and Fleming, then, are recentering the gender story of women in SNCC from black women's perspectives.[60]

Ruby Doris Smith Robinson's movement career illuminates one black woman's experiences in SNCC, particularly her attitudes toward white women during Freedom Summer. In fact, her biography is one of the few accounts about or by young black southern female SNCC activists. Robinson had opposed the summer project because she believed in a locally based, black-organized movement and was wary of an influx of northerners. She had joined the movement at seventeen and became a dedicated activist for the rest of her short life. From 1961 until Freedom Summer, she was involved in a myriad of militant civil rights actions, including sit-ins, Freedom Rides, and voter registration. Early on, she began to assume a great deal of responsibility in the SNCC office in Atlanta, working as the administrative assistant to Jim Forman, executive secretary, the highest position in SNCC. Not until she was named executive secretary of SNCC for a short time in 1966, when it was turning toward Black Power, did she become the only woman to that date with a formal position in SNCC.[61] She died the next year. Despite the lack of a formal position for many years, Kathleen Cleaver, SNCC activist and Black Panther party member, remarked, "Ruby Doris was essentially the heartbeat of SNCC."[62] Her biographer, Cynthia Griggs Fleming, characterized her as confrontational, sure of herself, powerful, and uncompromising in her dedication to SNCC. In white SNCC activist Dottie Zellner's words, Robinson was "very involved, she was very very smart, she was great, she was a legendary, fearless person. . . . She was tough as nails but wasn't just tough with white people, she was tough with everybody. . . . there were a lot of people who were really afraid of her."[63]

Robinson, like other female black SNCC organizers, believed that white women, particularly northern women, did not understand southern culture. Offended by the insensitivity of white women volunteers, she often found them frivolous and condescending. She was fearful that white women would put black people in danger and resented the confusion and pressure that white volunteers created in the movement, worrying especially about the threat of interracial affairs to the black community. But more than SNCC politics were involved in the tensions between white and black women. Robinson, who had little patience for weakness and ineptitude, grappled with issues of being a strong black woman in a society that preferred weak white women and in which standards of feminine beauty were white. Fleming pointed out that black SNCC women's "perceptions of proper morality" were shaped by the social stereotyping of black women as sexually loose and immoral. Middle-class-aspiring families taught "nice girls [to] carefully guard . . . their virtue and virginity." Black colleges reinforced these notions of creating black "ladies" and, Fleming remarked, "The pressure black women felt from their own communities to uphold such high standards was enormous and unremitting."[64] Admired beauty standards at black female institutions of higher education like Spelman College in Atlanta, which Robinson attended, mimicked white features. Robinson stated, "I spent three years hatin' white women so much it nearly made me crazy. It came from discovering how the whole world had this white idea of beauty." So offended was she by these unattainable beauty standards, "I just hated it so much that for three years I wouldn't speak to a white woman."[65]

Fleming underscored the burdens that black women faced in American society despite the new possibilities opened to them in SNCC. Her focus on one woman lends a more psychological and cultural interpretation to the trouble between black and white women. She would not disagree, however, with Robnett's suggestion that white women took center stage "in the feminist analyses of a black organization" and that white feminist concerns have shaped the story of SNCC in a way that emphasizes white/black relationships, particularly the tensions between women. "[T]he voices of Black women participants in SNCC have been mute," wrote Robnett.[66] Black female writers described the following: a black civil rights organization floundering and a freedom struggle that was moving toward race-based politics; black people and their relationships with each other as central to the movement, including romantic relationships between black women and black men; strong black women for whom gender issues were not compelling; sexism and interracial sex as insignificant in the larger picture of racist terror and racial inequality; irritation at white women and impatience at the sex and gender spotlight trained on the organization. Fleming noted, "[R]ace loyalty undoubtedly overshadowed gender issues in the minds of most African-American female civil rights activists of this era."[67] This was particularly true as the Black Power movement made headway among young black activists.

The debate in SNCC at the time and subsequently was also about sex. Ruby Doris Smith Robinson's concerns about the confusion that white women might bring to the project related in part to the specter of interracial romantic relationships. They were disruptive and hurtful to black women and dangerous for black men. And, of course, Carmichael's joke suggested that SNCC women should be available and prone for sex. Unsurprisingly, one of the most explosive boundaries tested during Freedom Summer was that of sexuality. In the midst of the danger and close proximity in which movement workers lived, heterosexual sexual attraction and curiosity thrived. Heterosexual romance and sexual involvements, particularly between black male southerners and white female volunteers, usually northern, generated tensions.[68] Interestingly, this is one of the few 1960s stories where white men are present but effectively absent or sidelined. White men undoubtedly had romantic attachments with black women, but I have found almost no written evidence.[69] Given white southerners' obsession with interracial sex, these romantic and sexual encounters represented real danger for civil rights workers and the people they were trying to organize. The history of this fixation on interracial sex, particularly black men's desire for white women, dates back to slavery when white slave owners imagined that their male slaves desired white women. The creation of ideologies in which African Americans were oversexed and desirous of whites obfuscated whites' oppression of and interest in blacks. Racist whites, particularly white men, developed a virtual panic and pathology about interracial sex, convinced that, above all, what black men wanted was "their" white women. Summarizing Freedom Summer volunteers' letters home, SNCC volunteer and author Elizabeth Sutherland wrote that southern whites were afraid of each other, afraid of Negroes, afraid of the volunteers, and haunted by sex and the nearness of whites and blacks: "Entwined with the fear was the obsession of sex; almost every conversation between the volunteers and local white people came around to that theme in the end. It seemed to run so deep that the Mississippians could not bear the sight of physical nearness between Negro and white even when the sexes were not mixed."[70]

Racial mores in the south enforced rigid segregation, and any breach was dangerous. One of the points of *Freedom on My Mind*, a film about the civil rights movement with a focus on Freedom Summer, is that the breakdown of racist etiquette was one of the central achievements of the movement. The deferential manner in which blacks addressed and encountered whites changed in those years: "The generations since the movement have not been taught to stay in their place or to understand that there is a certain way to walk and stand and look at and relate to white people."[71] With the sit-ins, young blacks began to reject submissive interactions. The transformation of everyday life, in which whites no longer had the power to control the public behavior of black people, was a hidden script of the civil rights movement whose overt goals were to end segregation, to gain voting rights, and to become equal citizens in America. Early SNCC workers had always attempted to avoid flouting interracial etiquette, which they knew would only inflame white southerners. The movement consciously adapted to southern norms, which among other things meant keeping white women out of public situations with black men because it was too dangerous.

White women were not, therefore, on the front lines and could not organize door to door. They were more likely to be found in offices and Freedom Schools, that is, engaged in traditional women's work. Since many of the earliest white female activists were from the South, they recognized the volatility of the situation. Interracial friendship and organizing were provocative, and contact between white women and black men was particularly so. Some Freedom Summer whites were unaware or less than sensitive about the peril they created for blacks.[72] SNCC organizers warned volunteers about interracial dating, and some forbade it in their projects because it endangered too many people. Sally Belfrage, a summer volunteer and a professional journalist, quoted Mrs. Amos, in whose home Belfrage and other white volunteers lived: "Jus' one boy touch a white girl's hand, he be in the river in two hours. We raise them up never to even look at one—they passes on the street, don't even look, that's the way down here."[73] A young black woman stated, "My mother told me to stay away from white men no matter what. If I see a white man dying on the street, I'll call the police or an ambulance or somethin' but I'm not goin' over there and help him out."[74]

Young southern blacks of this generation had grown up with a public taboo on interracial contact between black men and white women. The paranoid white suspicion of black men's sexual motives had been graphically driven home by the Emmett Till case. In 1955, fourteen-year-old Till, raised in the North and spending his summer vacation with relatives, had been brutally murdered in Mississippi for whistling at a white woman. The terrifying story and images of his lynching had burned themselves into the consciousness of young southern blacks. A photograph of his mutilated corpse was published in *Jet* magazine, which had a wide circulation among African Americans. One SNCC activist from Mississippi, Joyce Ladner, referred to this generation of youthful southern black civil rights activists, who came of age in the late 1950s, as the "Emmett Till generation." She stated, "I can name you ten SNCC workers who saw that picture [of Till's body] in *Jet* magazine, who remember it as the key thing about their youth that was emblazoned in their minds. . . . One of them told me how they saw it and thought that one day they would avenge his death."[75] Sam Block, one of SNCC's most successful organizers, recalled, "What made me realize that I had to do something was when Emmett Till was killed. And it happened right there by Leflore County. I was a teenager then." As he organized, he questioned young people about Till and found that "many of the kids were just as angry as I was but knew not what to do." Block explicitly chose to work in the county where Till was murdered.[76] SNCC organizer Cleveland Sellers also stated that this was the atrocity that affected him most deeply: "Emmett Till was only three years older than me and I identified with him." He wrote that the lynching affected everyone in the community: "there was something special about this one." The corpse held particular horror since the boy was brutally beaten and shot and then barbed wire was used to attach a heavy cotton-gin blower around his neck before he was dumped in the river. Sellers remembered the photos: "They showed terrible gashes and tears in the flesh. It gave the appearance of a ragged, rotting sponge."[77] Civil rights organizer Anne Moody wrote, "Before Emmett Till's murder, I had known fear of hunger, hell, and the Devil. But now there was a new fear known to me—the fear of being killed just because I was black. This was the worst of my fears. . . . I didn't know what one had to do or not to do as a Negro not to be killed. Probably just being a Negro period was enough, I thought." Upon learning that there was a long history of "Negroes being butchered and slaughtered by whites in the South," she said, "I felt like the lowest animal on earth. At least when other animals (hogs, cows, etc.) were killed by man, they were used as food. But when man was butchered or killed by man, in the case of the Negroes by whites, they were left lying on a road or floating in a river or something."[78] For Ladner, Block, Sellers, Moody, and "thousands of other black youths,

Emmett Till's gruesome murder and the photograph of his water-swollen body left an indelible impression on their minds."[79] Perhaps Elizabeth Alexander's words best sum it up:

> For Black writers of a certain age and, perhaps, of a certain region, a certain proximity to southern roots, Emmett Till's story is the touchstone, a rite of passage that indoctrinated these young people into understanding the vulnerability of their own black bodies, coming of age, and in the way in which their fate was interchangeable with that of Till. It was also a step in the consolidation of their understanding of themselves as black in America.[80]

Emmett Till's lynching represented a huge, unarticulated gulf between blacks and whites. Young whites never had to cope with the horror and shock. That terror could never touch whites the way it did blacks.[81] And while other African Americans had been lynched throughout history, in 1955, in the second half of the twentieth century, one year after the *Brown v. Board of Education* decision, during a postwar, self-satisfied, cold war celebration of American democracy and freedom, Till's murder terrified black adolescents in the South. Many white volunteers had probably never heard of Emmett Till and could not personally relate to this kind of terror. Years later, Chude Pam Allen, a white civil rights worker, wrote this account, based on an interview with an old local woman, who said that the "white men cut off his genitals and forced him to eat them before they killed him" and "that they cut his body open after he was found and his genitals were in his throat." Allen noted, "Whether or not Emmett Till was forced to eat his genitals, some blacks believed it" and reiterated that "Till's murder and the horror and outrage it generated is essential background to understanding the fear and sexual tensions on the Mississippi Summer Project."[82] The dread of the mutilated young black body, of his torture and murder, of a trial soon after in which his murderers, well-known white men in the community, were found innocent by an all-white jury, haunted young blacks, warning them of what could befall them and solidifying a determination to fight back. Less than ten years later, strains developed in their own organization about interracial sex and women's place that, unsurprisingly, generated deep feelings among SNCC activists, undoubtedly calling up memories of Till, an adolescent black male who had been murdered for whistling at a white woman by white men who explained that they had murdered him to protect white womanhood.

Another study of Freedom Summer stated simply, "White-black sexual relationships were . . . very bad for public relations; they were deeply resented by both the whites and the blacks in the Deep South."[83] In orientation sessions, volunteers were counseled not to engage in sexual relationships because they would endanger the projects. The open flouting of convention invited risk. Dave Dennis, a Freedom Rider and leader of CORE (the Congress of Racial Equality, a northern-based civil rights organization working in the South) in Mississippi, remarked that white southerners became enraged at seeing white women with black men and that projects "integrated both racially and sexually sometimes were attacked or harassed at least partially because white women and black men and, to a lesser extent, black women and white men were working together, not solely because they were doing civil rights work."[84] SNCC project director Ivanhoe Donaldson "was particularly emphatic about affairs between blacks and whites. He told us that he did not intend to have any interracial relationships between staff and members. In a very blunt and forceful manner, he told white females that they were to avoid all romantic entanglements with local black males." Interracial relationships, he said, would provide local whites with the excuse to kill them, and black people would question their political motives. Donaldson made it very clear that anyone who violated these rules would have to leave.[85]

Nonetheless, the theme of sexual liberation was a "subterranean current" running through white volunteers' accounts.[86] When interracial sex, "the most potent social taboo in the South," was based on mutual regard, "there was a sense in which the 'Beloved Community' of black and white together took on concrete reality in the intimacy of the bedroom," wrote Sara Evans.[87] The summer project was envisioned as the embodiment of a truly egalitarian community whose members were expected to be free, including free to truly love one another. For many volunteers, interracial sex became the ultimate expression of this ideology.[88] But, in Evans's words, "the struggle against racism brought together young, naive, sometimes insensitive, rebellious and idealistic white women with young, angry black men, some of whom had hardly been allowed to speak to white women before."[89]

In her study of Freedom Summer, Mary Aickin Rothschild suggests that white women volunteers were in a painful double bind. They faced a "sexual test": how to deal with sexual advances from black men. If they refused, they were called "racist" and became a focus of black men's hostility.[90] If, on the other hand, a white woman had sex with a black man, she was written off as an ineffectual worker and became the focal point for a great deal of anger from black women on the project. One black male project director commented, "Where I was project director we put white women out of the project within the first three weeks because they tried to screw themselves across the city." He agreed that the young black men were sexually aggressive—but that they never expected a positive response and blamed white women's behavior for undercutting the project's effectiveness.[91] Parenthetically, these reports never hold the men responsible; they assume that it was the women's responsibility to control sex. Ivanhoe Donaldson warned the women in the project but not the men. According to Rothschild, where there were sexual problems on a project, "for the most part young black women remained bitterly divided from white women, whom they saw as stealing their men." Rothschild overstated the case by suggesting that it was primarily sexual divisions that undermined black and white women's ability to work together as women. But she argued plausibly that "the hurt some black women felt as a result of their experiences with white women volunteers would remain long after the Freedom Summers were over."[92] African-American author Gloria Wade-Gayles expressed it this way: "The pain many black women in the movement experienced because of our invisibility as desired lovers was exacerbated by the male monopoly of decision-making power."[93]

Yet the problem as it was experienced at the time is difficult to get at more deeply because there are not many sources about interracial sex and what exists comes mostly from whites.[94] For white women who engaged in interracial sex, it was important—and thus it has been for their chroniclers. For black women, it was one more issue that created complications and hard feelings during a dangerous time. It is significant that almost no one who was involved in interracial sexual relationships has written about them, and few acknowledge ever having been involved.[95] One exception is white SNCC worker Penny Patch, who wrote in 2000:

> In retrospect, if I had known how my sexual relationship with a
> black man could affect black women, I hope I would have acted
> with greater sensitivity and discretion. It is, however, unlikely
> that I would have changed my behavior significantly. We were
> young, we were living in wartime conditions. We were always
> afraid; we never knew whether we would see one another again.

> We were ready, black and white, to break all taboos. SNCC men
> were handsome, they were brilliant, they were brave, and I was
> very much in love.[96]

Interracial relationships have found their way into some fiction, but interracial desire appears to be a taboo topic among SNCC members. Patch provided one explanation for the silence: "One thing was clearly changing by the end of 1964: interracial sexual relationships were no longer tolerated—black SNCC folk who took part openly in such relationships were subject to the charge of 'backsliding,' and those relationships, when they did occur, tended to be hidden from view." Another white organizer, Theresa Del Pozzo, wrote, "In 1965 it began to be politically incorrect in some movement circles . . . for blacks to be personally involved with whites, at least in public. Many interracial friendships and romances were cut off or went underground."[97] As racial politics shifted and Black Power influenced SNCC members, interracial relationships were less acceptable than they had been earlier. Perhaps talk about such relationships is still politically unacceptable, due in part to loyalty to SNCC and the betrayal it may imply of black women. Or, for some, it just wasn't that important in the scheme of things. In a discussion of heterosexual interracial relationships, African-American SNCC organizer Bernice Reagon remarked that they happened and that they were neither central to the movement nor to her experience in the movement.[98]

White and black southerners both believed that white women had a perverse sexual interest in black men. Writing about the experience of a Jewish woman working in the northern civil rights movement who was anonymously given a cruel poem, historian Debra Schultz noted, "The ditty underscores a projection that Jewish women civil rights activists would have to face throughout their movement tenure, especially in the South: that they were promiscuous, seeking, in particular, interracial sex."[99] Unlike black women, white women were outside their communities and less constrained by "nice girl" standards than were black women.

It was also the dawn of the sexual revolution. White volunteer Sally Belfrage noted, however, in a new preface written in 1990 for a reprinting of her 1965 book *Freedom Summer*, that she did not discuss sex originally because she failed to notice any sexual relationships. But, she remarked, alluding to the emotional debates, "there has been latter-day smoke indicating *some* sort of fire—specifically charges by feminist academics" that the sources of feminism lay in the victimization of white women by black men. She continued in a joking manner, "Even if anybody had ever offered to victimize me, there was simply no time or space; my single most plaintive wish was just once to be alone."[100] Like other SNCC women, Belfrage suggested that the sexual issue has been overblown and implied that white women's victimization by black men is a central tenet of an academic feminist argument in which she sees no merit.

During the summers of 1964 and 1965 and for years before, young black women worked alongside black men, even ran their own projects, and "were treated as one of the boys" during community and voter registration organizing. But when they would finally get back to some town "where we could relax and go out, the men went out with other women." That seemed to place us in "some category other than female," wrote black SNCC organizer Cynthia Washington.[101] Gwen Patton, another black SNCC worker, talked about how rough and frightening the organizing was, how tough you had to be in SNCC, and that such toughness in women exacted a personal toll: "Probably if you looked at all our personal lives, we've probably had a very difficult personal life in terms of relations with men. Many of us made decisions not to go with SNCC men because in some kind of way we didn't need to be fucked. . . . it was very confusing."[102] A bitter Mississippi Freedom Democratic party organizer remarked, "I've seen the Negro fellows run after white women. It's quite obvious that they're after a white woman, not this particular woman. And I'm quite disillusioned about that." In 1965, a young black woman stated, "The Movement is in worse shape now than a year ago. There's conflict between black and white on the staff. Negroes are not prepared for whites coming down. It takes on a sex thing. Most of the Negro men never have been close to a white girl before." According to one black SNCC staffer, "The Negro girls feel neglected because the white girls get the attention."[103] Put simply by African-American activist and writer Gloria Wade-Gayles, "Understandably, when romantic alliances between black men and white women became almost as common as cotton, we lost the harmony with which we had once sung, 'We Shall Overcome.'"[104]

The fraying of strong ties between long-time white and black women staff was only partially due to sexual relations between white female volunteers and black men. The exponential growth of the organization, the influx of whites, the difficulties of the summer, and the civil rights struggle that led to Black Power all contributed. Nevertheless, Mary King wondered whether "resistance to this pattern might not have contributed to the surge toward black nationalism in SNCC after . . . 1964" and ultimately to the expulsion of whites from SNCC and the development of an all-black and nationalist SNCC.[105] Doug McAdam, social movement sociologist and author of a book on Freedom Summer, stated that sexual tensions, particularly those generated by relations between white women and black men, were one of the most powerful pressures encouraging the expulsion of whites from SNCC.[106] Evans suggested that the white women's memo about sexism may have in part expressed their sadness at being excluded by blacks—in other words, it can be viewed as an overture to black women. By appealing to gender commonalties and the early SNCC organizational model, they hoped to repair their weakening relationships with black SNCC sisters. Race, gender, and sex complexly interacted so that in one interpretation sexual conflict led indirectly to a racial strategy, an all-black SNCC, and in another, racial conflict underlay concerns about gender inequality that led to a gender strategy: a memo about sexism and eventually the women's liberation movement.

Young SNCC organizers built an egalitarian alternative to the society in which they had grown up, but in the process they could not help but experience how race, sex, and class had shaped their lives and their organization. Struggling with these differences often meant struggling with one another.[107] It certainly meant a diminished idealism. In 1977, Cynthia Washington remarked, "I'm certain that our single-minded focus on the issues of racial discrimination and the black struggle for equality blinded us to other issues."[108] In the battle against racism, SNCC's sexism was less important to black women, particularly as the mood changed and a national black movement attracted young African Americans. White women were there because of their dedication to racial justice and integration which, it turns out, for most was not enough to create closeness with black women of their generation. Friendships developed, especially in the early years, but on balance the record indicates that distance prevailed.[109]

The SNCC sex and gender paper trail continues to generate powerful feelings among black and white women, among movement activists and their chroniclers. White writers have often been interpreted as unappreciative of SNCC's strengths or as emphasizing the wrong things, raising as much or more ire than there was when events unfolded. Just as black women accused whites of looking through retrospective feminist lenses, black women committed themselves to positions informed by racial politics defined by their dissimilarity to white feminism. For decades, Stokely Carmichael's jest, "The position of women in SNCC is prone!" has been invested with contradictory interpretations, a veritable gender/race Rorschach test. The texts continue to contribute to, reinscribe, even construct, differences between black and white women, making it difficult to connect the narratives of black women focused on civil rights and white women poised to found the women's liberation movement. Yet those narratives were—and are—connected.

Because white women were members of the dominant race, they had little allegiance to their men. For black women, this could not be a viable strategy. But like white women, black activist women were ambivalent about being seen as too strong and, sometimes, as asexual. Ruby Doris Smith Robinson's biographer wrote that black SNCC women wanted to lead, "but they did not wish to assert themselves at the expense of their men. Such a position was fraught with contradiction."[110] Young women of both races, raised in the postwar period, joined a social movement and in the process shared the experience of shedding gender constraints as they redefined femininity for themselves. Both were emerging from a narrow feminine domestic culture against which they struggled in order to become activists and, in the process, learn how they would live their lives as independent women. But it was difficult to recognize that they shared a great deal. SNCC opened up worlds for all of the women involved, transformed their lives, and empowered them. Every black and white woman has said this in some form or another.[111] The organization gave black and white women a chance to know one another and simultaneously highlighted their differences. In the process, their idealism was challenged. Their racial histories and cultures led them to move toward equality on distinct paths. The summer of 1964 and the following year changed the meaning of differences between black and white women, which earlier had been interesting and exhilarating. Their differences became threatening to the political solidarity and friendships they had achieved, highlighting, perhaps, how unusual, and how fragile, moments of interracial connection were in the United States. SNCC's hopeful and graphic visual symbol was a white and a black hand clasping, but the brave interracial nonviolent pact was unraveling as young activists looked toward the future.

> This is the era of liberation and because it is the era of
> liberation, the black man will be able to bring the woman along
> in our common struggle, so that we will not need a black
> women's liberation movement.
> —Nathan Hare, "Will the Real Black Man Please Stand Up?"
> (1971)

> I think this is *my time* now and I'm goin' to take it. Anybody'd
> be crazy not to take it. . . . I just don't care about anything
> else right now but takin' what my mother and my grandmother
> oughtta have had and they didn't get it.
> —Anonymous black woman interviewed by Josephine Carson,
> *Silent Voices: The Southern Negro Woman Today* (1969)

While optimistic early visions of an interracial movement as a path to racial equality gave way to racial separation in the mid- and late 1960s, idealism reappeared in different forms. Black women's expectations and hopes for racial justice remained high, as the words of the woman interviewed by Josephine Carson affirm. They embraced the Black Power movement as activists, organizers, and artists and were central to its accomplishments. Among the hopes that Black Power raised for women was the promise of solidarity between black women and black men. While the loyalty of women in the black liberation movement was primarily to their race, how that loyalty operated and the ways in which female activists' experiences as women changed them and the movements remains underexplored. Very simply, some of women's problems stemmed from the fact that men were the hub of attention and concern, considered by many to be more damaged by slavery and racism than were women and therefore more deserving of admiration and support. The racial solidarity for which women hoped, the community they imagined, was weakened by male dominance and sexism. The movement empowered women while simultaneously angering and disappointing them. This chapter presents a portrait of the Black Power movement followed by a consideration of women's experiences and reactions, one of the paths leading toward black feminism.

Black Power was a movement that "galvanized millions of black people in the broadest movement in African American history." It was enormously influential among black youth, female and male. Some organized political and artists' groups and others simply supported its ideas, but all were affected by black nationalism, a political and cultural movement that focused on achieving power, freedom, and affirmation for African Americans or, in the words of historian Komozi Woodard, "self-determination, self-respect, and self-defense."[1] A geographically diverse movement, it encompassed a range of cultural and political emphases, including the Black Arts movement, which articulated Black Power's cultural perspectives; the Black Panther party, the most well known political organization of the time; Malcolm X and the Nation of Islam, or the black Muslims; and black workers' organizations. Black nationalism is probably the most inclusive term for both the cultural and political aspects of the Black Power movement in the late 1960s and 1970s.

The anger that fueled the Black Power movement was generated by white vigilante violence against the civil rights movement and the government's lack of protection of African Americans and civil rights activists, organized state violence against the Black Panther party and other black militants, and the bloody war in Vietnam. Black Power developed in the South as a response to white supremacy—specifically out of traditions of black militancy and the disappointments of the civil rights movement— but the real base and power of the black nationalist movement was in the cities of the North.[2] Its political projects included black self-defense; a black nation; an end to colonialism, imperialism, and racism; and, ultimately, black freedom. The international situation, particularly anticolonial movements and the struggles for independent black states in Africa, the Chinese revolution, and the Cuban revolution deeply impressed black radicals of the international relevance of their cause and of their place in the world.[3] Many African Americans were persuaded by history and Islam as interpreted by the Nation of Islam.[4] Sometime around 1966, Black Power in the South, Malcolm X's influence in the North, Amiri Baraka and other Black Arts movement artists, Ron Karenga's organization US, the Black Panther party, and urban rebellions converged into a powerful social movement centered on black radicalism's insistence on self-determination and self-definition.[5] Poets, playwrights, and writers, in-

cluding James Baldwin, Julius Lester, LeRoi Jones (Amiri Baraka), Larry
Neal, Don L. Lee (Haki R. Madhubuti), Nikki Giovanni, Sonia Sanchez,
and scores of others created a body of literature that articulated the rage
and despair of black Americans.[6] They exhorted their listeners and readers to join the national black community, to see themselves as blacks and
no longer as Negroes.[7] They wrote to embrace blackness, celebrate black
culture and history, and express love for their formerly despised but newly
constructed selves. In the words of poet Larry Neal, the Black Arts movement conceived of itself as the "aesthetic and spiritual sister of the Black
Power concept," speaking directly to the "needs and aspirations of Black
America."[8] Defining the black aesthetic, Addison Gayle, Jr., wrote that the
artist's goal was to ask: "How far has the work gone in transforming an
American Negro into an African-American or black man?"[9]

Over and over again black political activists and artists, women and
men, articulated their bitterness, frustration, rage, and sadness at the failure of nonviolence and the apparent imperviousness of whites to morality. Young black civil rights supporters painfully turned away from the
peaceful and interracial vision of the early civil rights movement. In 1968,
Julius Lester wrote, "Now it is over. The days of singing Freedom Songs
and the days of combating bullets and billy clubs with Love. We Shall
Overcome (and we have overcome our blindness) sounds old, outdated.
. . . Too much love / Too much love / Nothing kills a nigger like / Too
much love."[10] According to Ron Karenga, leader of the black nationalist
organization US, "The only thing that non-violence proved was how sav-
age whites were."[11] And Don L. Lee's "No More Marching" poem begins:
"didn't I tell you / it would do no good / but you done gone / to school
and read all them books / now you is marchen / and singen / 'we shall
overcome'/ getten hit & / looken dumb / & smilen / holden that whi / te
girls hand pro / tecten her / that makes you / equal too??"[12] Female SNCC
activists articulated their changes: Anne Moody gave up God, rejected
nonviolence, and despaired of the violence ever ending while Jean Smith
"learned to feel black." Black Arts poet Nikki Giovanni wrote in her "Love
Poem (For Real)": "it's so hard to love / people / who will die soon / the
sixties have been one / long funeral day / the flag flew at half-mast / so frequently / seeing it up / i wondered what was wrong."[13]

Activists repudiated love, trust, hope, and integration, having learned
that politics were about power. Malcolm X, disenchanted SNCC workers,
and Black Panther party members, with all manner of activists, theorists,

and artists throughout the country, formulated analyses that ranged from critiques of institutional racism and individual bigotry to celebrations of black culture and its African roots, from visions of the beauty of blackness to arguments for a separate black nation.[14] By 1966, frustration at the federal government's lack of commitment to civil and voting rights, anger at white volunteers and the complications they brought with them, and sorrow at the death, destruction, and poverty surrounding them led southern civil rights workers to the notion of black people organizing themselves in order to create their own political institutions and to control their own communities. Racial self-determination was on the agenda.

In 1966, Stokely Carmichael, the new chair of SNCC, wrote, "The need for psychological equality is the reason why SNCC today believes that blacks must organize in the black community. Only black people can convey the revolutionary idea that black people are able to do things themselves."[15] The notion of psychological equality undoubtedly received a boost from Freedom Summer when blacks realized that whites, even supportive whites, unintentionally reproduced white supremacy through their position of power and domination in the larger society. Blacks recognized that self esteem, confidence, pride, skills, and resources were necessary to build a movement, and believed they had to do it alone. A celebration of African-American culture, bodies, and history, of self-determination, and an affirmation of black life that had been destroyed, discredited, and appropriated throughout American history were at the heart of the move to Black Power.[16] It was about hope too, a different kind of hope than that of the civil rights movement but hope just the same: for a better future in which freedom, pride, and self-determination would characterize the African-American community. Advocates of Black Power

> not only believed that African Americans had to challenge
> directly the state and its white citizens, they also maintained that
> a fundamental psychological and cultural conversion from their
> socialization as a subordinate people to a self-determining
> nation needed to take place. In other words, . . . a revolution
> of the mind was a prerequisite for the success of the black
> revolution.[17]

Many SNCC members were convinced that the organization "should be black-staffed, black-controlled, and black-financed." They stated, "If we are to proceed toward true liberation, we must cut ourselves off from white people. We must form our own institutions, credit unions, co-ops, political parties, write our own histories."[18] What bound all of the ideas and projects together was cultural nationalism. Central to its goals was changing the way that black people thought about themselves and their situations, the way they related to one another and to whites, and celebrating African-American history, culture, and bodies. A distinct black culture was spread through language, folk culture, religion, literature, and the performing arts.[19]

Speeches, essays, poetry, and plays often articulated antiwhite revulsion and violence. For some important Black Arts writers, a hatred of whites was a driving force.[20] Military images and preparedness and violent revolutionary rhetoric were not peculiar to black nationalists. Characteristic of late 1960s movement politics, they accompanied the desperation that grew in proportion to the government's intransigence, harassment, and provocation. In the case of the black nationalist movement, references to warriors, physical strength, virility, revenge, power, and nationhood were common. Ron Karenga, head of the Black Power organization US, explicitly challenged his followers: "When the word is given we'll see how tough you are. When it's 'burn,' let's see how much you burn. When it's 'kill,' let's see how much you kill. When it's 'blow up,' let's see how much you blow up. And when it's 'take that white girl's head, too,' we'll really see how tough you are."[21] Black Panther leader Eldridge Cleaver threatened, "We shall have our manhood. We shall have it or the earth will be leveled by our attempts to gain it."[22] Black Arts poet Larry Neal wrote that SNCC's attempts to use black and white organizers was a failure, that "intra-organizational strife, spiritual disunity, and operational co-option by white left wing youth were the result."[23] Many Black Power advocates "refused to even talk to white people," who sometimes ceased in their eyes to be people at all. Black Power writers felt most betrayed not by the Ku Klux Klan or overt racists but by those in whom they had placed their hope, particularly liberal whites and Jews, as well as the "Negroes" who worked with them.[24] A fury of resentment, a "rhetoric of excess and the fantasy of vengeance," informed much of the discourse.[25]

A central goal of the Black Power and black nationalist political movement was for the black man to recover the manhood that had been destroyed by racism, to transform himself from a Negro into a black man. "Man" and "manhood" were often employed as equivalents for the achievement of personhood, respect, and dignity.[26] The black male stood center stage, strong, proud, and furious, a crucial building block in the imagery of black nationalism. His rage anchored the movement.[27] The rejection of nonviolence and the Afrocentric celebration often took shape as a gendered politics that celebrated "black macho," in the words of writer Michele Wallace.[28] "[B]lack phallic power" or the glorification of the new black man's virility was a centerpiece of Black Power and "asserted black masculinity as coterminous with racial emancipation," wrote literary critic Robyn Weigman.[29] One example of this "one-dimensional masculine rhetoric," in the words of black intellectuals Kobena Mercer and Isaac Julien, is Larry Neal's attack on the Panthers for pandering to whites.[30] Combining antiwhite and masculinist imagery, he wrote of the Panthers as eunuchs who address themselves to and perform for whites, "[Y]ou have to become bitchy and perverted *'cause you ain't holding on to nothing*. You are being squeezed spermless, your seed scattered among ice and rocks."[31] In his essay "To All Black Women, from All Black Men," Cleaver referred repeatedly to the destruction of his masculinity in such formulations as "Across the naked abyss of negated masculinity, of four hundred years minus my Balls," "heal the wound of my Castration," and "I, the Black Eunuch, divested of my Balls, walked the earth with my mind locked in Cold Storage."[32]

Black Arts leader Amiri Baraka aligned femininity and feminization with whiteness and especially white men. Unabashedly homophobic, Baraka used homosexuality to denigrate white men. He dismissed their masculinity by questioning their heterosexuality: white men were perverted, effeminate, faggots; they were impotent.[33] Heterosexuality was the essential component of black virility. An anonymous editorial in the Howard University newspaper rejecting the Panthers' willingness to work with white activists claimed that such work allowed them to "to be controlled by 'white boys,' 'white fags and rejects,' who opposed nationalist sentiments."[34] Anxiety about and hostility toward gays was frequently expressed as a way to condemn black men who worked with white men. Those thought not to be strong black men were called white-identified effeminate Uncle Toms. English professor Philip Harper cited a Black Arts poem by Haki Madhubuti (Don L. Lee), which threatened homophobic violence and thereby reaffirmed the poet's virile masculinity.[35] Heterosexuality was equated with masculinity, and both were key to authentic blackness.

Affirming popular notions of the family, black nationalist men wanted to put black women in a traditional place they had never occupied.[36] Amiri Baraka wrote, for example, that cultural nationalists did not believe in the equality of men and women because they are different and complement one another. Each has separate functions, "which are more natural to us." He continued, "We say that a black woman must first be able to inspire her man, then she must be able to teach our children, and contribute to the social development of the nation." Baraka referred to those who advocated women's equality as "devils and the devilishly influenced."[37] Black Power writer Nathan Hare wrote, "The black woman is, can be, the black man's helper, an undying collaborator, standing up with him, beside her man."[38] Women's reproductive capacity and their helpmate role were celebrated in this literature, which advocated complementarity between the sexes—usually meaning the subordination of women.[39] Even as he was defending black women, the sociologist Robert Staples, a major contributor to impassioned debates about gender and sex in the black community, which appeared regularly in the journal *Black Scholar*, suggested that women's role was "to encourage the black man" and "to assist strongly but not dominate."[40] In general, the message was that women were expected to be supportive and understanding of their men in personal relationships and political life and were best suited for the bearing and care of children.

Unsurprisingly, inconsistencies between nationalist rhetoric and the reality of their lives plagued many activist women. They spent much time arguing with their male counterparts, refuting their political positions intellectually and in practice. Their delight in racial pride was tested by the chauvinism of their comrades. Women striving for equality and leadership positions faced double-binds, accused of being unfeminine and too strong.[41] As Black Panther party leader Elaine Brown explained, "A woman attempting the role of leadership was, to my proud black Brothers, making an alliance with the 'counter-revolutionary, man-hating, lesbian, feminist white bitches.' If a black woman assumed a role of leadership, she was said to be eroding black manhood, to be hindering the progress of the black race."[42] For black liberation leader Angela Davis, a constant problem of her political life was being criticized for doing a "man's job." There was "an unfortunate syndrome among Black male activists—namely to confuse their political activity with an assertion of their maleness. These men view[ed] strong Black women as a threat to the attainment of manhood—especially those Black women who take initiative and work to become leaders in their own right." Rather than assuming a leadership role, she was supposed to inspire men to leadership. In fact, according to Davis, it was women who kept the Los Angeles SNCC office running, and the women in SNCC and the Black Panther party—as well as the Communist party, to which she also belonged—had to struggle continuously for their right to be engaged on the front lines.[43] Davis stated that, in 1967, the Los Angeles SNCC chapter "fell apart, largely due to women's refusal to accept the masculinist posturing of the male leadership."[44] Female activists were expected to defer to men, who were extremely sensitive about women with "too" much power, according to Davis. The women were accused of being domineering and controlling, insufficiently submissive and feminine, of in effect castrating the men. They had to create the illusion that men were the source of all ideas and to "genuflect," in Panther leader Kathleen Cleaver's words, when trying to get their views across.[45] In meetings, Cleaver observed, things would get done only when men were the initiators: "But *if I suggested them* the suggestion might be rejected; if they were suggested by a man the suggestion would be implemented. The fact that the suggestion came from a woman gave it some lesser value. And it seemed that it had something to do with the egos of the men involved."[46]

Not only was black maleness celebrated, but critical assessments of the black woman accompanied the celebration. Much nationalist writing did not just marginalize or compartmentalize black women; it indicted them. Historian Paula Giddings wrote of the "tragic irony" in the attacks on black women by leading black thinkers: "Their chauvinism invested Black women with the same negative qualities that had been perpetuated upon them—and which they had fought against—for centuries."[47] Writer and civil rights activist Alice Walker summed up the sentiments of many female radicals: "a movement *backward* from the equalitarian goals of the sixties seems [to have been] a facet of nationalist groups."[48] Militant black men appeared to "embrace and endorse" a picture of a "domineering, emasculating black womanhood," a version of the controversial 1965 Moynihan Report, which argued that a black matriarchy undermined black men and black nuclear families.[49] Black nationalist writers underscored the Moynihan Report by targeting black women "as an active agent of the black man's economic and social emasculation." Often with the intention of criticizing Moynihan's black matriarchy thesis, they ended up reproducing it and indicting black women as the source of black men's troubles.[50] Ironically, many black women believed "that their men suffered more, and the Black women's duty . . . was to absorb their justifiable rage. Black women were proud that they were strong, that they were responsible, but wondered if they were too strong, both for the good of their men and the good of the race," suggested Paula Giddings.[51] The Moynihan Report exacerbated such thoughts, as did American white, middle-class, nuclear family politics. Prathia Hall of SNCC remarked that something happened after 1965:

> [T]here was a sense of the whole matriarchy thing, and wanting our family to look like what we were told white families looked like, and so many younger women at that point became very defensive about their strengths. And we have gone through a period of black women being extremely repressed, at least, in terms of ambivalence about strength, assuming a responsibility for the violation of the black man.[52]

An example of such nationalist gender politics was the female students at Howard University who formed a group called WOMB, a name chosen to indicate their dedication to black children and the black family. They were committed to the kind of "fertility and nurturing that is necessary" for community growth, "removing ourselves from a position of perpetual dominance to stand beside our men." They continued, "The white woman seeks to liberate herself by not doing things such as washing the dishes and taking care of her family. WOMB recognizes these things as a means of unifying the family and liberating black people."[53] A student at the time, historian E. Frances White, recalled meetings at her college in the late 1960s and early 1970s in which men and women argued about gender. Noting that those meetings were a wellspring of feminist ideas, she said, "Although a few of my sisters and I refused to be persuaded by the claim that black men needed to assert their masculinity at our expense, to my horror, some of my classmates at the all-women's college I attended began to argue that the time had come for black women to take a back seat to black men."[54] A study based on interviews of female militants, Inez Smith Reid's 1972 *"Together" Black Women*, echoed these nationalist sentiments. Reid quoted numerous women who believed that black women should stand by their men, bolster their egos, and support them in the movement. They said things like, "I think the woman should be behind the man"; "We should stand by our men and try not to take the leading role"; "She should make him feel like he is king or all important, that he is somebody"; and "I'm willing to make cookies, lemonade, and whatever," usually couched in the argument that this was black men's time and that they needed to be the leaders of the race.[55] Another said, "Men must be men and this is why I can admire the Panthers. At no time in history have Black men stood as tall as they are trying to stand now. I think Black women should do everything in their power to encourage this. I think we ought to take a back seat."[56]

Many female activists explicitly supported the argument that black men had been more damaged by racism than had black women and that women owed it to the men to support them. Panther Kathleen Cleaver explained that as "black men move to assert themselves, as black men move to regain a sense of dignity, to regain a sense of manhood, to regain a sense of humanity, and to become strong enough and powerful enough and manly enough to fight against the oppressor, they many times take out their resentment of their position against their own black women." In hindsight, Cleaver was critical of women's acceptance of black men's poor treatment of their women, including abusive and violent behavior, which she attributed to the historical colonization of the black man: "Unfortunately . . . too many of the black women are so brainwashed and anxious to help the men, as they always have been, in any way, that they go along with this and try to become overly submissive."[57] Gwen Patton, a former SNCC organizer, writing in Cade's *The Black Woman*, noted angrily that black women have had to be "cagey" and careful "for fear of deballing the needed and well-loved leaders. Black women have crouched in fear trying to do their thing."[58]

Heterosexual black women were and wanted to be loyal to black men, and they longed for black men to be loyal to them. But many men were not, and the women were hurt. In a poignantly titled essay in Cade's *The Black Woman*, "Who Will Revere the Black Woman?" Black Arts singer and actress Abbey Lincoln lamented that she had heard echoed by "too many Black full-grown males that Black womanhood is the downfall of the Black man in that she (the Black woman) is 'evil,' 'hard to get along with,' 'domineering,' 'suspicious,' and 'narrow-minded.' In short, a black, ugly, evil, you-know-what." Lincoln's rejoinder to the criticisms was, "Evil? Evil, you say? The Black woman is hurt, confused, frustrated, angry, resentful, frightened and evil! Who in this hell dares suggest that she should be otherwise?"[59] Whether they genuinely embraced a subordinate position or felt they had no choice, one of radical women's major challenges was to maneuver their way carefully through Black Power politics, and often they were wounded in the process.

Adding insult to injury, some male writers used the supposedly overbearing characteristics of the black woman to defend the black man's "escape" to the white woman. Black women's hurt, anger, confusion, and resentment crystallized around interracial liaisons between black men and white women. The continuity of this painful issue is striking as is its power to divide black and white women. It came up repeatedly as a source of bitterness. Radical black women were outraged about the public showing of Black Power bravado by men who would then leave meetings to join their white lovers or wives. One militant woman remarked that the black man chastised the black woman for "not having the kind of Black awareness and Black consciousness that can lead to liberation and yet at the same time consort with that individual whom he has just labeled the enemy of his liberation."[60] Lecturing and posturing about political rectitude, the men were seen as hypocritical and undermining of political solidarity. "What does it mean when a black man spurns his own women for outsiders? How can a black man lead black women to a black nation with white women as queens? What does this say to the black woman?" wrote educator Barbara Sizemore in an issue of the *Black Scholar*.[61] Nikki Giovanni remarked bitterly:

> I'm forced now to admit the white woman is obviously a natural
> and superior piece cause I have watched and am watching our
> men go ape shit to get it. Panthers coalescing and Communists
> communing are still talking about getting a white piece. And if it
> costs them their lives as it has been costing our men their cul-
> tural, emotional, spiritual and physical lives, that appears to be a
> small enough price to pay for it.[62]

Making matters worse, Abbey Lincoln suggested that black men seemed to want their women to know when they were with the white women she so disdained. She wrote angrily, "White female rejects and social misfits are flagrantly flaunted in our faces as the ultimate in feminine pulchritude. . . . At best we are made to feel that we are poor imitations and excuses for the white woman."[63]

In spite of all the aggressive egotistic masculinity, it is critical to recognize that there was often a discrepancy between the masculinist rhetoric of the Black Power and Black Arts movements and the experiences of women in those movements—and that throughout the 1970s men slowly abandoned their most chauvinist positions. Despite the sexist bombast of many male writers and activists, women were central to the maintenance of organizations and significant artistic contributors to the Black Arts oeuvre.[64] For example, Black Arts poets and writers Nikki Giovanni, Sonia Sanchez, and Toni Cade and political activists such as Angela Davis and Ericka Huggins, in the Black Panther party and other militant groups, were devoted and central players. Black Arts women wrote, spoke, and performed, sometimes about sex and gender, suggesting that they had a space, or made one, from which to create a conversation. Their work was published in Black Arts journals, and they read their poetry and spoke alongside the men.[65] Cheryl Clarke's study of women poets in the Black Arts movement explored the inspiration the movement provided to the writers and their ambivalent place within it. She showed how indebted black women writers of that generation were to the movement and suggested, "[I]t is sometimes difficult . . . to admit their debt to the Black Arts Movement because of its misogyny, heterosexism, and homophobia." The artistic space they found there created a base upon which to build a more diverse, open, feminist and lesbian cultural tradition in the coming years.[66] Despite ambivalent and sometimes hostile gender messages, the goal of black liberation kept radical black women inspired and active.

It is also critical to acknowledge that some radical women were simply unwilling to acquiesce to patriarchal politics. Influenced by the civil rights and Black Power movements, they became feminists early on and were part of white feminist groups or founded or joined small third world women's groups in the late 1960s and early 1970s that were the core of the black feminist movement. They rejected the movement's male chauvinism and saw no place for themselves in it. "Certain Black men are maintaining that they have been castrated by society but that Black women somehow escaped this persecution and even contributed to this emasculation," wrote Frances Beal, a black liberation activist who became an early feminist, in an often-reprinted essay, "Double Jeopardy: To Be Black and Female," in Toni Cade's 1970 book, *The Black Woman*.[67] Cade's landmark work in the development of black feminism included essays written by Black Power and Black Arts activists analyzing and lamenting the situation of black women in the movement and wider society. Cellestine

Ware, another early black feminist, wrote in 1970, "The black movement is so gratifying to these newly realized needs for group pride that black women have stayed in the black movement despite many injustices."[68] Black feminist and historian E. Frances White remarked that she read Black Power authors like Ron Karenga, whose opinions on women influenced her and other young black women "to turn away from the nationalist position."[69] They were unwilling to engage with men whose politics offended them.

Like the civil rights movement, there are cohort differences in the black liberation movement. Most of the voices we have just heard, women like Toni Cade, Kathleen Cleaver, and Nikki Giovanni, were part of the earliest Black Arts and Black Power generation. Although there were only a few years between them, younger women were often less directly engaged with Black Power and Black Arts movement male leaders. To give one example, Black Arts women were older than most Black Panther party recruits, many of whom were teenagers when they affiliated with the party. Other African-American female adolescents and young women were profoundly influenced by Black Power activists of all kinds, who were not much older than themselves, although the younger women did not necessarily affiliate with any organization. Writer Jill Nelson noted that her generation "listened, read, learned, soaked up the spirit of change from activists only a few years older than us," and while the younger women were not at the forefront of the movement, their lives were shaped by the 1960s.[70] Younger women were more likely to embrace feminism, but few women of any cohort have written accounts of their time in the Black Power movement.

An unwillingness to speak and write about their experiences is in part due to a desire to protect vulnerable organizations and members against outsiders. Remarking on the autobiographies of radical black activist women Angela Davis, Assata Shakur, and Elaine Brown, scholar Margo Perkins noted that in addition to silences about their personal lives, "their texts withhold other kinds of information, especially that which might undermine the image of the Movement or imperil the welfare of other activists."[71] Similar sentiments were noted by Black Panther party historians who interviewed former female members in the 1990s. Angela Brown observed that women were worried about talking about abuse by men in the party because there are so many people "who want to focus on that and cast a negative tint on the whole party. . . . there's a fear that that might implicate the party."[72] Historian Tracye Matthews wrote that many did not want to talk to an outsider about the gender and sexual politics of the organization. Others hadn't processed the experiences or still found the memories "too fresh and too painful to discuss." She noted that some people were "unconvinced that this was an appropriate, let alone, necessary or important line of historical inquiry."[73] Some objected that the Black Panther party was no more sexist than any other movement group or the larger society, and that by focusing on a negative issue, young African Americans would be distracted from learning about the positive contributions of organizations like the party.[74] Decades later, former activists are still reviewing their experiences and remain conflicted and often reluctant to talk about them. One former female Panther member said, "To this day I'm still sorting out what was the good part and what would I have done differently today."[75] Such comments suggest that these experiences, like those of feminist movement activists', are in a permanent state of transition. They are alive still, inflected with the present, unfinished in participants' minds. Movement activists' self-consciousness about how their history is told, particularly when they still feel intensely loyal, as in the Black Panther party, is striking. Black women have been particularly cautious, reflecting, perhaps, a pattern of male dominance from those years.

But male dominance was only part of the story. Like women in the civil rights, New Left, and antiwar movements, young female participants grew stronger personally and politically within movement environments despite conventional gender expectations. Often under great pressure, women and men worked, loved, and tried to fashion a new revolutionary life together. Custom was breached here, not so much in terms of the civil rights movement's empowerment of southern blacks in relation to whites, but in young black women's redefinition of themselves as beautiful, as warriors and leaders, by changing the way they saw themselves and were seen by others. The movement was alive with possibility and excitement. In contrast to early experiences of racism and fear, Black Power made young women feel proud, strong, and beautiful. Black consciousness reinforced black culture and black bodies, affirmed black skin, hair, and body shape. They let their hair grow out into Afros and presented themselves in new clothes, styles, and attitudes. Paula Giddings told of the 1966 response to the homecoming queen at Howard University who was political and the first to wear her hair in an Afro as she was presented on stage. The auditorium exploded when, before they could see her clearly, they saw the silhouette of her hair on stage and began chanting "Black Power."[76] Gloria Wade-Gayles noted that her "straightened hair became a weight pulling my head down when I wanted to hold it up. High." She decided to wear an Afro as "a badge, a symbol of my self-esteem and racial pride."[77] And Gloria Hull wrote:

> This decision to wear my hair in an Afro was, of course, a rejec-
> tion of one definition of gender/woman/the feminine in favor of
> another, a rejection of white for black. More suggestively, it
> could almost (though not quite) be read as a rejection of gender
> *for* race, and this indicates the crying need African American
> women have always had to think and feel both race and gender
> into one body/formulation/framework.[78]

Wearing an Afro empowered the women, but they noticed that radical men had not changed accordingly. Michele Wallace wrote that, in 1968 when she was sixteen, she started to wear her hair natural and to reshape her life: "Blackness meant . . . that I could finally be myself." She discarded all of her mainstream clothes and props and began to "think about being someone again. I thanked Malcolm and LeRoi—wasn't it their prescription that I was following?" She continued with the famous quotation, "It took me three years to fully understand that Stokely was serious when he'd said my position in the movement was 'prone,' three years to understand that the countless speeches that all began 'the black man' did not include me." She discovered that black men had strong ideas about the way that black women should look and behave, that "she was on probation as a black woman," and any signs that she was too independent or aggressive meant that she would end up alone since no black man would want her.[79] Assata Shakur, an imprisoned militant when she wrote this in 1978, recalled how liberated she was by the Black Power movement and at the same time bitterly recounted how she and her sisters dressed in African clothes and

> rejected our foremothers and ourselves as castrators. We did
> penance for robbing the brother of his manhood, as if we were
> the oppressor. I remember the days of the Panther party when
> we were "moderately liberated." When we were allowed to wear
> pants and expected to pick up the gun. The days when we gave

doe-eyed looks to our leaders. The days when we worked like
dogs and struggled desperately for the respect which they struggled desperately not to give us.[80]

Margaret Sloan, a future organizer and chair of the National Black Feminist Organization, participated in a rent strike at the age of fourteen. She
recalled "walking into that building and seeing women of different colors
in various either 'prone' positions or servile situations," making food and
taking care of the children while the men performed "the serious busi-
ness" of planning a demonstration. Sloan noted that, as a woman, no
matter how much you worked what really counted was your relationship
to the men: "It really mattered how well you performed at night. And who
you attached yourself to."[81] Women's observations are painfully contradictory: in the midst of a liberating political awakening, they recalled
their ambiguous position. They let their hair go natural and felt elated
about their new racial identities and perspectives but noticed that the
men were in charge and making the rules, even about what clothes Black
Panther women should wear.

Angela Davis was the first woman she wanted to be like, recalled author Jill Nelson: "She was smart, beautiful, political, outspoken, talented,
self-defined, single, and famous."[82] A political prisoner from 1970 to 1972,
Davis became an inspiring role model for eighteen-year-old Nelson and
other young black radical women.[83] Nelson "wore a 'Free Angela' button,
handed out leaflets, attended rallies of support. I devoured everything I
could find written by or about her, wanting to know what a Communist really was, how revolution worked." She wrote that Davis suggested that what
it meant to be a woman in America was not only physical but political.[84] As
a teenager, she was also attracted to the aggressive stance of SNCC leaders
Stokely Carmichael and H. Rap Brown: "When Stokely Carmichael terrifies
America by simply daring to combine the words black and power, we
cheer."[85] She and her friends styled themselves after activists slightly older
than they. She wrote of visiting the Black Panther party:

> I remember the men in the cramped office, dressed all in black,
> seemed much older than I was, incredibly intense, and vaguely
> threatening, the confluence of sex and revolutionary violence
> hung so thick around them I could smell it. I don't remember
> seeing any women around. Maybe they were in the back, taking
> care of business.[86]

Critical of the antifemale politics of nationalism despite the fact that she was seduced by its rhetoric and style, Nelson wrote, "Twenty years later, it is clear that not forcing the black nationalist movement to deal with its own patriarchy and chauvinism was a fatal mistake."[87]

Young women who joined the Black Panther party recounted stories of complicated observations and transformations as well. Tondalela Woolfolk, sixteen years old in 1966, told of going to a Black Panther party rally: "There was this feeling of excitement. These black guys [Black Panthers] came in. They were real black and big. They had a lot of pride about them. I found that to be exciting because white people were afraid of them."[88] In 1969, she joined the New York City chapter of the party, having been deeply moved by meeting Panther Ericka Huggins, a political prisoner in a New Haven jail whose Panther husband had been murdered in Los Angeles. But Woolfolk felt pressure to have sex with Panther men: "The brothers tried to put pressure on the sisters, saying that this was something that they were required to do. . . . The whole sex thing in the party was a little out of hand."[89] And the guns and police violence frightened her. She left New York and went to Chicago, where she had grown up and where party members were from her community. Fred Hampton, the chair there, had different ideas about sexual relations and women's role in the revolution: "It had nothing to do with being prone."[90] In the Chicago chapter, she didn't feel pressured and judged if she resisted men's advances.

Gloria Abernathy grew up in Northern California and was sixteen when she saw armed Panthers march into the California legislature in 1967. She joined the party in 1968 and became a political activist. All of her friends were in the party and she was totally involved in the group, selling Panther newspapers, community organizing, participating in military drills, and studying Marxism-Leninism. Unlike Woolfolk, she felt that life in the party was no different for men or women, that what you did was "determined by your own inclination and personality."[91] In the context of discussing how to use and clean guns, Abernathy said that she didn't believe that there "was discrimination based on sex, anymore than in the general community at the time." Abernathy saw herself as part of the third world struggle, connected to people around the globe who were against American imperialism. Eventually she became disillusioned by the drugs and violence of the members and by the fact that rank-and-file members were treated differently than the leadership, who didn't have to work and yet had more money, nicer clothes, and better places to live. She left in

1973 when she realized that the antidrug rules in the party were not observed and that leader Huey Newton was an addict. Both Abernathy and Woolfolk joined the Black Panther party to end police brutality; to feed, clothe, and educate the community; and to find other solutions to racism than nonviolent strategies. They shared a sense of excitement and romanticism that, in Woolfolk's words, led her to be willing "to die in the revolution, to die to make things right. . . . At least my life would be for something."[92] Both women "experienced the liberation of being totally committed and dedicated to a cause."[93] They have no regrets.

Regina Jennings became interested in the Black Panther party at sixteen and joined in 1968 because she wanted to "smash racism in America." A teenage runaway, she took a plane from Philadelphia to Oakland to join the party. She was "ready to become a Panther. Their mystique—the black pants, leather jackets, berets, guns, and their talk—aggressive and direct— attracted me and thousands more across America." She described herself as an angry, antiwhite young woman with a drug habit, "without race pride or self-respect." She saw Huey Newton and Bobby Seale speaking about race, defying racist oppression, and arguing for self-defense, saw the Panthers with guns at the California state capitol, and believed she "had finally found [her] calling."[94] She was deeply impressed by the courage of the party. Jennings was transformed as a Panther, kicked her drug habit, and became committed to the community, working in the programs the Panthers sponsored to provide free breakfasts for schoolchildren and other youth activities. She attended history classes, taught from an Afrocentric perspective, and political education classes where they studied revolution in the third world, read Mao, saw the film *The Battle of Algiers*, and went to exercise classes early each morning. They "blew" poetry of various Panther members "plus the precious words of Sonia Sanchez and Haki Madhubuti."[95]

Jennings said, "All I had ever wanted was to be a soldier. I did not want to be romantically linked with any of my comrades, and even though I gave my entire life to the party—my time, my energy, my will, my clothes, my money, and my skills," her (older) superior in the organization pursued her. He had been helpful and supportive but when she refused his advances, he made her life miserable: "I lacked maturity and the skill necessary to challenge authoritarian men so I searched for ways to circumvent the sexism of my captain." In the early years of the party, there were no procedures for challenging an officer. She tried to get help from

Black Panther party members at a political education class,
New York City, 1971. Stephen Shames. Polaris Images.

the Central Committee, but the all-male panel said that she should not
"behave as a bourgeois woman and bring such values to the party. They
believed that my attitude of sexual abstinence was both foolish and
counter-revolutionary." Although Jennings noted that "there were women
who came through the Party and would immediately leave because of the
vulgar male behavior," she and others held on because of the importance
of the organization. She recognized that not all male Panthers were sexist
and that the party was under siege, facing critical problems such as state
repression, political division, prison, exile, and police brutality. "Sexism
was a significant factor in weakening the structure of the Black Panther
Party," said Jennings. Nevertheless, she, like the other women, is still in
awe of the dedication of Panthers who spent every waking moment working for the people, who were willing to die for the people and sometimes
did.[96]

Influenced by African students from Columbia University whom she
met in New York City, Assata Shakur went to Manhattan Community
College and City College during the Black Power years, became a militant,
and briefly joined the New York chapter of the Black Panther party in 1969
or 1970. As a young woman, she changed her image of herself: no more

Black Panthers from Sacramento during a Free Huey rally
at Bobby Hutton Memorial Park, Oakland, California, 1968.
© 1968 Pirkle Jones.

"frying" her hair; she let it grow into an Afro as a way of affirming he
Africanness and blackness: "[I] think it's important for us to look and fee
like strong, proud Black men and women who are looking toward Afric
for guidance." She learned about slave rebellions and black resistance an
was ecstatic. "You couldn't catch me without a book in my hand. . . .
read everything from J. A. Rogers to Julius Lester. From Sonia Sanche
and Haki Madhubuti (Don L. Lee). I saw plays by Black playwrights lik
Amiri Baraka and Ed Bullins. It was amazing."[97] Although she had doub
about the New York chapter of the Black Panther party because of the a
rogant and disrespectful attitude of their spokesmen, she became an ac
tive member. She left the party because of the disorganization, chaos, irr
sponsibility, disloyalty, expulsions, and distance between the leadersh
and most of the members (although she continued to be involved in rad

cal black political work and was imprisoned for it). Nevertheless, she said she has been "blessed with meeting some of the kindest, most courageous, most principled, most informed and intelligent people on the face of the earth," and that "[t]he Black liberation movement has done more for me than i [sic] will ever be able to do for it."[98]

It is impossible not to be moved by the dedication and love these women felt for the Black Panther party. For them, as for other members, the party became their whole life. Women of the Black Power movement, and particularly those who belonged to organizations like the Black Panther party, often had to break with their families, who rejected their politics, for their new communal and movement families.[99] When the activity came to an end, their emotions echoed the devastated civil rights activists who felt they had lost the most meaningful part of their lives. Black Panther party historian Angela Brown said, "A lot of people tell me how difficult it was to transition, once they left the party, because the party was their life. What is it that you do once you're no longer part of this network that you considered family?"[100] A former female member explained, "What affected me most was being cut off from your whole life. All principles and everything you have lived for was just gone. . . . the comradeship, people in the party, and then feeling a part of a larger movement were the things I most valued in the party."[101] The movement became their world. Recognition and construction of a shared African-American culture generated meaningful connections among activists but left them in a void when they dropped out or the movement was no longer viable.[102]

Not only were young women changed by the Black Panther party, some pressed to change the party's gender boundaries. Tracye Matthews, a historian of the party, suggested that in the late 1960s and very early 1970s, struggle was under way that "forced a recognition of the sexism" in black organizations and that black women who organized around issues such as police brutality, racism, poverty, and imperialism significantly affected the development of gender consciousness at the time.[103] The women's liberation movement also played a part in Panther women's consciousness.[104] Female historians of the party, particularly Matthews and Robyn Spencer, argue that female Black Panther party members were "seeking to define a space for themselves in the movement that would value and enhance their potential power as women committed to revolutionary change."[105] Spencer wrote that just because the male leaders "were not ready to answer the question of women's participation doesn't mean that women at the time were not ready to pose it."[106] "Panther women . . . were continually evaluating and assessing the 'appropriate' role of women in the movement, and began doing so publicly in the pages of the Party newspaper as early as 1968."[107] Daily encounters in working and living together and with party leaders were the praxis of a developing, often contradictory, gender ideology. Female Panthers, who at first were called Pantherettes, were concerned about men's egos, and some liked the idea that men were taking charge, but many did not acquiesce, working out more egalitarian personal and political relationships on a daily basis. They walked a fine line between arguing for equality in the party and worrying about overstepping gender boundaries.

Panther politics supported class and national liberation struggles in which women fought alongside men. Panther women modeled themselves after Vietnamese women who were soldiers with men in a guerrilla army.[108] In line with Marxist and Maoist politics, Panther women argued that women were part of the proletarian and third world revolutions, that their liberation would coincide with a successful revolution for all men and women. About a 1970 Washington, D.C., Panther rally, the feminist newspaper *off our backs* reported, "Afeni Shakur, speaking about black women, said that they didn't need a separate women's liberation organization, but would be liberated within the context of their struggle as black people."[109] Nevertheless, Matthews suggested, "Although women in the BPP generally chose not to work in female-only organizations, and most did not think of themselves as feminists, this did not necessarily mean that they accepted male chauvinism or sexism. Most expected to be treated as equals, as revolutionary comrades, by their male counterparts."[110] The absence of feminist ideology, she argued, did not translate into an acceptance of inequality. Spencer's study of the sixteen-year history of the Oakland chapter acknowledged male chauvinism, a division of labor based on gender, and physical abuse of women, but by the 1970s, she suggested, the Panthers had transformed themselves.

Both Matthews and Spencer have argued that over time women became more prominent in the party, that the situation varied from chapter to chapter, and that some chapters had a good deal of contact with women's liberation organizations.[111] Women, for example, were central and respected in the Chicago chapter, partly because of the climate fostered by its young leader, Fred Hampton. Even after his murder, women were key to the growth of the Chicago and Illinois party.[112] Chroniclers of

Black Panther party members speak at Yale during a rally for Bobby Seale, chair of the Black Panther party, who was on trial in New Haven, Connecticut, 1970. Stephen Shames. Polaris Images.

the Black Panther party have remarked that women were the backbone of the daily programs, such as breakfast for children, community services, and schools which, by the 1970s, were all that remained of the party's activities. Matthews and Spencer did not want to claim Panther women as feminists, a label with which members would not have self-identified. But their research, along with that of historian Angela LeBlanc-Ernest, suggested that gender relations changed for the better in Oakland, particularly when, in Huey Newton's absence, Elaine Brown became chair in 1974, and more women got involved: "The increased presence of women, the shift from a paramilitary to a community service focus, the incarceration, assassination, and exile of key male leaders, and the increasing pressures of state-sponsored repression, all affected the internal dialogue about gender roles."[113]

The Black Panther party was more internationalist than nationalist,

Black Panther party free food giveaway, Oakland, California.
Stephen Shames. Polaris Images.

more Marxist and leftist politically, more willing to work with white radicals and to engage in issues relating to sexuality and gender than other Black Power groups. This ideological perspective differed from those who espoused black separatism and cultural nationalism in that the Panthers embraced international, anticolonial, third world, and class perspectives and were open to coalitions with whites. By the 1970s, even Huey Newton, at least nominally, supported women's liberation and the gay liberation movement.[114] Unlike most Black Power perspectives, which supported gender complementarity and keeping women and men in their respective places, the Panthers' Marxist/Maoist modernist ideology provided a language with which women could struggle to define new gender identities. Women expected more precisely because of the Panthers' revolutionary rhetoric, which was absent in more ideologically rigid cultural nationalist groups, such as those led by Amiri Baraka and Ron Karenga.[115]

There is a problem with these arguments, however. That proportionately more women were in the party and in leadership positions in the 1970s is not straightforward evidence of a less chauvinist organization. According to LeBlanc-Ernest, between 1972 and 1973, women were about 45 percent of the total membership and in the forefront of the party. Kathleen Cleaver suggested, however, that by 1974 the Black Panther party was decimated, with only a few branch offices left outside of Oakland. By then, according to Spencer, women ran almost everything in Oakland, but membership was fewer than 100. To say, then, that women and community programs had become central, indicating a progressive ideological gender shift in the 1970s, is misleading since by most accounts the party had fallen apart. It was less male-dominated because there were many fewer men. A number of factors, particularly the attrition of male leadership due to incarceration, murder, and exile, contributed to women's more prominent place in the organization after its heyday.[116] Black feminist Cellestine Ware put it bluntly, "The Black Panthers have hitherto allowed women little significant voice in strategy and communications. But the Panther men are now often in jails or in graveyards and, for the first time in many chapters, women are now as prominent as men."[117] Only when the party declined were women able to get ahead.

Even in its heyday, women's experiences were complex. Panther women were threatened and attacked by the police and were as brave as the men.[118] They were arrested alongside men and faced an equality of mistreatment in the streets and in prison. This, female Panther scholars have suggested, pressured the men in the party to change their views—to respect women more. Courageous Ericka Huggins, in jail and pregnant after her husband had been murdered by police, became a role model for women (including radical white women). Coincident with police brutality and the siege conditions in which they lived, women embraced a "macho style" in order to be heard and respected, as Elaine Brown showed in her autobiography, *A Taste of Power: A Black Woman's Story*. She and others adopted an aggressive, manipulative, and cool posture to challenge men's notions that community defense was a man's job and that women could not be warriors.[119] Many women didn't like the "arrogant fuck-you style"—in Assata Shakur's words—of the Panthers but conformed, nonetheless, in the face of police and FBI harassment and the military ideology of the early years.[120] The historians argue that the rise in Panther women's status as courageous police victims generated more egalitarian notions of comradeship in the party, an argument that makes violence and militarism a route to equality.

Black liberation heroine Angela Davis's retrospective thoughts on this issue are revealing. She remembered her own "responses to romanticized images of brothers (and sometimes sisters) with guns. And, in actuality, it was empowering to go to target practice and shoot—or break down a weapon—as well, or better, than a man."[121] Here Davis revealed the complexity of the time for women, in this case about the appeal of militarization and violent revolution.[122] While acknowledging a problem with masculine notions of revolution, she was simultaneously drawn to it. Davis recognized that she could do most things, whether it was taking political initiative or shooting a gun, as well as or better than a man, but had to fight to maintain her position. In a review of Black Panther Elaine Brown's autobiography, Davis wrote that Brown's story "reveals some of the myriad ways revolutionary practice was conceived as quintessentially masculinist."[123] Women fighters throughout the third world were inspiring to radical women. As the violence escalated, some American radicals, women among them, came to believe that armed revolution was inevitable. Guns, bombs, and military maneuvers occupied their minds and activities. "When women appeared in the radical imagination of the 1960s and 1970s, it was often as the iconic gun-slinging, baby-toting, Afro-coifed Amazon warrior."[124] Commenting on her involvement in black liberation groups, Davis said, "Eventually, I purchased a weapon myself and underwent serious training in its use. Like Masai, the father of Brown's child, I also found myself using funerals and shootings as the most obvious signposts of the passage of time."[125] That some women, those in the Black Panther party and the Weatherman faction of Students for a Democratic Society in particular, joined the militarization that has been called masculinist, complicates notions of expanding gender consciousness.[126]

Also complicating notions of growing gender equality are a number of women's stories, including Elaine Brown's, that tell of sexual abuse in the revolutionary organizations they joined. Many Black Panther party women were subjected to sexual harassment and pressured to have sex with male comrades, who argued that it was the women's revolutionary duty.[127] Regressive gender and sexual politics included an apparently liberated, nonpossessive sexuality in which no one "belonged" to any one person.[128] For women, this meant pressure to accept numerous partners, and, if they became pregnant, to be responsible for the children. Birth control was actively discouraged as a form of black genocide inflicted by the white power structure. In addition, women were encouraged to have babies who would become part of the black revolution.[129] Margo Perkins wrote that Elaine Brown's autobiography suggested "ways in which the spirit of sexual freedom and openness during the era was often manipulated to reinscribe patriarchal privilege."[130] Thus, even in a revolutionary movement (not uncommon in radical movements), some Panther women experienced a traditional and threatening version of the heterosexuality they had known prior to the movement. Nevertheless, as members of a dangerous organization, both because of its militant revolutionary politics and the state's efforts to cripple the party, they considered gender equality to be less critical than life-and-death issues.

Wherever their location, radical African-American women's accounts and histories attest to how they were changed by the Black Power movement: by objecting to Black Arts poets' male chauvinism, deciding to wear their hair naturally, discovering Afrocentricity, joining a revolutionary organization, analyzing capitalism, and thinking through and contending with gender. Many young, primarily northern, black women had grown up in segregation in working-class or poor families. The civil rights movement's goal of equality was formative, but it was southern and under way when they were still children. Black Power galvanized them, as did the urban rebellions. The cultural environment of the Black Arts movement, the poetry, manifestos, and theater along with the words and images of Malcolm X, Stokely Carmichael, Huey Newton, and Angela Davis, permeated their worlds. The movement inspired them to see themselves, their country, and their futures in a new way. Their lives were changed, although not entirely. The explicit male celebration and the centrality of the black man in Black Power politics replicated the gender politics of the dominant society. Many women, unaware of or supportive at first of the patriarchal current in nationalism, had no choice but to eventually confront the sexism. In the words of black activist Barbara Omolade: "Among themselves, sisters balked at being mere supporters and complained of male chauvinism—while maintaining a united front with men against white racism."[131]

Although many found family and home in the Black Power movement, their hopes of unambiguous cross-gender solidarity were unfulfilled—although high hopes for social reform and change were almost impossible to maintain by the late 1960s. All movement activists were shaken by the assassinations of President John F. Kennedy, Malcolm X, Dr. Martin Luther King, Jr., and presidential candidate Robert Kennedy; by the war in Vietnam; and by the escalating instability and violence at home. Reflecting back, writer Michele Wallace wrote poignantly, "Those years from 1966 to 1970 during which Black Power and Women's Liberation flowered were also the years in which the political and philosophical weight of the black woman was either erased or divided between black men and white women, who then proceeded to go their separate ways, pulling her apart in the process."[132] Solidarity fueled by hope, in this case cross-gender solidarity, frayed as many women realized they were unable to thoroughly rely on their brothers. Women shaped by Black Power learned the limits of that movement for women and inevitably had no choice but to relinquish visions of easy male and female solidarity. The movement's shift from an interracial ideal in the early 1960s to the goal of a separate black nation and culture was disrupted by intraracial tensions between women and men. Black women had begun this segment of their political journey for justice by substituting racial bonding for racial integration but gradually realized they were on their own, facing dilemmas peculiar to their sex and race.

Learning about Racism White Socialist Feminism

and Bread and Roses

> The trinity of race/class/gender that became the watchword of
> 1980s multiculturalism in fact had an early career in the
> women's liberation movement, which universalized women's
> experience yet also sought to pay attention to the impact of
> class, race and national oppressions. Popular pamphlets of
> the 1960s and 1970s described all women as subordinated
> and simultaneously emphasized the special oppression of
> women of color and working-class women.
> —Lise Vogel, *Woman Questions:*
> *Essays for a Materialist Feminism* (1995)

By the end of the 1960s, young, white radical women were streaming out of the New Left and anti–Vietnam War movement and enthusiastically organizing what was to become their own mass movement, feminism. Gender contradictions in society and experiences as political activists contributed to the development of the women's movement and its goal of achieving equality with men. The early women's liberation movement consisted of a number of political currents characterized as liberal, radical, and socialist feminist. Liberal feminism had begun earlier in the postwar period and was the most accessible and effective wing in its focus on combating legal aspects of inequality and eliminating government and workplace sex discrimination. Many participants were professionals with careers. Radical and socialist feminists, younger than liberal feminists, were more closely linked to the New Left and antiwar movement. Based on their critiques of men and capitalism, they were not interested in assimilating into the male-dominated capitalist system. Although these feminists were all political radicals, the term *radical feminism* came to mean women who believed that men were the problem—men controlled the power, were the source of women's subordination, and benefited from women's secondary status in all political and economic systems. Radical feminists were less likely to struggle with men, finding it easier to leave men behind or form all-women's groups to achieve their goals. Socialist feminists were anticapitalists whose political goal was a socialist and feminist society. They did not believe that women could achieve equality in a capitalist system, but saw men as their comrades in the movements and were more attached to the mixed movements than were radical feminists. The most politically leftist, they are the feminists in whom we are most interested.

Some socialist feminists had been SNCC activists, and most were involved in radical politics. Even if they had not been directly involved in the civil rights movement, they were inspired by it and came to feminism with ideals about an interracial movement. By the mid- and late 1960s, their ideals had been tested. They had seen the Black Power movement organize itself on the basis of race and leave sympathetic whites behind. They noted male chauvinism among their male comrades and, over time, painfully withdrew from men to organize their own movement. White women were experiencing difficult losses but continued to organize and think about how to build a united white and black women's movement. It didn't happen in the early years but not for lack of white women trying. They had to revise their ideas and understanding, including their ideals, as the reality of race and difference sank in. Their hopes had been heightened by the promise of the civil rights movement, but they were rejected by black women who were more interested in black solidarity than in white women's liberation, who could not find a place for themselves in the white socialist feminist movement.

One of the most unacknowledged and important factors that kept white socialist feminists from successfully connecting with black women is that most black women were on another path and simply were not interested in white feminism in the late 1960s. Many were still engaged with the Black Power movement. In 1968, civil rights activist and feminist Chude Pam Allen noted, "[W]e are very aware of the fact that a lot of middle class black women want nothing to do with us because we are white and it is very difficult to see any potential for alliance."[1] Another feminist activist, Jo Freeman, angrily recalled, "Our contacts with minority women were few, despite our roots in the Civil Rights Movement and community organizing projects. The message white women got from black activists was to stay away; our presence, our ideas, our whiteness was oppressive."[2] About her feminist movement experiences, historian Sara Evans wrote that race became more and more important in white women's minds, "though, to be honest, in those Black Power years we were mostly waiting for black women to tell us what to think about them."[3] They made efforts nonetheless and waited for signals from black women that did not come; they reached out to them and were met with indifference or anger. Most radical black women's attention was focused on black nationalist politics and culture. They were angry at white women and wary of them and the white women's liberation movement. An intricate racial dynamic operated in which the disconnect came from both sides.

Despite the fact that these years were filled with separations that strained movement visions of solidarity, white women were exhilarated by activism, which created a sense of purpose and community in primarily white groups. Through it all, a version of idealism, of universalism, continued to vie with the racial and gender realities white feminists faced. As they deepened their understanding of racial and gender politics, interracial visions did not disappear but assumed new contours. The rest of this book considers the development of white and black socialist feminism separately and together. This chapter presents the ideas and activities of white socialist feminists with close attention to Bread and Roses, a Boston socialist feminist organization formed in 1969. Numerous such groups appeared around the same time throughout the country, primarily in urban areas and college towns. The next chapter examines the politics of black socialist feminism, with a focus on the Combahee River Collective, also located in Boston.

The controversial memos censuring sexism in the movements and society that white SNCC organizers Mary King and Casey Hayden had written in 1964 and particularly the 1965 memo that they sent not only to SNCC women but to activist women in SDS, the National Student Association, the Northern Student Movement, and the Student Peace Union, had repercussions throughout the movements.[4] Most black female civil rights workers criticized the memos as irrelevant to their concerns, but Hayden and King's 1965 "Sex and Caste: A Kind of Memo" stimulated white activist women in the North to act on male chauvinism in the movement. In historian Sara Evans's analysis of the development of feminist consciousness from the civil rights movement to SDS and into the flowering of radical, youthful, second wave feminism, she considered an early 1965 SDS workshop, directly inspired by the Hayden and King memo and convened by women to discuss women in the movement and society, to be "the real embryo of the new feminist revolt." She noted that it took two years for the new insurgency to come to fruition, during which time gender consciousness percolated among white women activists in SDS and ERAP (the Economic Research and Action Project), SDS's community organizing projects, and the antiwar, draft resistance, and student movements.[5]

At the April 1967 national council meeting of SDS, women's liberation became a public and explosive issue in the New Left. In Evans's words, "The Dam Breaks" in 1967, when a generation of young women in the New Left, building on experiences in SNCC, ERAP, and other movement organizations, began to recognize and reject male chauvinism.[6] They publicly objected to women's subordinate status in the movement and society, challenging movement men to recognize sexism as a significant political issue. After two years of sporadic debate, the issue came to the fore at the National Conference for a New Politics (NCNP) in August 1967, which was an attempt to unify numerous New Left organizations into a more coherent movement.

According to feminist historians, during the meeting of more than 2,000 leftists, white women found white men overly deferential to Black Power activists and platforms while they were contemptuous of women's demands.[7] Drawing on the model of the black caucus and of Black Power, women demanded acknowledgment of and action on women's issues, including proportional representation on committees. They were ignored and demeaned. Convinced that women should organize themselves separately around their own oppression, they immediately convened a women's liberation meeting in Chicago. Writing about that time, Chicago movement activist and early women's liberationist Vivian Rothstein reflected:

> Building an American women's liberation movement was a matter of survival for politically conscious and skilled women in the late 1960s. We were smart, we were dedicated, we had revolutionary ideas—but who besides ourselves gave a damn? We had hit the glass ceiling on the left and there was nowhere for us to go. We were hungry for political discussion with others who took us seriously, and we slowly began to find each other.[8]

The Chicago group wrote a call in 1967, "To Women of the Left," arguing against male chauvinism and for justice and equality for women. They wrote that women must not make "the same mistake the blacks did at first of allowing others (whites in their case, men in ours) to define our issues, methods and goals. Only we can and must define the terms of our struggle."[9] Sara Evans reflected:

> [T]he new flood of self-conscious feminism flowed into the channels left by seven years of movement activity. Through a network of personal friendship, organized media and events the word spread until within a year there was hardly a major city without one or more "women's liberation groups," as they called themselves.[10]

Women who had been friends or acquaintances, usually through movement participation, convened in major cities such as New York, Boston, Baltimore, Washington, and San Francisco, and in college towns across the United States; the response was astonishing. White movement women began to organize an independent women's movement.

Around the country, women who shared a New Left history enthusiastically created the radical, anticapitalist, and socialist feminist women's liberation movement. Despite the socialist feminist groups' variations in their emphases, for example, on how activist, theoretical, divided by lesbianism, or inclined toward organizing they were, it was the first time they were able to talk about themselves, and they were thrilled to recognize that their issues were politically legitimate. And talk they did. Nancy Hawley, an early Bread and Roses member, described a dinner where women got together for the first time:

> The flood broke loose gradually and then more swiftly. We talked about our families, our mothers, our fathers, our siblings; we talked about our men; we talked about school; we talked about "the movement" (which meant new left men). For hours we talked and unburdened our souls and left feeling high and planning to meet again the following week.[11]

Movement activist and feminist Jo Freeman wrote that the small groups that were the basis of the movement "form and dissolve at such a rate that no one can keep track of them."[12] One early Chicago women's liberation organizer stated, "I have never known anything as easy as organizing women's groups—as easy and as exciting and as dramatic."[13]

Movement women were the organizers of socialist feminism, although others joined almost immediately, as they joined all branches of feminism. Growing recognition of sexism led them to reject the roles they had been assigned in the movements and their treatment by movement men. Women began to meet without men to explore their situations and in these settings made connections between capitalism and male dominance, eventually rejecting the idea that female equality, or racial equality, could be achieved in a capitalist society. For years, they had been devoted members of New Left groups. Bread and Roses historian Ann Popkin wrote, "For many, the new left was their hope as the agent of change; it was their community, and their 'family,'" a point that echoes Black Panther women's sentiments about the powerful place they had found in the movement.[14] Like women in the civil rights and Black Power movements, they struggled with ties to men and movements that had been fundamental to their political consciousness and activism. Goaded by male criticism that they were weakening the struggle for socialism by focusing on their own issues, they initiated a rupture from the movements which had shaped them. Despite feelings of ambivalence, articulated in volatile relationships with mixed leftist groups, particularly the antiwar movement, growing numbers of women began to realize that an autonomous women's movement was necessary. They were angry that movement men did not recognize and take seriously the significance of women's subordination and that they were accused of fragmenting and weakening the New Left by being selfishly self-indulgent (bourgeois) in their (middle-class) concerns.

Like radical black women, socialist feminists struggled to define themselves in relation to the mixed or male Left. Leslie Cagan, an activist in New York City and subsequently in Boston, stated:

> We had to deal with the fact that the Panthers were being shot down, we couldn't ignore the war in Vietnam. I didn't know how to do it, how to pull it all together. So I felt and acted as if I were several different people all at once; I was an anti-war activist; I was a Panther support person; I was a feminist and my women's group probably had the biggest impact on me.[15]

Complex commitments and divided loyalties characterized early socialist feminist politics. "Emerging from an active social movement meant that younger feminists had to work to separate themselves from their parent movement," wrote Benita Roth in her analysis and explanation of the concurrent links and divisions feminist women faced as they disconnected from the New Left. Their experiences in the civil rights movement and New Left had provided them with tools, skills, and networks they could apply to their own organizations, but they were understandably ambivalent about dropping their long-standing connections to the New Left.[16] Women divided between those who believed that capitalism was at the heart of women's oppression, which meant that they maintained their connections to the male Left, while the feminists, who ultimately prevailed, argued that women should not continue their subordination in the Left, that not only capitalism but also male supremacy were responsible for women's oppression. This is often referred to as the politico/feminist split.[17] Bread and Roses members maintained ties to the Left but recognized the significance of patriarchy and became increasingly feminist over time. They spent a great deal of time and energy analyzing their relationship to the New Left, torn about whether an autonomous women's movement was necessary.

In the words of two Bread and Roses members, "We have tried to voice our opinions as members of male-dominated organizations. We are tired of trying to out-argue men. . . . Sexist attitudes are so deeply ingrained in even movement males that our words are not strong enough to change their thought processes or actions." They complained, "We were usually relegated to positions of typists, office clerks, janitors, and flunkeys [sic] in these organizations; our opinions were seldom asked for and rarely heard. The processes and priorities of the male Left alienated us."[18] When they did break away to form autonomous groups, they were often thrilled. A Chicago activist wrote years later, in 1998, "So after years of feeling judged and humiliated by the male heavies of the new left, I finally felt that I had political comrades—people with whom I could develop ideas without feeling judged or dismissed. . . . Suddenly and jubilantly, I was released from the need for the approval of the male left establishment." Instead of the "heterosexual chill" of the New Left, Naomi Weisstein described her exhilaration: "All of a sudden we were no longer inaudible! I can hardly describe the joy! Unbelievable!"[19] They organized, too, because women's equality was on the social and political agenda in the postwar period due to women's growing labor-force participation. Profound contradictions existed in the culture in which they had grown up between domestic expectations and growing opportunities available to women.

Many articulated their rage in verbal attacks on movement men.

Feminist writer and activist Robin Morgan's manifesto "Goodbye to All That" expressed fury at white men, "the friends, brothers, lovers in the counterfeit male-dominated left" who degraded and destroyed women and ran and ruined the world. She concluded:

> Women are the real left. We are rising, powerful in our unclean bodies; bright glowing mad in our inferior brains; wild hair flying, wild eyes staring, wild voices keening: undaunted by blood we hemorrhage every twenty-eight days; laughing at our own beauty we who have lost our sense of humor; mourning for all each precious one of us might have been in this one living time-place had she not been born a woman; stuffing fingers into our mouths to stop the screams of fear and hate and pity for men who we have loved and love still; tears in our eyes and bitterness in our mouths for children we couldn't have, or couldn't *not* have, or didn't want, or didn't want *yet*, or wanted and had in this place and this time of horror. . . . POWER TO ALL THE PEOPLE OR TO NONE.[20]

Author Marge Piercy's widely read "The Grand Coolie Damn" stated bitterly, "Movement men are generally interested in women occasionally as bed partners, as domestic-servants-mother-surrogates, and constantly as economic producers: as in other patriarchal societies, one's wealth in the Movement can be measured in terms of the people whose labor one can possess and direct on one's projects."[21] And she wrote even more bitterly: "Fucking a staff into existence is only the extreme form of what passes for common practice in many places. A man can bring a woman into an organization by sleeping with her and remove her by ceasing to do so."[22] Feminist writer Ellen Willis wrote, "All around me I see men who consider themselves dedicated revolutionaries, yet exploit their wives and girlfriends shamefully without ever noticing a contradiction."[23]

Radical white movement women noted a decrease in their sexual capital, as did black women, if they were self-assured organizers and leaders. "[A] woman's acceptance in the movement still depends on her attractiveness, and men do not find women attractive when they are strong-minded and argue like men," wrote female movement activists.[24] Heterosexual women in the civil rights, New Left, and student movements all remark about organizers not being chosen by men as their sexual partners.[25] This was one of several similar experiences that white and black women had in the mixed movements, which they were unable to share because of the racial divide. No matter how many gendered experiences they had in common—for example, providing the labor for the daily routine of organizations, having their contributions and ideas go unheard, and being overlooked as romantic partners, they had no context in which to share them. Both groups faced pressures as they moved out of the mixed movements. There was more at stake for black women who wanted to maintain racial unity, but for both groups the necessity of organizing on their own behalf created divided loyalties. As the 1970s progressed, fractured commitments were not as characteristic of younger feminist activists, who had been less deeply involved with the New Left or the Black Power and Black Arts movements.

African-American and white women both recognized, too, that a social and political system of male supremacy was as much to blame as were individual men. Piercy wrote, "There is much anger here at Movement men, but I know they have been warped and programmed by the same society that has damn near crippled us. My anger is because they have created in the Movement a microcosm of that oppression and are proud of it."[26] The resentment directed at white movement men, and more generally at white men who used their power and influence to maintain inequality and exploit women and poor people, contrasts with the more anguished and ambivalent position of many radical heterosexual black women, who could not afford and often were not inclined to alienate and reject black men. Their anger was combined with sorrow and longing that many white women did not experience. Although heterosexual relationships in the New Left were difficult to negotiate and often broke up painfully, radical white feminists believed they were building a new community of women, which could sustain them personally and politically.

The new social world they would create was not based on stereotyped notions of femininity (or masculinity). Women's liberationists enthusiastically exposed the constricting ideas behind feminine socialization. It dawned on them that they were socialized as girls not to succeed so well that men would not want them, were expected to become wives and mothers and not pursue careers, and were directed for years in school and at work toward feminine pursuits and discouraged from subjects, aspirations, and achievements that were typically masculine. Young, white, middle-class women were taught that their futures depended on a man while they were simultaneously empowered by their experiences of growing up in prosperous postwar America, by encouragement in school and university, sometimes by their families, and by their movement activism. They eventually rejected the narrow gender expectations that Betty Friedan dubbed "the feminine mystique."[27] This was especially true for movement women, a good many of whom had grown up in liberal homes or as red-diaper babies—their parents had been communists or sympathetic to the Communist party—and had been encouraged to achieve and to be actively involved in oppositional and unpopular social movements. Meredith Tax, a Bread and Roses leader, wrote:

> The total structure of a woman's life—her parents, her schooling, the attitudes she absorbs from the mass media, doctors, the law, the men she knows, her job opportunities—all combine to give her a sense of her utter unimportance as a human being. She is dispensible [sic]: a decorative object, a replaceable part, a service station. Her destiny and her sense of herself are both dependent upon men, or a man. She is convinced that it is her place to serve, to efface herself, to live for and through others— brothers, husbands, children.[28]

This statement is not unique for political second wavers. Yet it is extraordinary in its contradictions. Tax suggests that society's communication to young women is of their "utter unimportance," but this is belied by their activism, confidence, anger, indeed by the statement itself. The forceful and indignant articulations of women like Tax were evidence of power they did not know they possessed.[29]

The feminine socialization that young white feminists dismissed was shaped by their race and class positions. Working-class women and women of color were not easily able to imagine themselves as full-time housewives and mothers. The feminine mystique was irrelevant to them. The women around them worked. Marriage was usually not a ticket out of the labor force for any generation. Their socialization could not help but include a recognition of race and class as barriers to the leisurely way of life for which middle-class white girls were being prepared. Echoes of the SNCC debates about the role of women can be heard here. Black SNCC women argued that, unlike white female volunteers, their role models were strong black women, often their mothers, and that they had the self-confidence to tackle almost anything. In contrast, white women worried about narrow gender issues, such as being dependent on a man, not being permitted to work, and being expected to perform stereotypically feminine services, issues that were not of great concern to black women. Feminine socialization was not homogenous across race and class, something that white feminists did not clearly recognize at first.

Another issue that distanced black and white women was whites' analysis of the nuclear family. Women's liberationists undertook a "vehement . . . rhetorical crusade against the nuclear family," suggesting that it was the "catch-all source of all women's oppression, because it seemed that it was primarily through their roles as wives, mothers and daughters that women were 'kept in their place,'" noted historian of Bread and Roses Ann Popkin.[30] Radical feminist Ellen Willis wrote, "[W]ithin the family system, men function as a ruling class, women as an exploited class. Historically, women and their children have been the property of men."[31] "A Proclamation of the Rights of Women," written by Bread and Roses members, made their position clear:

> Our goal is the abolition of the family as an economic unit and as the only socially sanctioned living unit of society. We encourage people to experiment freely with alternate living arrangements. Central to the liberation of women is the provision of alternatives to the present pattern of rearing children in isolation, which results in each mother bearing virtually the entire responsibility for her children. Such alternatives would eliminate the untenable choice most women must make between bearing children and developing independent adult work.

In this document, Bread and Roses members demanded free, community-controlled, round-the-clock childcare centers and good, reasonably priced housing with provisions for communal childcare, cooking, and housekeeping. The proclamation argued, "The state should not interfere in interpersonal relationships between consenting adults" and called for the abolition of all laws concerning marriage and divorce, sexual behavior between consenting persons, and legal distinctions between legitimate and illegitimate children:

> Children should have a choice of living arrangements with relatives, nonrelated adults, other children and any combination of these possibilities. Any number of adults should be able to make legal contracts between themselves, other than marriage

ceremonies, that will concern mutual responsibilities for each other and for children.[32]

Linda Gordon of Bread and Roses outlined the manner in which the nuclear family "harnessed men to provide sustenance for children on the basis of each man providing for his own biological children" and freed men to work by "harnessing women to raise children, each woman with one man's children." The family repressed sexuality, making reproduction its main purpose, and separated "people into small isolated units, unable to join together for common interests." It exploited women in the work force by "training them to look upon their work outside the home as peripheral to their 'true' role" and "chained women to their reproduction function," particularly by assigning them full responsibility for child rearing. Among its other characteristics, the family made private property of children, created families as the central institution of rigid socialization into feminine and masculine sex roles, and trained children to believe that the nuclear family is the "only model for adult life." While all of this is extremely complicated, she concluded, "it is absolutely clear that the nuclear family is an institution of privatization and exploitative division of labor which could not coexist with the kind of true socialism that the women's liberation movement envisions. The nuclear family must be destroyed, and people must find better ways of living together."[33] Her views were echoed in an even more distilled form in a section on the family in a "Draft of Political Program for Bread and Roses, November 1970," which contains the following: "The nuclear family in our society is oppressive; it is a prison to women and children. But it is still the most human thing in many people's lives because it is the only group on which they can *depend*." While condemning the nuclear family, Bread and Roses members simultaneously recognized its significance by suggesting, "We all need a group to come to when we need help, warmth, love, and security. Such a group should not be restricted to biological relatives." To give some idea of the revolutionary nature of their ideas for a new feminist society, they argued that Bread and Roses should set up emergency childcare; organize cooperative childcare centers staffed by men and women and the old and young; struggle to obtain city, state, and corporate tax support for these centers; break down sex roles in the family; seek control of women's bodies; demand paid maternity and paternity leave; and create coops to share food, housekeeping, and appliances.[34]

These almost clinical analyses of the oppression created by the nuclear family are jarring. No shred of sentimentality can be discerned in revolutionary socialist feminist critiques of the family; personal relationships did not intervene in their straightforward political condemnation of the family as the site of women's—and children's—oppression.[35] This did not mean, however, that wrenching family confrontations with parents, siblings, and partners were absent from their lives, but, they argued, more liberating and communal forms of personal life had to be invented that would free everyone, including men, from the coercive nature of sex roles and the family. To put these ideas into practice, some women lived in communes. "Our commune formed in 1971 when social change was in the air and young feminists were questioning the ground rules of marriage, monogamy, and heterosexual relationships. If the conventional family looked like an oppressive institution for women, we would come up with a more workable alternative," wrote socialist feminist Vivian Rothstein retrospectively. She described the Chicago commune in which members shared finances, childcare, and sometimes beds. What seemed at first a hopeful alternative to the traditional family ultimately made her unhappy and doubtful about whether communal living and sisterhood could overcome obstacles such as sexual possessiveness, which had propelled her and her friends into experimenting in the first place. Nevertheless, as she looked back on her commune experience, she still felt "proud of our fearless and serious ambitions. With our own lives we tried to create new social forms that would foster women's autonomy and transcend the isolations imposed by the nuclear family."[36]

In contrast to working-class radical black women who often saw their task as protecting the family as a unique site of resistance to the ravages wrought by racism, white feminists were mechanical and cold in their writings about the family. They were certainly out of touch with the concerns and inclinations of many black and working-class women. Like their characterization of oppressive sex roles, their interpretations of the family were shaped by their middle-class whiteness. As young, privileged, white women, they were not protective of the family and developed an analysis that identified women as its victims, often criticizing their own mothers for accepting a subordinate status. They did not feel that they needed their families of origin, which enabled them to advocate alternative support systems. For black women who had grown up in lower-income families, this was not a helpful critique. It alienated them from white feminists who did not initially appear to absorb the fact that views on gender and families were complicated by race and class. The family was an institution that radical black women admired because parents sacrificed to protect and nurture children in a harsh racist world. Women were often the backbone of the family, and younger women believed that the older women deserved recognition for this. The confident attack on the family by white socialist feminists displayed their unfamiliarity with people different from themselves.

Consciousness-raising (CR) groups were the central organizational form of the new radical movement.[37] Here, too, race and class shaped political ideas and forms. Characterized by "a conscious lack of formal structure, an emphasis on participation by everyone, sharing of tasks, and the exclusion of men," small groups of women met to discuss politics and personal life, in the process changing their consciousness and their lives.[38] Wrote Anita Shreve in her book on the women's movement:

> [W]ithout CR, the movement simply would not have been as powerful. It would not have entered so quickly into the mainstream, nor would it have harnessed the large numbers of middle-class women that it did. In the year 1973 alone, some 100,000 women belonged to CR groups nationwide—making it one of the largest ever educational and support movements of its kind for women in the history of this country.[39]

Forging close bonds with other group members through sharing personal experiences and feelings, women recognized that the problems they faced were social and not simply personal. Writer Vivian Gornick explained, "[A] group of women sitting in a circle discussing their emotional experiences as though they were material for cultural analysis was political dynamite."[40] Each person in the group talked, wrote Ann Popkin about Bread and Roses groups:

> We shared the hurt, confusion, and anger that each of us had harbored inside, and the excitement and relief that came with the act of sharing. Time and again we said, "You too? Whew! I thought it was just me!" We also shared the hope that maybe, just maybe, we could, all together, *do* something to change the world around us so that women would no longer be treated as second-class human beings.[41]

Many in Bread and Roses believed that the way to change one's personal life was not through individual solutions—the consciousness-raising groups were, rather, considered a vehicle that led toward women's activism—but by transforming the structures of society.[42]

One of the slogans associated with the radical women's movement was "the personal is political"—the idea that individual lives were not simply personal and private but were shaped by society, politics, economics, and culture. The goal of consciousness-raising groups was to recognize the political in the private. Margot Adler remembered, "But it wasn't until I was in the company of women, in one of the many hundreds, perhaps thousands, of consciousness raising groups . . . and was listening to the stories of women and telling my own, that I began to understand how similar were many of the threads in our tales." She continued, "I realized that almost every 'weird' thought or feeling I had carried around inside, convinced that it was the product of some personal defect, was shared by millions of other women."[43] Women began to recognize how profoundly shaped they were by notions of femininity that were linked to subordinate status. The idea of psychological oppression was new to young women, who had "deeply internalized the norms of the society" and had "come to think less of ourselves and other women than we did of men. Each woman reproduced the society's power relationships and the values placed on the different sexes in her own psyche and in her own relationships."[44] They learned that even though they were superficially different, there was a similarity in their experiences. One woman described going to a group in which she seemed to have nothing in common with the others. But when they delved more deeply, she discovered that "they all feel pretty much the way I feel. . . . When I saw that what I always felt was my personal hangup was as true for every other woman in that room as it was for me! Well, that's when my consciousness was raised!"[45] The realization that institutionalized male dominance could explain what had appeared to be painful personal shortcomings, that women as a group shared experiences, led to intense feelings of relief and created deep allegiances to feminism.[46] The small group experiences also confirmed the possibility of gender solidarity and bonding. Moments of togetherness made their participants imagine that all women could join and feel connected since they were not yet fully conscious that their whiteness, as well as their gender, made such bonding possible.

As radical as these groups were and as inclusive as their members aimed to be, they did exclude women. Years later, in 1998, feminist writer Shirley Goek-lin Lim bitterly criticized the account of second wave feminism that Sara Evans gave in her 1979 book *Personal Politics*, arguing that the white women who were involved had social capital and networks to which only they belonged: "By social capital I mean the old-girls network, the same-o, same-o circles, telephone trees, college connections." She continued, "The condition that makes possible the intimacy and mutuality so celebrated as core values in Evans's history is exclusivity." Women of color, immigrant women, and blue-collar women did not have the time to participate in consciousness-raising groups and were not comfortable sharing intimate details about their lives: "To say that early consciousness-raising groups 'formed almost instinctively' is to reveal that the members of these groups were unaware that what they saw as universal ideas and cultural experiences were thoroughly alien to masses of other women. Class and race norms, not instinct, fused the unity described as movement strength."[47] In Anita Shreve's book *Women Together, Women Alone*, about the centrality of consciousness-raising groups for second wave feminism, one of the women in a fictional group taking part in a reunion fifteen years later is African American. The narrator remarks that the black woman, JJ, always had more global concerns than the rest of the group and always reminded them of the bigger picture, arguing that consciousness raising and the women's liberation movement did not help most black women. JJ asserts, "Women's Liberation was never intended for women of the underclass. Well, maybe on paper it was, but not in reality. For the most part, solidarity among women refers to women of the middle class, maybe some white women of the working class. That's it."[48]

Both women, one real and one fictional, question the relevance and availability to women of color of the consciousness-raising groups, "rap groups" in Jo Freeman's words, the small groups that were the backbone of the youthful women's movement. White feminists were aware of the issue: "While trying to reach out to women different than ourselves, we still did not basically change the nature of our group. Instead we required that they become more like us to participate."[49] Without question, the success of early consciousness-raising groups was based on the participation of like-minded women.[50] Their participants were primarily white and middle class and, if they were working class, college educated. The experiences they shared as women were shaped by race, class, and education. In addition to networks and shared histories, a common culture facilitated their closeness. The groups certainly would have not worked so easily, even magically in some cases, if they had been more diverse: "Not all women felt comfortable openly discussing sexual topics, nor did all women feel as articulate as the university-trained white women who, for the most part, made up the groups."[51] Consciousness-raising groups were not comfortable for women who were not white and middle class, especially in mixed class and race groups, nor were they part of the networks from which women were invited to join.

White socialist feminists' ability to cut ties with men and families, to focus primarily on gender, and to create intimate, inward-focused groups as the basis of their movement networks revealed their movement's strengths and weaknesses. Wildly energetic, political, active, and open to questioning everything related to the status of women, they were effective in building a grassroots women's liberation movement. As socialist inter-racialists, they intellectually recognized class and race as barriers to feminist solidarity but were not yet fully aware that their politics were unwelcoming, even irrelevant, to African-American women, that their middle-class whiteness inflected their politics as profoundly as race did black women's politics. Their learning curve about race, class, and gender was enormous in the next ten years. But in the late 1960s and early 1970s, white movement feminists' unambivalent anger at men, their willingness to leave their New Left and antiwar communities behind, and their interest in personal issues perpetuated divisions between young white and black women.

Prior to the establishment of Bread and Roses, several regional meetings took place in 1968, one in August in Sandy Springs, Maryland, and another in November in Chicago which, with less than a month's notice, drew more than 200 women from twenty states and Canada. The small conference held in Sandy Springs, with attendees primarily from cities that already had women's liberation groups, such as Boston, New York, Chicago, Washington, D.C., Baltimore, and Gainesville, Florida, has taken on an infamous significance because of white women's discussion of black women.[52] In an appendix to her 1989 book, *Daring to Be Bad: Radical Feminism in America, 1967–1975*, historian Alice Echols published the section of the proceedings devoted to how the fledgling women's liberation movement should relate to African-American women, which has become another contested movement text, part of the story of the women's movement. A historian of black feminism, Kimberly Springer, wrote that the transcript is "riddled with misguided ideas about Black women and feminism." It demonstrated white women's mistrust of black feminists, based on beliefs that they were not really feminists or that they would be disruptive. That white women "refused to recognize the complexity of race and gender oppression" was manifest.[53]

The conference discussion articulated white women's confusion and apprehension about how to include black women, particularly as the white women doubted black women's interest. In her account of this meeting, feminist activist Roxanne Dunbar wrote that she and all of the other, mainly middle-class, women there were "troubled . . . that we were uniformly white-identified." She continued, "I was also bothered that the women at the Sandy Springs meeting said that they believed black women and other minority women would reject women's liberation and accuse white radical women of racism and selfishness for talking about 'our own personal problems.' " Dunbar noted, too, that the women seemed to want the approval of important black women, discussing whose endorsement or presence they could obtain.[54] In Echols's words, "[T]he drama would be played out many times in the future, for the issue of black women's relationship to women's liberation continued to haunt the movement." In retrospect, she believes that "the decision against making overtures to black women was, of course, a terrible mistake." It would have made the situation much more confusing, but, in her words, "[T]his is precisely why black women should have been invited. Had the black women participated, white women would have been less inclined to rely solely on their own experiences when theorizing about women's oppression."[55] Echols continued that it is not clear how black women would have benefited from being there: "[T]hey would have been in the position of having to explain to white women that some of the experiences that they were claiming as common to all women were more particularistic than universal."[56] The small Sandy Springs conference discussion—and its whiteness—foretold racial trouble in early socialist feminism.

Many who attended the Sandy Springs meeting had known each other through movement work, and they went on to Chicago a few months later. An enthusiastic response greeted Boston attendees who returned from Chicago to report on the development of a national women's movement, and local meetings were organized.[57] They discussed the formation of an autonomous women's movement, unaffiliated with the male or mixed movement. Although the women's liberation groups that were forming around the country focused their energies on their own towns and cities, from 1967 on they planned to organize a national women's movement.[58] At the 1968 Chicago meeting, the "discussions were intense, disagreements sharp, and debates often discouraging, but the women returned to their cities turned on by the *idea* of women's liberation, to organize more and more groups."[59] By early 1969, women in Boston were forming groups of all kinds, writing position papers, rejecting their subordinate positions in the antiwar movement and New Left, becoming increasingly active and noticeable, and informally communicating through meetings, conferences, and personal connections to feminists throughout the country. In May 1969, a Female Liberation Conference was organized at Emmanuel College in Boston by a number of informal women's groups of varying perspectives. To the surprise of the organizers, 500 women attended. That summer, large meetings were organized by and for the women who would eventually form Bread and Roses. Bread and Roses members announced its formation in Boston in the early fall of 1969, the "first socialist women's organization," according to women's liberation movement historian Alice Echols.[60] Indicating their identification with working women, the organization was named after the women textile workers' slogan of the Lawrence, Massachusetts, strike of 1912. Other new women's groups in Boston, particularly young radical feminists, formed an important part of the feminist landscape as well. In 1968, several women organized a group called Cell 16/Female Liberation and within the year put out the influential first issue of their journal *No More Fun and Games*.[61] Before and after the formation of formally identified groups, women overlapped in meetings and activities around the city.

Bread and Roses members' median age was twenty-five, and they were highly educated: most had finished college, and a good number had some graduate education or graduate degrees. They were almost all white; many came from liberal families with at least one professional parent; and they grew up under segregated conditions in East Coast urban areas.[62] Most were single and/or childless.[63] They were well educated, articulate, politically experienced, confident, and able to utilize and create movement distribution networks.[64] After the formation of the organization:

> For over two years, about six hundred women met, talked,
> wrote, made posters, yelled, designed courses, organized, made
> speeches, learned Karate, had conferences, marched, wrote

songs, sang, change[d] public opinion, changed their lives, changed their sexuality, changed jobs, taught, wrote pamphlets, sent out newsletters, talked to workers, talked to high school students, talked to housewives, talked to their men, demanded, changed laws, changed tradition, changed expectations, changed themselves.[65]

As early as 1967, women in Cambridge, Massachusetts, had begun meeting in a variety of settings to discuss and write about women's subordination, particularly by movement men. Many had already identified themselves as socialists and were struggling with the concept of socialist feminism—how to combine the ideas of socialism and/or Marxism with those of feminism. A first draft of the Bread and Roses statement of purpose read as follows:

Bread and Roses is an organization of socialist women. We believe that a socialist revolution is a necessary precondition to the liberation of women, although we know that we will not be liberated unless we continually fight against the oppression of women. For this reason we believe that a woman's movement must be autonomous in order to fight against male supremacy as it exists in all institutions, and in its structural basis, the bourgeois family. We believe that capitalism has to be overthrown to create a socialist society, which means one free of all forms of exploitation, racism, imperialism and male supremacy.[66]

Bread and Roses members met often in their collectives or consciousness-raising groups, in larger organizational meetings, and in groups focused on particular issues, such as health or the media. Perhaps because so many of the women were college graduates and intellectually inclined, their political projects included a great deal of writing. They invented new analyses about the relationship of capitalism to patriarchy and about how male dominance, capitalism, and racism operated to discriminate against women. Papers and discussions were devoted to linking the two theories of subordination and social change, Marxism and feminism, and to ensuring that gender, race, and class were recognized as central explanatory factors in women's exploitation. Some women focused primarily on organizing and outreach, but the work was always fluid as women, usually anchored in collectives, worked on a multitude of projects.

From Bread and Roses' founding statement to their support for the Black Panther party to their concern with outreach to poor and working-class women, they articulated a consciousness that was broader than their own personal fulfillment or equality with men. "Among politicos and socialist feminists, the mandate to respond to the material situations of black women had always been emphasized, at least in writing," wrote feminist historian Lauri Umansky. She noted that in 1970 Bread and Roses' concerns included population control that concentrated on nonwhites; an education system that miseducated about women, working people, and people of color; and establishing admissions policies at schools and universities that gave preferential treatment to women from races and classes that had been discriminated against.[67] In addition, a national network of socialist feminist publications and connections expanded, bringing Bread and Roses news of other American socialist feminist activity and theory. All were engaged with issues of gender, capitalism, imperialism, race, and class from a structural perspective, influenced by the New Left and Marxism. As Bread and Roses leader Meredith Tax emphasized, "We can not talk of sisterhood without realizing that the objective position in society of most of us is different from that of welfare mothers, of the black maids of our white mothers, and of women in 3rd World countries. Sisterhood means not *saying* their fight is our fight, but *making* it our fight." She argued that they had to do consciousness raising about class and race, as well as sex, and integrate it into their politics:

> We have to make the fight of all 3rd World peoples, people on
> welfare, and others who are oppressed *our* fight. Which means,
> part of our everyday life. . . . Class and race are involved in all
> propaganda and organizing around childcare, abortion, and every-
> thing else; and should be dealt with openly and specifically.[68]

Bread and Roses women wrote, "Women today are being told by the male movement that our oppression is nothing compared to that of blacks and third world people, without these men's [*sic*] realizing the basic connection of the oppression of all three groups—by a few rich white men."[69] About another important socialist feminist organization, the Chicago Women's Liberation Union (CWLU), Margaret Strobel wrote, "Their evolving ideology embraced antisexist, antiracist, and anticapitalist sentiments and affirmed lesbian rights. Thus, CWLU activists envisioned societal, not only personal, transformation."[70]

Women's liberation demonstration to legalize abortion and end sterilization abuse, Boston Common, 1972. Courtesy of the Boston Public Library, Print Department. Courtesy *Boston Herald*.

Bread and Roses members contributed to a Boston *Women's Liberation Newsletter* that announced political activity and study groups. These listings ranged from committees to locate a space for a women's center, for compiling information about how doctors treated female patients, and for action against racism; to classes on karate, auto mechanics, Marxism, and the history of women.[71] Another issue announced groups to organize clerical workers, repeal antiabortion laws, and form a children's coop.[72] Across two pages of another is a statement by feminist Charlotte Bunch-Weeks of Washington, D.C., Women's Liberation, "Revolution Is a

Symphony of Liberations," with announcements of all sorts, including one for the November 22, 1969, New Haven rally "planned by women (men are invited) to support Black Panther women in jail," and another announcing a November rally to support anti-imperialist antiwar actions at MIT where a Black Panther sister spoke, as did Diane Balser and Linda Gordon of Bread and Roses.[73] Expressing similar ideas, a flyer written at the time stated, "Abortion is our Right!" and continued, "One woman can not be liberated without the liberation of all women. Good abortion is now the privilege of the few. 90% of the women who get legal abortions are white . . . private patients. 75% of the women who die from abortions are non-white. . . . We demand: the repeal of all abortion laws! Free abortions to women on demand."[74]

Members of Bread and Roses were involved in antiwar activity, particularly draft counseling, support for the Black Panthers, developing health groups concerned with women's treatment, providing mental and physical health services and information, campaigning for the legalization of abortion and against sterilization abuse, raising consciousness about violence against women, reclaiming and celebrating International Women's Day, organizing secretaries and childcare centers, picketing and demonstrating against institutions that discriminated against women, researching and publicizing information about women's sexuality, living communally, and writing for and publishing newspapers and newsletters. Collectives, which were both consciousness-raising and action groups, often chose political issues on which to focus their energies. One collective involved in helping to start Bread and Roses functioned as an outreach committee: "We spoke to classes and meetings. We gave little talks with facts and charts showing how women were paid 60 percent of the wages of men. We argued that the prevailing images of women as emotional, sexual, and illogical and of men as rational, nonsexual, and logical served discrimination. All of this was news to everyone."[75] Some of the collectives were devoted to organizing women different from their mostly middle-class selves—working-class women, high school girls, women of color.

Bread and Roses' most dramatic action was organizing a feminist takeover of a Harvard University building at 888 Memorial Drive in Cambridge on International Women's Day 1971, which attracted a good deal of media attention. They occupied the building for ten days, demanding that Harvard provide space for a women's center for all women, community as well as university. Because Harvard was a major employer of female staff and had increasingly expanded its property holdings into low-income minority neighborhoods in Cambridge, Bread and Roses women believed that the institution owed the community, particularly women, resources and services. They met with African-American women from the surrounding community who had been involved in a campaign to force Harvard to provide low-cost housing in the neighborhood and reiterated their support for the housing. They explained that the proposed women's center would be available to all women. By the following year, as a direct result of the occupation, the Cambridge Women's Center had been set up,

The Harvard University–owned building at 888 Memorial Drive that Bread and Roses members occupied for ten days in March 1971. They were demanding the establishment of a women's center and that Harvard contribute to the building of affordable low-income housing in the community into which the university was expanding. "Free Ericka" refers to imprisoned Black Panther Ericka Huggins. Courtesy of the Boston Public Library, Print Department. Courtesy *Boston Herald*.

albeit with no help from Harvard.[76] It is the longest-running women's center in the United States, a space where hundreds of women's groups have met.

In March 1972, women from Bread and Roses founded the Women's School, which gave classes at the new women's center. Run by a collective with volunteer instructors, the school offered such courses as "In America They Call Us Dykes," "Her Story" (women's history), "History of Black Struggle and White Racial Response," "Jewish History and Culture," "Fix-It," "The Capitalist System," "Marriage and the Family," "Native American Women: An Historical Perspective," "The War in Indochina," "Lesbianism," "China," and "Introduction to Black History." The successful book *Our Bodies, Ourselves* grew out of a course called "Women and Their Bodies" first offered at the school by a Bread and Roses group that had been meeting prior to the establishment of the school.[77] In an account of the Women's School, activists wrote:

> The school's selection of courses would reflect a particular set of politics—that we needed to explore our personal lives and look further at the historical development to our present social and economic relation[s]. Our task is to change society, we needed to look at the past forces of change that were embodied in labor, Black and women's struggles, as well as Europe, Vietnam, China and Cuba.

After recognizing how they were oppressed as women, their task "was to examine why, to begin to explain the deeper reins [sic] society has over the individual, a look at the nature of capitalism, the role of the family and others."[78]

In a mimeographed document, "To Students and Teachers in the Women's School," that begins, "Dear Sisters," the authors give some history of the Women's School, including how they came up with courses, what they wanted to achieve, and how they attempted to offer topics that were not taught in formal schools. They didn't offer some courses, they stated, because they were available elsewhere:

> On the other hand, we continued to offer Black History even though relatively few women signed up for it the first couple of terms. This is because we believe the struggle of black people is our struggle, too. There is a lot the women's movement needs to

> learn and do in order to bring ourselves into a more conscious
> and active alliance with the black liberation movement and
> learning black history is one step in this direction.[79]

A course description of "The Black Struggle and the White Radical Response" stated that it was vitally important for the women's movement to study the history of black people and the roots of white racism: "In an effort to reach women of different ages and backgrounds, Third World, Black and working class women, in 1972 and 1973 the school offered extension courses in three neighboring communities." They continued, "[W]e have always made free child care available, believing that children are society's, not an individual's responsibility and to allow mothers to take courses."[80] Another mimeo discussed offering a course on the black struggle:

> The relationship of the women's movement to the black struggle
> is not just an abstract question of morals or principles. The failure to eradicate racism has crippled nearly every radical movement in Amerika's past, including feminism. Right here in the
> women's center, we have hardly begun to discuss, much less resolve, the questions of our relationship to the black liberation
> movement in Boston, to our black sisters (very few of whom
> come to the center) and to the nearby black community (even
> though that community played a role in our getting the center
> in the first place.)[81]

It is evident that while socialist feminists focused on their own subordination and efforts to liberate themselves as individuals and women, they were also committed to larger political issues, especially race. "The most burning controversial issues of the fall [1970] were racism and relating to the Panthers, Imperialism and what it means to be international, and the smoldering controversy over lesbianism," wrote D.C. socialist feminists, suggesting how inextricably the political and the personal were bound.[82] In fact, white socialist feminists' antiracist politics, based on equality for women of all classes and races and sexual orientations, have gotten lost in the telling.[83] Feminist philosopher and movement participant Marilyn Frye reflected:

> [M]emory and research both attest to the fact that various differences among women were very salient indeed, from the mo-

ment solidarity among women was conceived. To mention just a few examples: there were issues both about class and sexuality articulated within (and from without) the National Organization of [sic] Women in the early 1970s; the Furies Collective battled out class issues; more leftist women's groups such as Bread and Roses attended actively to issues of race and class; black women, in and out of the Black Power and Black Muslim movements, were discussing the relations of feminism and black women to those movements.[84]

Bread and Roses members and other white socialist feminists were aware and active in their efforts to combat racism within their own ranks and to integrate race and class into their politics. Even amid the thrill of sisterhood and solidarity, activists recognized differences among women. The most immediate and difficult difference they faced among themselves was sexual preference. Especially significant after the Stonewall Rebellion in 1969, lesbianism created tensions within the primarily heterosexual socialist feminist movement, making its relationship to lesbians almost as wrenching as the conflict between the male Left and feminism. Differences in sexual preference prompted straight women's fears that the issue would divide and discredit the young women's liberation movement. Socialist feminist lesbians came out publicly and demanded to be acknowledged by their sisters but reported homophobic reactions. So much energy was devoted to sexual orientation that those outside the movement often saw sexuality and lesbianism as its major preoccupations. Some members attempted to organize a separate lesbian feminist movement, arguing that lesbianism was the ultimate feminism, a version of political solidarity among women that heterosexual women could never achieve.[85] They created new identities and confronted straight women about their dependence on and connections to men.

The gap between lesbians and straight women in the women's movement appeared large and potentially dangerous to feminist solidarity. Although historian Alice Echols believed that the "gay-straight split," in particular, "crippled" the movement, which was reluctant to explore women's differences, this did not hold true for all organizations. It was not true for Bread and Roses, for example, although there were strains. Straight women and lesbians worked together in Boston. In Washington, D.C., however, a lesbian group, the Furies, split off from the women's liberation movement.

The particularities of leadership, personalities, and political inclinations meant that lesbianism ruptured some groups, created anger and divisions in others, and was absorbed in some, although not without a great deal of talk and confrontation.[86] White socialist feminists' gender analyses inclined them toward smoothing over differences among women, but they knew better. As antiracist and anticapitalist socialists, they understood that power differences had their source in race, class, and gender inequality. They did not ignore differences but they, like most others of that time, were not particularly successful in negotiating them. Socialist feminists believed that, by coming out, women became stronger and truer to themselves and created a women's community that would include and care for everyone, but Bread and Roses chronicler Popkin noted complex feelings, "The mixed immediate emotional effects in the women's community were exhilaration, excitement, and fear. Some women felt that their sexuality and lifestyle were being challenged."[87] Coping with differences while attempting to build a collective movement was among the greatest challenges feminists faced and, for white women, lesbianism was their most immediate and concrete experience of difference.

Another marker of difference, class, was less divisive than race but significant nonetheless. Women of color and white working-class feminists could not help but notice that the movement was composed primarily of middle- or upper-middle-class white women or women who were highly educated. Often higher education divided women, and college graduates frequently became the unofficial leaders, people whom the media anointed, or who seemed to gravitate to leadership positions. It was not uncommon for working-class and lower-middle-class women to feel uncomfortable or unacknowledged.[88] But despite their socialist politics, for the majority of activists, class was never as significant as race or sexual preference. Ann Popkin wrote, "The issue of class, however, remained enshrouded in middle-class guilt during much of this period, and this kind of analysis was never systematically pursued within the organization." In part, this was a reaction to the male Left's privileging of race and class over gender.[89] The compelling and desperate nature of the black freedom movement and of third world revolution internationally, with the war in Vietnam always on activists' minds, also contributed to the attention to race at the expense of class.

There were, however, endless debates about class. In discussions of class, socialist feminists were usually referring to white working-class women, although most black women were working class. (The separation of categories, in this case working-class women and black women, highlights a profound weakness in early socialist feminist thinking, one that African-American feminists adamantly corrected.) Statements like this one from the Bay Area Women's Union were numerous: "A real alliance between black and white women should take place and will greatly strengthen the movement of blacks and women towards their liberation but this alliance must take place on the basis of clear working class politics."[90] In a doctrinaire statement of working-class politics that condemned feminists, D.C. lesbian feminists Colletta Reid and Charlotte Bunch wrote at the time, "Women's Liberation was middle class and that's bad. . . . We never looked at how working class women within our movement were oppressed." They knew that class divisions should be eliminated in the women's movement. After an enormous effort to comprehend the problem, Bunch recognized that "much of my behavior came from being raised middle class and was oppressive to working class women. . . . When middle class women carry their attitudes and ways of behaving into the movement, it oppresses working class women." They concluded with the recognition, "Bringing down the male supremacist system in this country will not be a possibility until we stop acting out our class supremacist attitudes on the women with whom we're building a movement."[91]

Much of the written record of class politics is similarly moralistic and judgmental. Organizers recognized that the feminist movement had to include a range of women and chastised white, middle-class feminists for not being more successful in changing their middle-class assumptions and behavior. Such a position led to guilt and remorse, among other emotions, parallel to the feelings evoked by accusations of racism. Guilt, as many black feminists later pointed out, is not a constructive response, although it was not uncommon among white, middle-class movement women. White feminists who were linked to Marxist politics were the most likely to use this kind of language and to abstractly exhort other feminists to cease oppressing working-class women. Others, too, were deeply concerned and unsure of how to proceed. They became more conscious of class problems within their own movement as well—how personal networks operated, who were leaders and speakers, who felt excluded. But recognizing issues of class and how it created power differences among women did not lead to obvious strategies for how to achieve a mixed-class movement. The emphasis varied from locale to locale and person to person. Some individuals and groups used their energy to admonish and theorize abstractly, while other women focused on activities, such as eliminating sterilization abuse, improving the conditions and pay of working women, and fighting domestic violence, which linked women across class and race. And there were combinations of both theory and practice. In Bread and Roses and subsequent Boston socialist feminist organizations in the 1970s, most political activity that included community women revolved around the Cambridge Women's Center, Women's School, and Rape Crisis Center; campaigns against sterilization abuse, for legalizing abortion, for women's control of their bodies, for tenants' rights, and for childcare; providing services for women who were victims of domestic violence; and community organizing in white working-class neighborhoods, though Bread and Roses was not particularly successful in organizing working-class women.

Nor was the group successful in attracting black women. Bread and Roses members were committed to understanding racial differences among women. Their goal was to build a multiracial movement. They theorized and organized with the goal of connecting to and attracting black and minority women to feminism. They wrote an enormous number of position papers, flyers, underground newspaper articles, and statements about racial discrimination against black women and race in feminism. Black women were consistently on members' minds, but in these early years their theory was more interracial and racially sensitive than was their practice. That practice involved opposing racism, usually in the form of supporting radical black groups.

One Bread and Roses document began with a poem: "Four revolutionary sisters / Erika [sic] Huggins / Rose Smith / Margaret Huggins / Frances Carter / 344 days of confinement / no trial yet." This was part of a flyer for the November 22, 1969, New Haven women's march and rally to protest the imprisonment of the Panther women, one of the first large-scale militant demonstrations of the women's liberation movement. The Panther women were being held without bail in a New Haven prison with thirteen other Panthers charged with murder, conspiracy, and kidnapping. Six of the prisoners were women and three were pregnant. Ericka Huggins, whose husband, Panther John Huggins, had recently been murdered in Los Angeles, was one of the imprisoned women, and she became a kind of socialist feminist icon due to her courage and militancy. The flyer ends with the famous slogan, "Sisterhood Is Powerful." A flyer for a 1970 Panther support rally, signed by "Sisters from women's liberation in New Haven, Boston and New York," began, "To Our Sisters: Women in the women's liberation movement have come to New Haven to support the Black Panther Party's struggle for liberation." They noted that "the system that keeps black people down is the same system that keeps women down," and "the women's liberation movement has developed a deeper understanding of racism through its experience of sexism." During the day of demonstrations, for which day care was provided, meetings at the New Haven Women's Center were organized around topics such as racism and sexism, anti-imperialism, childcare, the Venceremos Brigade—the leftist organization that went to Cuba to help in the harvest of sugar cane—and abortion/genocide/birth control/population control.[92]

Much of the focus on race during the Bread and Roses years took the form of Black Panther party support work, which meant primarily working with the black male leaders to organize and participate in demonstrations.[93] There was only a small Black Panther party and a relatively small black population in Boston, but there were trials and rallies in New Haven and New York. Support for the Panthers was one of the only tangible ways for white radicals to articulate antiracist politics since it was one of the only Black Power groups that encouraged white support and was willing to work with whites. There were female Panthers, of course, and white women were especially sensitive to the plight of those in jail, but they inevitably worked primarily with the male leadership. White socialist feminists rarely had contact with Panther women, and when they did their efforts to raise feminist issues did not prove fruitful. They were disappointed in the two 1970 Revolutionary People's Constitutional Conventions in Philadelphia and Washington, D.C., called by the Panthers and attended by thousands of radicals. Although an earlier speech by Panther leader Huey Newton urged Panthers to see gays and women as oppressed groups with whom Panthers should work, and D.C. feminists and gay men were intensively involved in organizing the events, the meetings disillusioned women liberationists. D.C. feminists had urged other feminists to attend because "through our contacts and experiences with third world liberation struggles we become more conscious of our racism and privilege—we intend that third world contact with revolutionary women will enable them to become more conscious of sexism." At both conventions, the Panthers were unfriendly to white feminists and at neither were

Rally for Black Panther party and women's liberation at Yale,
New Haven, Connecticut, 1970. Stephen Shames. Polaris Images.

links created between white and black women. The Panthers were suspicious of separate women's groups and of lesbians, slighted women in their speeches, and generally created a hostile environment for feminists.[94]

Channeling support for black people through the Panthers raised complicated issues. One mimeographed letter to Bread and Roses members put it this way: "It seems to us critical to find other ways of relating to black people—specifically black women—than coming to Panther support rallies." The authors were critical of themselves for accepting the egotism and chauvinism of Panther leaders, suggesting that this situation has "positively held back our development of new ways to fight racism."[95] And a heartfelt editorial in the *Old Mole*, a Cambridge underground newspaper where a group of Bread and Roses women worked, entitled "The Panthers and White Radicals," said, "One of the ways the white movement has been racist is in being afraid to criticize the Panther Party, pretending to agree with everything they say," and proceeded to talk about "the way the Panthers glorify a few individual leaders, especially heroes used to project a feeling of black strength and dignity through a masculine image. This reflects a male chauvinism that is also present in frequent Panther statements which attack the autonomous women's movement." They argued that whites should support the Panthers, who were suffering from state repression, but should not drop their other work or become a "reflection of the Panthers."[96]

Many white radicals had a romantic vision of the Panthers and third world revolutionaries as the threatened vanguard of the revolution. A kind of "third-worldism" characterized the politics of many late 1960s white radicals. "[A] true revolution can only be led by the most oppressed peoples—blacks, third world people, and women," stated Boston University women's liberationists.[97] Some feminist women supported a position that verged on the sycophantic and/or the adulation of third-world revolutionaries. Discussing her participation in the 1968 Democratic Party National Convention demonstrations for peace and freedom in Chicago, African-American Combahee River Collective member Barbara Smith reported ironically on hearing Black Panther leader Bobby Seale at a rally in Lincoln Park: "It is always curious to me to see a certain type of white person receive with such enthusiasm the promise of the destruction of their society by Black people."[98] The enthusiasm was an earnest but uncritical, often guilty, recognition by whites of the heroism of third-world freedom fighters, often fueled by a denial of their white and middle-class backgrounds. The notion of "white skin privilege" was generated by and used to generate guilt.[99] "We are white and we have, of course, all of the guilt feelings and all of the problems of racism that any white group has and when we talk about blacks and say we have similarities with the black movement it seems to be an attempt to solve the guilt by saying that we're oppressed too and therefore not really responsible," remarked feminist Pam Allen.[100]

Glorified images of female freedom fighters from around the globe permeated the American New Left. The use of such images often carried an implicit criticism of white American feminism, yet white radical women both participated in this idealization and were critical of it. Angela Davis noted the same phenomenon among black women—an idealized military ideal in which armed black women would meet their men's needs, nurture their children, and fight a guerrilla war. A white socialist feminist described the distinctions that male activists made between revolutionary third world women and movement women, who were expected to provide support work and services, including having their babies and doing their typing: "Such a man will sit at his desk with his feet up and point to the poster on his wall of a Vietnamese woman with her rifle on her back, telling you, 'Now that is a truly liberated woman. When I see you in that role, I'll believe you're a revolutionary.'" She continued, "When I am told day in and day out to shut up because our oppression pales beside the oppression of colonized peoples and blacks, I remember half of them are women too. . . . We are told that our sense of oppression is not legitimate."[101] In an account of her second wave political evolution, activist Leslie Rabine remarked that the Marxist version of feminism was of a third world woman nursing a baby while carrying a rifle on her back. Rabine recounted how New Left Marxist men argued, "Women's oppression is a secondary contradiction; it's a bourgeois question; and Third World women are more oppressed than white women, proletarian women more oppressed than bourgeois women."[102] Indeed, many socialist feminists considered themselves Marxists and glorified the cultural revolution in China and women's international revolutionary struggles. Rabine accepted these politics and joined a sectarian Marxist group: "I wanted to support the struggle of Third World Women, and it seemed to me that my only chance for doing so was through the Maoist organization that was leading the Movement at Stanford."[103] Meredith Tax went from Bread and Roses to join a "Marxist-Leninist 'pre-party formation'" because of her belief that whites had to concentrate their political attention on third world revolutions and working-class people of color. Eventually, she was "expelled" for asking too many questions about the group's position on women and other policies.[104]

Third world politics meant that socialist feminists closely identified with international freedom movements. New Left women chose the term *women's liberation* both in a genuine effort to name themselves and in order to legitimate themselves in terms of the male Left. As one leader of the Chicago women's liberation movement recalled, "We were afraid to call ourselves feminists, since in the New Left that was hopelessly 'bourgeois.' We finally came up with 'women's liberation,' an analogy with Third World struggles (since we couldn't yet imagine the legitimacy of our own)."[105] Feminist Ellen Willis suggested that the denigration of women's issues by New Left men led women to embrace a revolutionary version of feminism linked to third world people: "The main reason that 60s feminists relied so heavily on comparisons between sexism and racism is that white male politicos recognized the issue as morally legitimate, while dismissing feminism as 'a bunch of chicks with personal problems.'" The women wanted the men to feel as guilty about sexism as they did about racism.[106] The analogy of women's oppression with third world and African-American oppression was made often. The 1967 "SDS Statement on the Liberation of Women" had drawn an explicit connection: "As we analyze the position of women in capitalist society and especially the United States we find that women are in a colonial relationship to men and we recognize ourselves as part of the Third World." The authors acknowledged difficulties raised by the third world analogy but agreed that "the importance of the analogy was its placing of the problem of male chauvinism within a clear social and political context."[107] There were as many criticisms of this analogy as there were statements of it, including women identifying themselves as "niggers."[108] White feminists who used the black or third world analogy were grasping at straws in an effort to describe and legitimize themselves, but in the process displayed their arrogance and insensitivity to the situation of African Americans.[109] Radical black women were outraged that white, middle-class women would compare their situation with that of black people. But white women demurred too. Many were uncomfortable with suggesting equivalency between mostly middle-class women's social, economic, and political situation and that of African Americans or third world people. For example, in her "Toward a Female Liberation Movement," Beverly Jones criticized the SDS statement's language as immoral.[110] And movement activist Pam Allen stated, "I objected to women using analogies to the black movement because I feel that we have to deal with racism in ourselves. We can't allow any way of getting around the fact that we are racist; we are part of a racist society."[111]

Identification with people of color by radical whites had its source in the recognition of racism.[112] A central accomplishment of the civil rights movement was to educate Americans about racism, and radicals took those lessons to heart. Young whites looked to black social movements and black culture in order to make sense of American society and whites' place in it. Supporting the Panthers and third world revolutions, especially the Vietnamese fighting the United States, was one version of antiracist politics in a racially divided world. Identifying with other races was a critical part of white youth's creation of oppositional identities in the 1960s and 1970s. In the words of cultural theorist Kobena Mercer, whites were involved in a "collective dis-affiliation with the American Dream" in which they distanced themselves from whiteness in a racist system. Their search for new identities through Black Power and the Black Panther party empowered and radicalized them and created new forms of solidarity.[113] Aware of racism, young whites were ambivalent about their whiteness and drawn to blacks and black culture not only as appropriation but also as a way to find meaning for their own lives. Their search for an identity and a just racial politics easily veered into presumptuousness and sycophancy in its worship of black liberation leaders, particularly the Panthers. White support of and identification with the Panthers was often based on politically unwise and unconscious motivations, but it also represented a recognition of the centrality of whiteness and privilege in maintaining racism in the United States (as well as the vulnerability of the Panthers to state-sponsored repression).

The evidence makes abundantly clear that Bread and Roses members, like other socialist feminists, embraced antiracist politics. Yet their support, while genuine, was abstract. It was not rooted in actual experiences with black women. As white socialist feminists moved toward an analysis of women's subordination, they accused white men of abstract politics but were unconscious of their own abstractness in relation to black women and racism. Bread and Roses members Linda Gordon and Ann Popkin claimed: "Because our analysis is derived from our concrete, everyday experience it is less likely to become rigidified into 'correct political lines'—a problem of the male left whose program is based primarily on theoretical perceptions of people's oppression."[114] In reality, they had little actual experience with black women except for those who had been in the South in the civil rights movement. Segregation in American society impeded white socialist feminists' ability to break out of their class and race positions. Bread and Roses' Ann Popkin wrote, "[E]ven among women who thought themselves conscious, without solid grounding in intimate knowledge of the lives of the women involved, the attraction would at times be romanticization."[115] Demonstrations for the Panther women and other gestures of support, including making sure that major women's liberation anthologies included work by black feminists, were not particularly effective in reaching white feminists' goal of a multiracial and multiclass movement. Outreach to black women proved to be confusing and difficult. Feminist author Lauri Umansky wrote:

> Whereas single gestures toward solidarity, like the Panther demonstration, carried symbolic power, many feminist groups agonizingly sought to develop a gender politics that would recognize the specific, material needs of black women rather than simply appropriate and render symbolic the pathos of those needs. With the belief that a mass movement must be built "from the ground up," these groups altered their own priorities in search of a more genuine dialogue with black women.[116]

Despite their desire, and their ideals, early white socialist feminists' efforts to build an interracial movement foundered on their inevitable abstractness. Notwithstanding relatively sophisticated understandings of class and race, they conceptualized women as an undifferentiated oppressed group. Paradoxically, these contradictory themes of recognizing racial difference and embracing gender universality persisted alongside one another. Feminist historian Margaret Strobel noted that Heather Booth of the Chicago Women's Liberation Union, who had been active in the civil rights movement, SDS, and community organizing, "clearly transferred her understanding of the oppression of blacks and the urban poor to women as a group."[117] Numerous published and unpublished socialist feminist documents universalized gender by conceptualizing women as a homogenous category, provoking black women, who were invisible in such analyses and who considered them racist. Black women insisted on the centrality of race and class in conjunction with gender as the basis for feminist theory and action, but in socialist feminism's initial years white women obscured differences among women. Identifying gender as an all-encompassing category was a first step in separating their identity from movement men, positioning all women as a relatively powerless group in contrast to men as a powerful group.[118] Ironically, then, for women's liberationists, the universalist notion that all women experienced similar oppression stemmed from both an unfamiliarity with and an insensitivity to differences between black women and themselves and the powerful desire to include all women—the antithesis of racism from white women's perspective. Universalism, a concept with which they had grown up, was a way to naturally, and abstractly, include all women in feminism. In the process of learning about differences, once again their hopes for solidarity were threatened, their idealism dealt another blow. Sisterhood was not a simple powerful bond that connected all women across race.

The Black movement needs its women in
a position of struggle, not prone.
—Linda La Rue, "The Black Movement and
Women's Liberation" (1970)

What do black women feel about Women's Lib? Distrust.
It is white, therefore suspect. . . . They look at
white women and see them as the enemy.
—Toni Morrison, "What the Black Woman
Thinks about Women's Lib" (1971)

Black feminism developed slowly. More cautious and less expansive than white feminism, radical black feminism had to contend with Black Power's attractive notions of racial solidarity and pride in contrast to which feminism was viewed as divisive and as a betrayal of black men and the black community. It also had to contend with the mushrooming white women's movement. The need for black women to build their own movement became compelling, even urgent, in the 1970s, but it never became a mass grassroots movement like the white women's movement. Radical black women, influenced by the civil rights, Black Power, and women's liberation movements, generated feminist analyses in papers, articles, and several books, including, of course, Toni Cade's *The Black Woman.* They also organized primarily local, feminist political groups in the late 1960s and throughout the 1970s, though later and on a smaller scale than the white women's liberation movement. A groundswell of black feminism in the United States never developed. Nevertheless, black feminism developed on its own track, in reaction to black nationalism and white feminism, with major insights and contributions of its own.[1] Through their writings, the media, and political activities, white and black feminists interacted and profoundly influenced one another.

African-American scholar Beverly Guy-Sheftall views 1970 as a critical year for African-American feminism due to the publication of several path-breaking books—Toni Cade's *The Black Woman*, writings by Toni Morrison and Audre Lorde, and the autobiography of Shirley Chisholm—which "signaled a literary awakening among black women and the beginning of a clearly defined black women's liberation movement that would have priorities different from those of white feminists, and generate considerable debate, even hostility, within the black community."[2] The Cade anthology included some of the earliest African-American feminist statements. Among them were Frances Beal's "Double Jeopardy: To Be Black and Female," which linked racism and sexism and was one of the first public essays by a black woman to explicitly connect black women's experiences to feminism. Appearing in this critical year for black feminism were other pieces linking sexism, racism, and feminism, including Linda La Rue's "The Black Movement and Women's Liberation," Pauli Murray's "The Liberation of Black Women," Mary Ann Weathers's "An Argument for Black Women's Liberation as a Revolutionary Force," and Patricia Haden, Donna Middleton, and Patricia Robinson's "A Historical and Critical Essay for Black Women."[3]

The foundations of early black socialist feminism can also be traced back to several political groups. Years after SNCC had become a Black Power organization, Frances Beal of the New York City SNCC chapter organized a group that came to be known as the Third World Women's Alliance (TWWA).[4] As one of the earliest manifestations of second wave, black, socialist feminism, the emergence of TWWA from SNCC, albeit a northern version, is important because it delineates the rise of black feminist consciousness out of the civil rights movement.[5] Beal had long been aware of gender issues in SNCC, including those elucidated in 1964 by Mary King and Casey Hayden's memos about sexism in the organization. She and others had first formed the SNCC Black Women's Liberation Committee in 1968 to discuss the contradictions between the politics of freedom and conventional expectations of women. Initially oriented toward consciousness raising as they explored their situations as black women, they began to formulate a gender, class, and racial interpretation of black women's position. While SNCC provided them with a space to function, they were criticized as being too influenced by white women.

In 1969, they became independent, first calling themselves the Black Women's Alliance and then the Third World Women's Alliance when other women of color joined them. Influenced by Marxism, they articulated a socialist racial and gender politics in which third world women struggle against capitalism, racism, and sexism. Members argued that Black Power's gender positions were regressive and imported from white middle-class culture. Opposed to patriarchy everywhere, they considered themselves a third world women's anti-imperialist group. Beal's "Double Jeopardy" essay announced that any feminists who did not have an antiracist and anti-imperialist ideology shared nothing with the black woman's struggle. The group contested the claim that black men had been more oppressed in slavery and throughout African-American history than had black women. They believed they were stronger by joining forces with all third world women, who, as its victims, were logical opponents of imperialism.[6] The Marxist, anti-imperialist, third world, and feminist politics of TWWA spread from New York to other cities. A Bay Area chapter was set up by a woman who had been involved in New York and who had gone to Cuba with the Venceremos Brigades, young Americans sympathetic to Cuba who helped to harvest sugarcane and learned about socialism there. The West Coast branch had close ties with the Communist party and was dedicated to supporting Cuba and the Committee to Free Angela Davis. New York City TWWA members joined a number of white feminist–organized demonstrations, participated in political activity to free Angela Davis and other political prisoners, were involved in the anti–Vietnam War movement, held consciousness-raising sessions, and wrote position papers. Mostly, they focused their attention on their newspaper, *Triple Jeopardy*, aimed at third world working-class men and women.[7]

In 1973, five years after the appearance of the TWWA, the National Black Feminist Organization (NBFO), a larger black feminist group with national aspirations, was founded. It lasted from 1973 to 1975.[8] Although small black socialist feminist groups and significant black socialist feminist writing preceded NBFO, not until the mid-1970s did black women in any numbers identify as feminists. The group was begun in New York City primarily by educated professionals, most of whom had participated in white feminist organizations, including the National Organization for Women (NOW) and *Ms.* magazine. Involved from the outset were important radical African-American women, including Shirley Chisholm, Alice Walker, Jane Galvin-Lewis, Eleanor Holmes Norton, Flo Kennedy, and Margaret Sloan. They wanted to define black women's relationship to feminism and create an organization that would make the connections among gender, race, and class, thereby including black women and poor women. Historian Deborah Gray White concluded that "more than any organization in the century," it launched "a frontal assault on sexism and racism."[9]

Margaret Sloan, a founding editor of *Ms.* magazine and a founder and chair of NBFO, had noted a strong black women's interest in feminism. Throughout this period and subsequently, polls regularly showed that black women supported feminist goals.[10] She and other women organized the first meeting of about thirty women in *Ms.* magazine's New York offices. At that August founding meeting and press conference, Sloan stated, "Black women have suffered cruelly in this society from living the phenomenon of being Black and female in a country that is both racist and sexist. The women's group . . . will remind the Black liberation movement that there can't be liberation for half of a race."[11] They announced a black feminist conference in the winter and the formation of NBFO—at that point, more a concept than a reality. The media focused on the unique appearance of a national black feminist organization, which generated calls from all over the country from women offering to come to the winter meeting and to set up chapters.[12] Brenda Eichelberger offered to found a chapter in Chicago. She wrote Sloan, who had written an article in *Ms.* about the NBFO, that "prior to reading that article, I thought I was the only black woman on the planet Earth who felt the way I felt," saying that the black women with whom she came into contact were male-identified and wanted only to get married.[13] Eichelberger called an NBFO meeting in Chicago that eventually spun off into another early black feminist organization, the National Alliance of Black Feminists (NABF).[14]

The NBFO Eastern Regional Conference of about 400 women took place in New York at the end of November and was successful in reaching black women from all walks of life. Organizers argued that black feminism would contribute to empowering the entire black community and highlighted economic survival issues important to black and working-class women. African-American women's concerns, such as welfare, day care, employment discrimination, reproductive rights, rape, and sexual orientation were on the agenda, and consciousness-raising sessions were held. The sexism of the Black Power movement was criticized. Above all, the founders wanted to persuade black women that feminism was relevant to their lives and that a feminist organization would strengthen their position in society.

Sloan recorded women's grateful reactions to the organization: "You will forever have my eternal gratitude for sponsoring the NBFO Conference. Never before have I felt such genuine sisterhood with other black women. A longtime feminist, I have often felt I was a pariah, since very few black women I knew ever admitted sharing my views."[15] Local chapters were established despite irregular communication with the national office. Within a year of its founding, the NBFO had a membership of 2,000 women in ten chapters, although the original New York chapter lasted only two years. (Most feminist organizations did not last long.)[16] Local chapters survived or reinvented themselves in places such as Chicago and the Bay Area. For some, the NBFO was the impetus to organize their own groups. One of these was the Combahee River Collective.

In 1974, the Combahee River women began to meet in Boston. The group was always small and fluid, with no more than fifteen active women in Boston, but was nevertheless the most important black socialist feminist group of the time. The collective is most well known for its declaration "A Black Feminist Statement," a widely cited and influential document of radical black feminism—in fact, a founding document of black feminism. A unique articulation of a black lesbian socialist feminist politics, the "Statement" has been reprinted in numerous women's studies and feminist anthologies since its initial publication. The Combahee River Collective's central contribution to black socialist feminism was intellectual and theoretical; they were as much a study group as anything else. A starting point was existing feminist analyses that, in the words of collective member Demita Frazier, "did not look closely at the issues of race, color, caste, and class" and that "created frustration and tension."[17] After the dissolution of Bread and Roses in the early 1970s, socialist feminism was still flourishing in Boston. Other, primarily white, socialist feminist organizations, which included many former Bread and Roses members, were synchronous with Combahee.

The collective brought together a small number of young radical black women who were political activists and intellectuals in Boston and were developing political analyses based on their movement experiences, including white feminism. In 1978, Combahee member Barbara Smith wrote in the Boston women's newspaper *Sojourner*, "Despite the fact that the majority of Black women have not joined the second wave of feminist political action, the current women's movement has affected their lives in *direct* and indirect ways and a Black feminist movement is now evolving."[18] The women of the Combahee River Collective named themselves after the campaign led by Harriet Tubman, who freed 750 slaves near the Combahee River in South Carolina in 1863.[19] Barbara Smith, a key founder along with her sister Beverly, became politically active in the civil rights movement in high school in Cleveland and then in black student organizing, civil rights movement support work, and the anti–Vietnam War movement in college. She recalled that at the University of Pittsburgh in 1969 black students were critical of her involvement in white politics, namely, the antiwar movement. She said that she graduated from college at the height of black nationalism and that she couldn't be the kind of woman whose job it was "to have babies for the Nation and to walk seven paces behind a man and basically be a maid/servant."[20] About Black Power politics, she remarked: "I actually imagined that I would never be politically active again because nationalism and patriarchal attitudes within Black organizing was *so* strong—we're talking early '70s now."[21] Demita Frazier, another founder, said, "[M]any of us were refugees from other political movements—civil rights, the antiwar movement, the labor movement—where we found ourselves in conflict with the lack of a feminist analysis and, in many cases, we were left feeling divided against ourselves." Frazier remembered that in some of the political groups with which they were allied as nascent feminists, they were branded as "troublemakers, brainwashed by the 'man-hating white feminists.'"[22]

By the late 1960s, a backlash to the social movements, particularly the civil rights, Black Power, and antiwar movements, had begun to develop. In Boston, the 1970s was the time of the busing crisis where, under court order, black students were sent out of their neighborhoods in buses to white schools and whites to black schools as a way of redressing segregated education, an outcome of the civil rights movement and specifically the 1954 Supreme Court *Brown v. Board of Education* decision.[23] Racial tension was high in the city, creating a frightening and threatening environment for African Americans, especially in South Boston. Combahee Collective members worked in this fraught context. They came together and worked in an array of political activities at a time of heightened racial tensions in Boston, making the accomplishments of this small group all the more impressive. In Frazier's words, Combahee was "instrumental in founding a local battered women's shelter. We worked in coalition with community activists, women and men, lesbian and straight folks. We were very active in the reproductive rights movement, even though, at the time, most of us were lesbians. We found ourselves involved in coalition with the labor movement." She continued that they understood how important coalitions were both to their own political survival and in creating a viable political opposition.[24] Throughout the period of their existence, they were particularly interested in getting involved in political issues that involved sex, race, and class. They worked as individuals and together on political issues such as sterilization abuse, reproductive rights, battered women, rape, and a number of cases that involved ensuring the hiring of black workers; defending Kenneth Edelin, a black Boston doctor who had been arrested for performing a legal abortion; and national campaigns to defend unfairly imprisoned black women, including a local female prisoner who had killed a guard who had sexually assaulted her. They also ran workshops on black feminism at schools and conferences.[25]

The original Combahee members came together out of the 1973 National Black Feminist Organization meeting in New York. Barbara Smith and others convened the first Boston NBFO meeting in Roxbury and later

Joanne Little was tried and acquitted of killing a prison guard who attempted to rape her in a North Carolina prison cell. Here, she is speaking at Northeastern University in Boston, 1975. © Ellen Shub.

meetings took place at the Cambridge Women's Center, which had been established by Bread and Roses. Members who were leftists and Marxists influenced the politics of the group, moving them in the direction of an explicit socialist and class-oriented politics More radical and less mainstream than NBFO in their anticapitalist position and their explicit concerns about class and homophobia, they decided to "become an independent collective since we have serious disagreements with NBFO's bourgeois-feminist stance and their lack of a clear political focus."[26] The Combahee Collective was a small core group that met for years, reading, writing, and organizing in Boston. "As the only Black lesbian, socialist, feminist organization in the Boston area, Combahee was at the vanguard of articulating the parameters of Black feminism."[27] They were political activists, produced the Combahee River Collective statement in 1977, and organized periodic retreats in the Northeast between 1977 and 1980 for about twenty to thirty black feminists.

Founding members have noted how difficult it is to convey what it was like in the mid-1970s to do black feminist and lesbian organizing when they had no role models. Smith quoted Frazier as saying, "This is not a mix cake. We have got to make it up from scratch"[28] In Smith's words, "I was very aware that we were doing something new. . . . It was absolutely daunting work. It was depressing. It was frightening. It was exhausting."[29] Member Margo Okazawa-Rey remarked in an interview that it was amazing going to early meetings, simply a thrill—they were anti-imperialist, socialist, black, feminist, and lesbian.[30] Despite the development of several black leftist or liberal feminist groups in the late 1960s and early 1970s, including the National Black Feminist Organization, the Combahee women were self-conscious about their aloneness and sense of embarking on a new kind of politics. Demita Frazier recalled that, for a change:

> We weren't having to apologize for being smart. We weren't
> having to apologize for being intellectuals. We weren't having to
> apologize for feeling that we had a right to say what we saw and
> to speak the truth about what we saw. It was very powerful. And
> also because we recognized that it was powerful because we were
> standing at the cross roads of our own identity. We were not
> going to give up being female or being Black. We wanted a
> synthesis.[31]

The collective rapidly became an important feminist presence in Boston. Combahee member Mercedes Tompkins remarked, "Within Boston people looked to Combahee for anchoring around things— around the whole issue of race and culture. So that if you touch[ed] base with us or we were involved in giving support to a certain position, it almost gave them a rubber stamp."[32] In Okazawa-Rey's words, "[I]t kind of created the base line for thinking about black feminism, radical black feminism . . . a feminism that is radical: anti-imperialist, socialist, and is made up of black women—black lesbians in particular. And it kind of made us really visible and our politics was [sic] complex."[33]

The retreats were a "way for people who were separated to be in the same place and do some political work with each other."[34] But the retreats were more than that too: they were a way to connect to other black feminists, to learn and change, explore, celebrate, and organize. A good many of the women who participated—between twenty and thirty—were already or became well-known radical black feminists. The lesbian writer and activist Audre Lorde participated in them, and her involvement moved many of the younger women. Lorde's work was outspoken about racism, sexism, and heterosexism, and both her talent and courage inspired young feminists. Poet Cheryl Clarke recalled being at retreats with her: "Audre Lorde was an incredible inspiration. . . . hearing her talk about writing, the act of writing, and what it meant to her, was very inspiring for me and liberating." Clarke recounted how fearless Lorde and other women in the group were, how forbidden it was for black women to write, and how she began to write poetry as a result of the retreats.[35] Smith said:

> I used to feel like if only Lorraine [Hansberry] hadn't died so
> early then there would be someone who is older than me who is
> trying to carve out the territory. Audre [Lorde] was important to
> me in that way. Being able to look over to and up to someone
> who had been here more years than I, who shared the same kind
> of vision in politics.[36]

Many Combahee attendees were writers or aspiring writers who admired African-American women who had been persistent and brave enough to express themselves. A major contribution of the Combahee Collective and its retreats was to encourage women writers. In historian Miriam Lynell Harris's words, for these black women writing was an "act of resistance."[37]

Poet Pat Parker
reading at the Varied
Voices of Black
Women: An Evening
of Words and Music
concert, Boston
University, 1978.
© Ellen Shub.

Collective member Gloria Hull recalled:

> At the retreats we tried out our creative and critical work on
> each other; shared our latest reading; discussed books, music,
> and films. Planned (and sometimes executed) ways to spread
> Black feminism among Black women; formed nucleus groups
> for politically and culturally active projects; talked about
> ourselves and our lives, and engaged in stringent social critique
> and analysis. I probably do not need to say that we also
> drummed, danced, loved, laughed a lot, did rituals and made
> gorgeous meals.[38]

Smith recalled how exciting the retreats were, with people coming from
all over. She said that they had been organizing by that time for a couple
of years and were feeling isolated and hungry for more: "It was risky to be

a feminist in the Black community. We realized it was risky and there we were, all these risk takers, all these ground breakers."[39] Letters from young black feminists written to and by Barbara and Beverly Smith in the 1970s express all manner of need, excitement, discouragement, and discovery as they defined themselves, came out as lesbians, and looked for others with whom to create a black feminist movement.[40]

Most of the founding women were out lesbians or were in the process of coming out. Smith said that "the women who were integral to organizing Combahee were Lesbians," although there were also bisexual and straight women in the group.[41] She remarked that it was not an accident that most of them were lesbians or bisexual since they had less to lose in staking out a radical feminist antihomophobic or prolesbian politics and added, "In that era, many heterosexual black women did not want to work with open lesbians."[42] Radical black heterosexual feminists risked the disdain of men and the black community, of losing intimate relationships with men, of marginalizing themselves by calling themselves feminists. To call oneself a lesbian feminist in an era of nationalism in which the black community and heterosexuality were idealized was to place oneself outside that community. Given the homophobia of the country, including the radical movements, and, in Audre Lorde's words, the "hysterical rejection of lesbians in the black community," the Combahee River Collective's antiheterosexist black feminist politics explains their feelings of exhilaration, fear, and fatigue.[43] Founders of and activists in the NBFO, Combahee, and other pioneering black feminist groups, authors, founders of journals and a publishing company, Kitchen Table: Women of Color Press, in 1981—in which Barbara Smith was central—lesbians have been key black feminists.[44]

Intellectually, the Combahee River Collective built on Cade's *The Black Woman* as well as the work of activists and writers such as Ella Baker, Fannie Lou Hamer, Lorraine Hansberry, Pauli Murray, Alice Walker, Angela Davis, and Audre Lorde, women affiliated with the Black Arts movement, and numerous other movement activists and cultural workers. As a writer and an outspoken radical lesbian, Lorde's influence on young radical lesbians was enormous. Neither can the significance of Cade's *The Black Woman* be overestimated. About her own life, historian E. Frances White wrote, "This was a book I carried around with me during college as a political badge of honor. It marked me as a feminist within the black student movement."[45] Combahee member Gloria Hull remembered:

> Among . . . early formative reading, the most precious of all
> for me was *The Black Woman: An Anthology* . . . which I
> acquired in October 1970, the year it was published. . . . It gave
> me theory, analyses of current issues and cultural works, poetry
> and fiction. . . . In its uncompromisingly radical female and
> racial perspectives, *The Black Woman* taught me how our posi-
> tion could be both thoroughly feminist and for-real Black.

Indicating the wide influence of black and white writing on feminists,
Hull also wrote:

> Even with my current knowledge of all that is lacking in
> Friedan's analysis, I have to admit that her work deeply affected
> me (as it did other Black and Chicano women my age and
> slightly older). Looking at it now, I am still struck by its clear
> passion and radical persuasion. . . . It goes without saying
> that, because of my education, feminist tendencies, social
> positioning, and personal circumstances, I could identify with
> what Friedan was saying.[46]

Barbara Smith, Beverly Smith, and Demita Frazier were the authors
of the influential Combahee document, "A Black Feminist Statement,"
published in 1977. Barbara Smith was the most visible leader of the Combahee Collective, the most public representative of the group, and the primary author of their writings. In the document, they explicitly articulated
an anticapitalist and socialist perspective and made clear that race, class,
and sexual oppression are linked and cannot be prioritized:

> [W]e are actively committed to struggling against racial,
> sexual, heterosexual, and class oppression and see as our par-
> ticular task the development of integrated analysis and practice
> based upon the fact that the major systems of oppression are
> interlocking. The synthesis of these oppressions creates the
> conditions of our lives. As Black women we see Black feminism
> as the logical political movement to combat the manifold and
> simultaneous oppressions that all women of color face.[47]

Their experiences in the movements had led to Combahee: "It was our experience and disillusionment within these liberation movements, as well
as experience on the periphery of the white male left, that led to the need

to develop a politics that was anti-racist, unlike those of white women, and anti-sexist, unlike those of Black and white men."[48] They were the first or one of the first political groups to use the term *identity politics*, which appeared in their statement: "This focusing upon our own oppression is embodied in the concept of identity politics. We believe that the most profound and potentially the most radical politics come directly out of our identity, as opposed to working to end somebody else's oppression."[49] In an interview, Smith said, "I think we came up with the term. . . . I never really saw it anywhere else and I would suggest that people if they really want to find the origin of the term that they try to find it in any place earlier than in the Combahee River Collective statement. I don't remember seeing it anywhere else."[50]

The collective stated that sexism is as pervasive in black women's lives as is class and race and that they cannot be separated. They nonetheless declared racial solidarity with black men:

> Although we are feminists and lesbians, we feel solidarity with
> progressive Black men and do not advocate the fractionalization
> that white women who are separatists demand. Our situation as
> Black people necessitates that we have solidarity around the fact
> of race, which white women of course do not need to have with
> white men, unless it is their negative solidarity as racial
> oppressors. We struggle together with Black men against racism,
> while we also struggle with Black men about sexism.

At the same time, they argued, "Accusations that Black feminism divides the Black struggle are powerful deterrents to the growth of an autonomous Black women's movement." They clearly articulated a leftist politics: "We realize that the liberation of all oppressed peoples necessitates the destruction of the political-economic systems of capitalism and imperialism as well as patriarchy. We are socialists because we believe that work must be organized for the collective benefit of those who do the work and create the products and not for the profit of the bosses." The Combahee women were also critical of and deeply disappointed by white women's lack of effort to understand and struggle against racism in the feminist movement. Eliminating racism in the white women's movement is white women's work but, they said, they would continue to point out the white women's movement's racism.

From the moment "A Black Feminist Statement" was first published, it was hailed by black feminists. In the recent words of historian Robin D. G. Kelley, "The Combahee River Collective's 'Statement' remains one of the most important documents of the black radical movement in the twentieth century."[51] It clearly articulated a black socialist feminist position that argued that race, class, and gender intersected and had to be considered together if the oppressed situation of black women was to be understood, identified black women as a separate group with its own issues that could not be subsumed under the guise of the black community or within white feminism, criticized patriarchal politics in society and the Black Power movement but eschewed separatist politics, argued that capitalism oppressed people, and poignantly defined African-American women as damaged by the system but fighting for their freedom. Inspiring to generations of feminists around the country, white and of color, the Combahee River Collective's most important contribution was its "Statement."

Unsurprisingly, within the small Boston group, there were tensions. They worked to negotiate differences among themselves, but Combahee member Demita Frazier remarked that they had trouble coming to grips with class. The group had an anticapitalist critique of American society and embraced a socialist analysis and goals, but "many women felt excluded because they felt they didn't have the educational background and privilege of the leadership. We also had women feeling, rightfully so—women who were educated and who had struggled to get an education—that they didn't want to be told yet another time to hide that dimension of themselves." She continued that most of them had uncomfortable experiences due to class differences and "recognized that it was almost a taboo subject within the Black community," a divisive issue that was expected to be downplayed in the name of racial unity. "Even though we were primarily from poor and working-class backgrounds, somehow we were seen as aggressively articulate, educationally privileged, middle-class women, without an understanding of the issues of the 'average' Black woman." They had a class analysis that was, in retrospect, not sophisticated enough: "[T]he fact is that many of us who began life in poverty or as the children of working-class parents moved into the lower-, middle-, and upper-middle classes via education, professional attainment, and life experience." She suggested that they "were fairly naive about the depth of pain and anger the lack of consciousness about class privilege caused within the Black community."[52] As a fictional character in a book about consciousness raising reflected, "You scratch the surface of most of us middle-class black women and you're going to find we're first generation or at best second generation out of the ghetto or off the farm. Our ties to our families are deep, and we never forget where we come from, and where most of them still are."[53] Noting that most feminists assumed an unproblematic relationship between themselves and other African-American women, historian E. Frances White stated, "In part, this assumption derives from the working-class background of many feminists. Dealing with the transition to middle-class status may feel dangerously close to accepting charges that we are traitors to the race."[54]

The Boston Combahee group struggled with exactly such tensions around educational achievement and the kinds of interests achievement generated. Several group members were pursuing graduate degrees and were more intellectual and less activist than others. They read together and discussed what they read, but there were differences in approach and inclination. "Some Combahee members' acculturation into academic culture ran counter to other members' concepts of class struggle and grass-roots activism," wrote feminist historian Kimberly Springer.[55] Springer suggested that this was in part a debate about whether theorizing and writing counted as activism: "[B]ook knowledge and street knowledge were falsely opposed as aspects of Combahee members' Black feminist collective identity."[56] Margo Okazawa-Rey noted that the group had a class analysis but was really middle class, which meant that the members had few strong links to the neighborhoods and the black community. She wanted to be more activist and based in the community, and although individual members of the group were, Combahee was never really an activist group. Agreeing with Okazawa-Rey, member Mercedes Tompkins said, "I wanted to move outside of just talking about it. I wanted to do it."[57] Barbara Smith, on the other hand, noted that some Combahee women "used to make fun of the fact that I was pursuing a graduate degree. . . . That was really difficult for me because I loved what I did. I loved the literature and I valued education and learning."[58] Their diverse inclinations toward intellectual work and organizing in the black community raised issues of class identity that were emotionally loaded for women in the women's movement and particularly for African-American women.

Ironically, a moving statement by Demita Frazier described how when they organized Combahee, they finally felt that they did not have to apologize for being smart or intellectual, a theme in both black and white women's accounts of growing up in the 1950s and 1960s. Barbara Smith wrote that she "fits neither society's stereotypes nor Black men's expectations" and adds, "We are supposed to be telephone operators or bourgeois housewives . . . and not intellectuals which face it is what we are."[59] Combahee women were relieved and proud not to apologize to the outside world for their interests but, inevitably, within the group tensions arose about upward mobility, class, education, and their relationship to the community. A kind of anti-intellectualism pervaded all of the movements of the 1960s, including white and black feminism, leading activists to question education and theorizing. Suspicion of or impatience with intellectuals and theory were often linked to working-class or community politics where the goal was to become, or remain, a proletarian or community person oneself. By shedding one's privilege, the argument went, an activist was better able to organize the disadvantaged or to maintain links to the community, which might be undone by education. Young black radical women feared that upward mobility would fracture their connection to the community and the race, a concern that led to downplaying the benefits of graduate degrees and questioning those who were pursuing them. Other members of the Combahee River Collective were simply more inclined toward activism and impatient with theorizing and talk. They knew that their constituency was black women, and they wanted to organize them. While their class origins were not so different, their education and inclinations created differences, perceived in class terms, among them.

Similar questions arose over sexual preference. Combahee member Demita Frazier said that although they were dedicated to empowering all black women, they became identified as a black feminist lesbian organization. The Combahee River Collective bravely announced itself as opposed to "heterosexual oppression," and in the forging of their politics, straight women were often excluded. They were fighting rampant homophobia in their lives and dealing with the issue of race with white lesbians, but they did not address issues of concern to heterosexual or bisexual women: "[S]traight women who came to our organization had to struggle to find a place and a voice for themselves." Frazier noted that they weren't separatists, that they worked with progressive men in coalition: "But I never felt that we truly confronted . . . this tension between straight Black feminists and Black lesbians." At the same time, she pointed out, it was extremely important to emphasize what it meant to stand up and say, "I am a black lesbian feminist" in 1974—an act of bravery that "made it possible for women to live proud and authentic lives." They talked about sexual politics in the African-American community, not just lesbian sexuality, because "in our history of a people in this country, sexuality is so charged and so fraught with meaning. It was important to raise the issue of women's sexuality and lesbian sexuality just as a way of breaking the silence."[60] As in white feminist organizations, Combahee members negotiated the issue of sexuality in relation to the homophobia of the society as well as its expression within their own group. Primarily lesbians, they did not experience the wrenching internal divisions over sexual difference that Bread and Roses women had several years earlier, but when they organized in the community they were extremely sensitive to differences between themselves and other African-American women. Despite their concern that their lesbianism would discredit them, they were committed to truly acknowledging who they were.

Both the Combahee River Collective and Bread and Roses discovered that differences lay not just between the races but within them. Lesbianism divided women. Class and education divided them. Class and sexuality remained the perennial stumbling blocks of black women's national organizing and made solidarity difficult, as it did for white feminists. Black women learned that they had to address the class backgrounds and aspirations and sexual orientations that could divide them. Ironically, conflicts between women were often more bitter than struggles with male chauvinism, sexism, patriarchal institutions, and specific men. Black feminists faced multiple jeopardies in the world they inhabited and, sometimes even more disturbing, myriad complications within the organizations they were building.

I want to interrupt the story here to explore the time gap between the development of the radical white women's liberation movement in the late 1960s and the subsequent appearance of black feminism, an issue that comes up regularly in studies of multiracial feminism. Black feminist groups appeared in the late 1960s and 1970s, but despite black women's political support for feminist goals of equality of pay and of opportunity, they did not embrace black feminism in substantial numbers. Black feminism was never a grass roots movement; black feminists did not create or join many organizations. Indicating that she did not consider a black feminist movement imminent, Cellestine Ware, the black feminist author of the 1970 book *Woman Power* wrote, "It is not unlikely that five years from now a wave of lower-class and college-educated black women, disillusioned by their oppression in the black militant movement (much like white women from radical student organizations in feminism now) will be coming into the feminist movement." She pointed out that white feminists were "unable to attract black women to the female liberation cause."[61] And years later, in 1979, Combahee River Collective member Barbara Smith stated that white women in general do not grasp that

> the Black feminist movement is in a very different period
> historically than the white feminist movement, even though
> the participants in these movements are each other's
> contemporaries. I have been constantly aware of this "time-lag"
> during my seven years of involvement in Black feminist politics.
> If measured by the closedness of the Black community to
> feminism, the still relatively small number of Black women who
> identify themselves as feminists, and the lack of Black feminist
> institutions Black women have, our movement is still in its early
> stages.

White women should recognize this and "not assume that it means the same thing for us to be feminists and lesbians as it does [for] them to be feminists and lesbians."[62]

Most writing by black feminists at this time chronicled a hostile rejection by black women. Recall, too, the unsympathetic responses of both men and women to Black Arts and Panther women who raised issues of sexual politics and gender equality. The Combahee women felt alone in 1974 in their identification as radical, black, antiheterosexist feminists. "When I first became a feminist, my black friends used to cast pitying eyes upon me and say, 'That's whitey's thing,'" wrote feminist author Michele Wallace.[63] As late as 1981, feminist authors Gloria Joseph and Jill Lewis noted that black women did not get involved in feminism: "Indeed, they barely did at all."[64] Many black women were reluctant to consider themselves feminists in part, of course, because of its association with white feminism and the fear that it would split the black community.

Evaluations of black women's disinterest in feminism were often gauged in terms of recruitment to white feminist groups—not an accurate criterion since black women were unlikely to join them. But even between black women, feminism was not an easy topic. Letters written in 1975 to Barbara and Beverly Smith of the Combahee River Collective worried that "the relatively small number of Black feminists today" is due to a "deliberate avoidance" of feminism, and another wrote, "everywhere I went women of color looked at me with empty eyes. We really do not know. We really have no movement of our own. It really scares me because the need is so obvious in the eyes of these women for some direction."[65] In 1989, well-known black feminist writer bell hooks remarked that black feminism had had little impact: "Small groups of black feminist theorists and activists who use the term 'black feminism' (the Combahee River Collective is one example) have not had much success in organizing large groups of black women, or stimulating widespread interest in [a] feminist movement."[66] In the minds of most black feminists, black feminism was not a grassroots movement primarily because it was more controversial in the black community than among whites.

But there is debate about chronology. Scholars are revising the white, second wave feminist history with which we are familiar, placing black feminism at its beginning and even its center and, in some cases, suggesting that the wave analogy is not pertinent to women of color feminism. They argue that the development of black feminist organizations—as well as other feminisms of color—paralleled the development of white feminist organizations. Historian E. Frances White wrote that the "authoritative view of the rise of the feminist movement" ignores the early experiences and resistance of black women in the antiwar and black nationalist movements, presenting the movement as stemming exclusively from white women's experiences in SNCC and SDS, with black women solely concerned with race: "In contrast, I propose that there was always a small but vital group of black feminists in the mainstream women's movement and there were also feminists in the black liberation movement." White criticized feminist history for not being interested in the "early rumblings of black feminism" and cited Toni Cade's *The Black Woman* as proof of early black feminism: "Clearly, black feminists were active at the end of the 1960s and in dialogue with each other."[67] Kimberly Springer said that, despite commonly accepted ideas, black women *were* interested in feminism, "black women did call themselves feminists," and they "played significant leadership roles in the mainstream and radical branches of the women's movement."[68] African-American women were ambivalent about white women's liberation, but their "general hostility to feminism has been greatly exaggerated."[69] These authors have suggested that black feminism developed as early as white feminism in the 1960s but has been historically eclipsed by the rapid and successful growth of white feminism. Separate feminisms developed out of different contexts and conditions, but "Black feminist organizing began roughly when white feminist organizing did, albeit in smaller numbers. Scholars have conflated the timing of Black feminist emergence with the separate analytical problem of the numbers of Black women involved in feminist groups," wrote Benita Roth, and playing the "numbers game" obscures the "simultaneity and *interrelatedness* of Black and white feminist emergence, the very mutual influence that some feminists had on one another across racial lines." If we "stop expecting large numbers of Black feminists to flock to white organizations, we can see that second-wave feminism was *at its roots* the creation of Black and white women."[70]

What appears to be at stake is dating black feminism further back than has heretofore been acknowledged in order to recognize its significant place in feminist history.[71] Second wave feminism has been studied primarily as a white movement, and these authors correct the record by pointing out that there were black feminists, although not in large numbers, active in the early years of the second wave (perhaps even more in the liberal wing) and, most important, that white, black, and Chicana feminisms mutually influenced one another. Their work, along with others who have made similar points over the past thirty years, points to active African-American feminists in the early years of the second wave. They err, however, in overemphasizing the formation of a black feminist movement in the late 1960s and early 1970s.[72] Theirs are organizational histories that downplay the particularly unfriendly climate in which black feminism developed and the animosity of radical black women toward white feminism. Racial discrimination and black nationalism meant that black women were much less likely than young white women to become feminist political activists. There was a good deal of overt hostility toward black feminism by women influenced by the Black Power movement who thought that it was divisive in the black community, criticized black men, and exacerbated difficulties in heterosexual relationships. Young white women were decidedly more receptive to the feminist movement than were black women. White movement women's logical trajectory led directly out of the New Left toward feminism. Race was not a direct issue for them. The TWWA, NBFO, Combahee River Collective, and other groups represented the stirrings of a separate black feminist movement that did not make its presence felt until the late 1970s and 1980s, and even then there was never a mass movement. Rather, the importance of the timing debate lies in its recuperation of black and multiracial feminism from within the dominant white narrative of second wave feminism. It teaches women, especially white women who have been feminism's primary chroniclers and audience, that the seeds of radical black feminism were sown early.

Organizational studies, particularly those tracking origins, often overlook the political and cultural context in which early black feminism developed, thereby ignoring one of the strongest incentives behind black feminism: black feminists' hard feelings toward white women and white feminism, which provides a framework for making sense of an important factor in the development of Combahee and other black feminist groups. Their anger indicates a continuity of radical black women's concerns from the mid-1960s SNCC days to the end of the 1970s. It was within this setting that the Combahee River Collective formed, and it helps to explain why an interracial feminism did not develop. In contrast to white feminists, women of the dominant racial group who did not have to respond to other women and whose movement was large and powerful, black feminists inevitably reacted to white feminism. In Benita Roth's formulation, white feminists' class privilege and relative advantages became the reference point to be challenged by women of color feminists.[73] Strains between white and black women and between black women and black men are part of the story of black feminism; black feminism formed in the midst of angry debates and feelings and, in some cases, was inspired by them. Black Power and white women's liberation left radical black women disappointed and alone, struggling to build their own movement. Hope and ideals were no longer focused on the larger movement communities but on themselves. The Combahee women were excited to find each other, as were women of the NBFO and other groups, but black feminist anger is not irrelevant to the story of the development of separate feminisms; it contributed to the shape of the trouble between white and black women. Tensions stemming from black feminists' intense feelings about race and class politics and from sexual politics between women and men provide a sense of the environment in which black feminism developed. One of the most important dynamics was black women's rejection of white feminism.

The pervasive explanation for the development of black feminism, by black and white feminists alike, including the Combahee River Collective was, simply, the racism of the white women's liberation movement. According to historian E. Frances White:

> Many black feminists sought out white feminists in what at first seemed like a natural alliance: womanhood. Feminism made all women more aware of themselves as women and extended support to black women as they confronted the sexism of black men. Serious divisions among women were temporarily obscured by the call for women to unite. Black women entered alliances with white women with the expectation that a raised consciousness of female oppression led to a constructive sensitivity towards other forms of subordinating oppressions. When many white feminists remained blind to major class and race differences, black feminists felt betrayed.[74]

In the first pages of her 1984 book, *Feminist Theory: From Margin to Center*, bell hooks stated:

> [W]hite women who dominate feminist discourse today rarely question whether or not their perspective on women's reality is true to the lived experience of women as a collective group. Nor are they aware of the extent to which their perspectives reflect race and class biases. . . . Racism abounds in the writings of white feminists, reinforcing white supremacy and negating the possibility that women will bond politically across ethnic and racial boundaries.[75]

She and many other black feminists have been vocal in their bitterness. Academic and activist Barbara Omolade wrote that black feminists were "always being contained, discouraged, and limited by white women who in spite of their so-called 'feminist politics' replicated existing power relationships, which minimized and subordinated us because of our race."[76] Writer doris davenport echoed her, "[W]e experience white feminists and their organizations as elitist, crudely insensitive, and condescending. Most of the feminist groups in this country are examples of this elitism."[77] Combahee member Lorraine Bethel's poem title says it simply, "What Chou Mean *We*, White Girl? Or, the Cullud Lesbian Feminist Declaration of Independence (Dedicated to the Proposition that All Women are Not Equal, i.e., identical/ly Oppressed.)"[78] Black women questioned white women's notion of sisterhood, noting that the "sister" was almost always white and middle class and that women of color were invisible or mistreated in feminist practice.

Commenting on the racist and "self-indulgent politics of the sisterhood," educator and activist Sheila Radford-Hill remarked that she began to understand that "white feminists' fixation on patriarchal dominance masked their culpability for black women's oppression and for their own."[79] White women did not develop a view of the relationship of racism and sexism; they did not acknowledge their white skin privilege and racism.[80] Anthropologist Leith Mullings wrote, "My own ambivalence toward the mainstream women's movement was rooted in issues of race and class."[81] In 1988, sociologist Deborah K. King wrote of the failings of the feminist movement. While black women were supposedly included in the sisterhood, "[t]he assertion of commonality, indeed of the universality and primacy of female oppression, denies the other structured inequalities of race, class, religion, and nationality, as well as denying the diverse cultural heritages that affect the lives of many women." Feminism has neglected, misunderstood, or ignored the politics of race and class that directly affect the lives of black women.[82] Historian Deborah Gray White bluntly summed it up: "Few African-American women thought black and white women had anything in common."[83] Many, many feminists of color have made these points; this selection gives a sense of the widespread convergence of their critiques.

The following incident illustrates the racial divide. In August 1970, there was a large feminist demonstration in New York City. Frances Beal of the Third World Women's Alliance, along with other black women, were carrying placards about the imprisoned Angela Davis. "We had signs reading 'Hands Off Angela Davis,'" Beal recalled, "and one of the leaders of NOW ran up to us and said angrily, 'Angela Davis has nothing to do with the women's liberation.'" "It has nothing to do with the kind of liberation you're talking about," retorted Beal, "but it has everything to do with the kind of liberation we're talking about."[84] The incident reveals the differences between white liberal and socialist feminism since liberals were more narrowly focused on gender issues but, more important, the encounter articulates black radical women's sense of the indivisibility of race and sex, of the distance between white and black notions of feminism. Whether or not she was a feminist, from radical black women's perspective, Davis was a militant leftist, female, African-American political prisoner, a heroine and symbol for them of racial oppression. Racial divisions between feminists were reinforced by some women's liberationists' inability to recognize that the intersections of race and class with sex put women of color at risk in American society and that, from black women's perspective, defending Davis was a feminist act. All black commentators agree on the weakness or irrelevance of white feminist analyses for black women. Black feminism developed on its own path in part because black women were not subordinated solely through their sex. White feminism appeared to separate race and racial justice struggles from their feminist analyses, unable to consider race, class, and gender together as feminist issues.

Black women felt betrayed and enraged. Their statements convey deep feelings that white, middle-class feminists were blind to any women's situation but their own. The way they saw it, white feminists did not genuinely seek out black women on their own terms. They invited them to be speakers at their meetings, conferences, and demonstrations more as tokens than as integral participants. They often only included black women in their political analyses—or meetings—in order to make themselves feel less guilty for being white. Their understanding of the black woman's situation was superficial, and they did little to remedy it. Thus black feminists could not look to the white women's liberation movement for solutions to the problems in their lives.

In a class-related explanation of why "most black women stayed away" from white feminism, historian Deborah Gray White wrote, "The white woman's demand for a more 'meaningful' existence was not taken seriously by African-American women who had more experience as the domestic employees of these women than as their political allies."[85] White women were too advantaged to be oppressed. Barbara Smith and her sister Beverly "both talked about how we thought these people were just crazy because we couldn't understand what white women had to complain about."[86] Black militant Assata Shakur, in jail at the time, wrote, "Most of us rejected the white women's movement. Miss ann was still Miss ann to us whether she burned her bras or not. We could not muster sympathy for the fact that she was trapped in her mansion and oppressed by her husband." She continued, "[W]e had no desire to sit in some consciousness raising group with white women and bare our souls."[87] In the words of Angela Davis, "Feminism was not a popular subject among most black women in revolutionary organizations. While many of us may have detested the overt sexism of male leaders, we tended to associate feminism with middle-class white women who could not understand our battles against racism."[88] Reflecting their privilege, white women exhibited insensitivity about structural differences by often emphasizing gender above race and class. Put simply, white women's privileging of gender in an image of a universal sisterhood undercut the possibility of women of color feeling part of that sisterhood.

One argument by black women has maintained that they rejected feminism because of white racism and class privilege. Another line of argument has suggested that black women were already liberated in ways that white women were not and thus did not need feminism. In the words of Barbara Smith, "The popular assumptions about this question are that Black women are not interested in 'women's lib' [*sic*] and that they have *never* been interested in it and that they are *already* liberated."[89] Black feminist Michele Wallace put it this way: "Hardly a week passed during the late sixties and early seventies when there wasn't an article on how black women felt that women's liberation was irrelevant to them because they were already liberated."[90] She refers to articles in black magazines and journals, speeches, and statements by Black Power advocates. Implicated in the idea of the irrelevance of white feminism was some black women's wish, usually deeply influenced by nationalist gender politics, not to reject black men. In a 1972 report prepared for the Black Women's Community Development Foundation about militant black women, Inez Smith Reid found three general reactions to feminism. The women she interviewed expressed concern that feminism would undermine relationships between black women and men, a fear that the women's movement would co-opt the black movement, and empathy for particular goals of women's liberation, especially those connected with improving women's economic position and employment opportunities.[91] "The recurring point of contention that black women have with feminism is its impact on Black male/female relationships. Many times, Black feminists in the 1970s spent so much time reaffirming their commitment to Black men and the Black community that their gender critiques and actions to end sexism fell by the wayside," wrote Kimberly Springer in her study of black feminism.[92]

In the midst of these sentiments, we know that radical African-American women, those who were most receptive to feminism, deplored the male chauvinism of the black liberation movement. "Black women, particularly those who founded Black feminist organizations, were less ambivalent than some civil rights forerunners and nationalist women about the importance of gender struggles in Black communities," wrote Springer.[93] Barbara Smith said simply that she was turned off by the sexism of black nationalism.[94] Frances Beal wrote that when it came to women, the black male in the Black Power movement "seems to take his guidelines from the pages of the *Ladies Home Journal.* Certain black men are maintaining that they have been castrated by society but that Black women somehow escaped this persecution and even contributed to this emasculation."[95] Historian E. Frances White recalled contentious meetings with black nationalist men and women about the assertion of black men's "masculinity at our expense" and suggested, "These meetings were one of the immediate sources of black feminism."[96] The fragility of the black community, the notions that black women needed to strengthen and support black men and that complementary roles suited black traditions, the importance of loyalty to the race—all of these ideas affected even black women who rejected the sexism of the Black Power movement, women who were sympathetic to feminism. "The combination . . . of the pressure to maintain (at least outwardly) racial solidarity with Black men and of alienation from the agenda of the predominantly white middle-class women's movement account, historically, for Black women's reluctance to identify as feminist," wrote Margo Perkins, a scholar of militant black women's 1960s activism.[97] Black feminists were unique in their defiance of such pressure.

Romantic and sexual relationships between black men and white women played a part in black women's wariness of white feminism, as they had during Freedom Summer and in SNCC. Black women, particularly in the Black Arts movement, some of whom contributed to Toni Cade's *The Black Woman*, were bitter about black men's interest in white women and their unflattering portraits of black women. Brenda Eichelberger, chair of the Chicago NBFO and later of the National Alliance of Black Feminists that grew out of NBFO, mentioned that one of the central issues that came up in discussions in Chicago was interracial relationships: "This problem is a thorn in the side of the black women, the fact that some black men date and marry white women, especially when there are so many fewer black men than black women to begin with."[98] At the height of black militancy, riots, and enormous racial turmoil, during her teenage years, Michele Wallace noted, "That same fall the streets of New York witnessed the grand coming-out of black male/white female couples. Frankly, I found this confusing. . . . In '67, black was angry, anywhere from vaguely to militantly anti-white; black was sexy and had unlimited potential. What did the black man want with a white woman now?"[99] In her study of militant black women, Inez Smith Reid wrote about the "heated responses" that the subject of black men and white women evoked, making a "Black woman ready to spit fire."[100] She related black men's derogatory remarks about black women, why they preferred white women, and black women's angry and confused feelings about interracial relationships and summarized: "It is not erroneous to assert that most Black women eagerly look forward to the day when all ties and relationships between Black males and White females will be severed." They viewed these relationships as "incorrect."[101] An article in *Essence*, "Men on Women," by a male college instructor, concluded, "[T]hese sisters, who champion the cause of Black female liberation and security, see themselves as tragic figures, . . . damned to inevitable frustration and loneliness because they are a new species without sane, responsive and relevant mates." They felt that too many black men chose white women as partners.[102] Toni Morrison referred to the "growing rage of black women over unions of black men and white women. . . . Clearly there are more and more of these unions, for there is clearly more anger about it." She bitterly remarked that black women consider themselves to be superior to white women and regard the black man's choice of a white woman to be an inferior one. Black women are always asking each other why black men choose the dumb, ugly, flat "nobodies of the race? Why no real women? The answer, of course, is obvious. What would such a man who preferred white women do with a real woman? And would a white woman who is looking for black exotica ever be a complete woman?"[103] Feminist activist and lawyer Eleanor Holmes Norton argued that one of the reasons that some black women attacked the women's movement, a reason that "no one likes to discuss, is that many Black women associate the women's movement with white women's ability to steal our men."[104]

These many reflections were part of an intense discussion in the late 1960s and 1970s about relationships between black women and black men, black matriarchy, sexism in the black community, and the black family—all of which played a part in shaping the concerns of black feminism. Black women, especially feminists, were on the defensive as they worked to construct a strong and independent image of themselves. The Moynihan Report had revived old controversies about strong women and weak men, men who couldn't or wouldn't protect and care for their families, women who took over as a result and were too strong, and the effects on sons and black progress. The debates unfolded in the pages of the *Black Scholar*, which had articles and issues devoted to black sexism, the black man, the black woman, the black family, black women and feminism, and black women's critique of black men. Academics and intellectuals explored black men's interest in white women, the lack of appropriate partners for black women due to a sex ratio imbalance and higher education among women, whether there was a black matriarchy or if it was in the interest of men, white and black, to portray the black family in this manner, the vulnerability that black men felt due to racist structures that prevented them from succeeding, the hurt and anger that both men and women felt. Black feminists were particular targets of black men. In 1979, Robert Staples wrote "The Myth of Black Macho: A Response to Angry Black Feminists," an attack on ntozake shange's poignantly titled play "for colored girls who have considered suicide" and black feminist Michele Wallace's book *Black Macho and the Myth of the Superwoman*, both of which had received a great deal of negative attention because they were considered inflammatory and controversial in their portrayals of black women as suffering and black men as sexist. Staples deplored the absence of a male voice in shange's and Wallace's work and suggested that they were attacking black malehood, which had always been undermined in this racist, capitalist society. He criticized women for not being supportive and feminine enough and agreed with Wallace about heterosexual difficulties: "Ms. Wallace is, oh, so correct when she says that the last 50 years has [*sic*] seen a growing distrust, even hatred, between black men and women."[105] The next issue of the *Black Scholar*, "The Black Sexism Debate," was filled with responses.

The rawness of the discussion, similar to Black Arts movement women's laments and criticisms of men and the men's reactions, is startling.[106] Almost all of the writers confirm Staples's conclusion of a growing estrangement between African-American women and men. (One has to question whether heterosexual relationships were so much better among whites.) Psychiatrist Alvin Poussaint wondered whether black feminists shange and Wallace were not cooperating with white feminists in order to keep the black male in his place. In his view, the black woman had joined white society in scapegoating the black male. Black male and black female contributors to the response issue of the *Black Scholar*, including Audre Lorde, June Jordan, and Julianne Malveaux, who entitled her piece "The Sexual Politics of Black People: Angry Black Women, Angry Black Men," almost all agreed that regardless of the merit of the work being debated, there were problems between black women and black men that had to be acknowledged and addressed. Sexual politics were discussed publicly, often rancorously. Unlike white men, black men were directly engaged in dialogue with the women. Most, but not all, of those involved in these debates were heterosexuals and were convinced that a great deal was at stake in their relationships and families. The bitterness of the discussion also revealed how deeply participants believed that the future of the black community was implicated in the divisions between women and men and that feminists exacerbated the divide. Most lesbian feminists were obviously less concerned with male/female relationships, but all young black radical women were affected by these opinions and had to fight desperately to forge an autonomous, authentic political position for themselves. A separate black movement was threatening to men and to community solidarity. Over time, with more and younger feminist lesbians involved, both the black and white feminist movements became less focused on men, but in the 1970s, black feminists were isolated and unpopular.

Another factor that generated distrust was that women's liberationists credited Black Power with the inspiration for their own political activity. Latinos, Asian Americans, women, and gays all modeled their movements on the Black Power movement. Historian of feminism Alice Echols stated, "Black Power enabled them to argue that it was valid for women to organize around their own oppression and to define the terms of their struggle."[107] Echols also suggested that Black Power had different consequences for white and black women. While it conferred masculine privilege and women's subordination in the Black Power movement, it fostered feminist consciousness among white women.[108] White women embraced it as a way to defend themselves against the criticism of white men for separating from the mixed New Left. They argued that they had to set their own agendas and goals, distinct from men. But in the view of many black women, the women's movement "coincided with the deterioration of the Black movement," and "it appeared that the predominantly White women's movement was going to reap the benefits that the Black movement had sown. Comparing the status of women to that of Blacks was particularly upsetting."[109] In 1970, Linda La Rue wrote in the *Black Scholar*: "[O]ne can argue that Women's liberation has not only attached itself to the Black movement but has done so with only marginal concern for Black women and Black liberation."[110] And in Toni Morrison's words, "[T]oo many movements and organizations have made deliberate overtures to enroll blacks and have ended up by rolling them. They don't want to be used again to help somebody gain power."[111] Radical black activists were suspicious of the women's liberation movement for what they interpreted as its piggybacking on Black Power and dividing black women and men. Barbara Omolade wrote of activist black women: "Many have chosen to ignore or condemn the call of feminists to join them in fighting sexist oppression, as a ploy to sidetrack them from the larger issue of racism."[112] Most African Americans felt that white women had neither fought and sacrificed as had blacks, nor had they proven themselves. Like spoiled children, they had gained something for nothing. "As the 1970s progressed, and the women's movement got stronger, while the black movement was attacked and weakened, these feelings only deepened," wrote historian Deborah Gray White.[113]

At the moment that the Black Power movement waned, white women were blamed for the success of the women's liberation movement. Interpreting the link between the two events is complex, but it is fair to say that identity politics were enthusiastically embraced by many subordinate groups in this period, not just white women, and analyses of which groups were successful and how to define success are not simple. Black socialist feminists were also inspired by the idea of organizing themselves and that impetus came from Black Power, white feminism, and gay liberation. While it may have appeared that white feminism was appropriating the energy of the Black Power movement, it was not purposeful, and feminism's success had more to do with social and economic conditions and social movement energy that had been building throughout the decade. The decline of the Black Power movement cannot be attributed to the success of the women' liberation movement. It was, nevertheless, one more issue that contributed to black women's mistrust of white feminism.

In short, feminism was controversial. According to bell hooks, any "black woman who uses the term risks being seen as a race traitor," a phrase that recurs in discussions of black feminism.[114] Historian E. Frances White noted that, for black women, upward mobility and becoming middle class could mean that they would be targeted as traitors to the race. Moving out of the community, class, and family into feminism was fraught with accusations of treachery that, for the most part, white middle-class women did not have to face. Regardless of these charges and challenges, radical black women formed organizations and wrote about the precarious situation of black women in a racist and sexist society. Often black feminists were angry and frustrated, but they saw the desperate need for feminism and persevered. They formed mostly local radical groups whose goals included encouraging black women to become feminists, organizing them into political action, and theorizing about their subordinate position in the United States. Absorbing lessons from the movements all around them, radical black women's organizations, with Combahee prominent among them, were determined to articulate a politics based on who they were.

Organizing on the basis of one's own identity was the only strategy that made sense by then to many political activists.[115] Interracial feminism was not viable, at least for African-American women. As the Combahee River Collective wrote, "We believe that the most profound and potentially the most radical politics come directly out of our own identity, as opposed to working to end somebody else's oppression."[116] Several years later, Barbara Smith reiterated, "Anything we do is informed by our identity. 'Identity politics' is really a very substantial concept for what we practice. In other words we practice a politics that mesh with our real physical identities."[117] White and black women felt liberated by being able to focus on their own situations. But, and this is a crucial difference, for white women this did not mean just women within their own racial group, but all women. By the mid-1970s, black women, however, saw no other path than to center themselves.

Benita Roth's study of second wave feminism suggested:

> [The] ethos of organizing one's own was accepted by feminists
> in each racial/ethnic community, leading to a consensus
> whereby feminists agreed among themselves that it was
> impossible for them to organize across lines of race and
> ethnicity. When feminists did talk to each other across color
> lines, they frequently found common ground on just how
> impossible it would be for them to work closely together.

Their vision was more of "separate movements in some sort of vaguely defined future alliance."[118] She argued that, in the late 1960s and 1970s, identity politics led women of all races and ethnicities to organize within their own groups. From this perspective, white women's lack of success in building an interracial feminist movement can be viewed as due, in part, to black women's lack of interest in joining white feminism. Compelling racial identity politics in the Black Power movement and the invisibility of black women's issues in the white women's movement led black feminists to concentrate on themselves. (Organizing one's own also can help to explain white women's sense that black women were not interested in feminism or were more interested in their differences from white women, which was expressed at the 1968 Sandy Springs socialist feminist conference and by white women throughout the period.)

But, while this is an accurate description of black feminist politics, it is not an accurate description of white socialist feminist politics. White women did not participate in a consensus in which women of different races agreed not to organize one another. Despite the encouragement that white socialist feminists found in identity politics to separate from the New Left and the antiwar movement, it was men from whom they wished to separate, not black women. They were committed to building an interracial movement. White women built an autonomous women's movement but were simultaneously inspired by ideas of sisterhood across races and ethnicities. Most black women were not. Disappointment shaped the politics of both Bread and Roses and subsequent Boston white socialist feminists as it did the Combahee River Collective as they looked toward one another—whites hoping to join together with blacks and blacks disengaging because classism and racism were apparently not high priorities for white feminists. Identity politics operated differently for each group.

The Combahee River Collective's "Statement" remains the group's central contribution. In member Demita Frazier's words, the most important part of her feminist journey was the empowerment it had fostered in her:

> The strength that, as young Black women, we found in
> supporting one another, in defying the myths about who we
> were and could be; the delight we took in our intellectuality; the
> permission we gave each other to express, as activists, the power
> we knew in our hearts was a legacy from our foremothers, not
> some superficial affront to the egos of men; all these things
> made it possible for me to explore the world, secure in the
> knowledge that I have a place within it, with my own gifts to
> share.[119]

The Combahee River Collective, in conjunction with other black socialist feminists of the time, brought home to all feminists that race, class, and gender were indivisible in understanding the lives of the oppressed, a central tenet of radical second wave feminism. By articulating a theory that located themselves socially and politically, they insisted that the real lives of black women had to be taken into account, that *they* would have to be taken into account. Little more than a decade after it appeared, black (and women of color) feminism had established its presence, particularly its insistence that race was central to feminism, so that no feminists could easily assume a universal sisterhood. Not numerous in these years but powerfully persuasive, black socialist feminists, building on the civil rights and Black Power movements, alerted white feminists to the seriousness of race and class and transformed feminist thinking.

Apart and Together Boston, Race, and **5**

Feminism in the 1970s and Early 1980s

> As women, we have been taught either to ignore our
> differences or to view them as causes for separation and
> suspicion rather than as forces for change.
> —Audre Lorde, "The Master's Tools Will Never
> Dismantle the Master's House" (1979)

> If then we begin to recognize what the separation of black
> and white women means, it must become clear
> that it means separation from ourselves.
> —Adrienne Rich, "Disloyal to Civilization: Feminism,
> Racism, Gynephobia" (1979)

By the mid-1970s and early 1980s, second wave feminism was a tidal wave at its crest, evident locally and nationally in the thousands of activities and projects initiated by feminists.[1] Every aspect of American life was shaken and transformed. Black feminism was part of the mix, gathering steam, generating challenges to whites, particularly white feminists, and to the black community. In the accelerating energy to build an autonomous black feminist movement, black feminists initiated projects; wrote papers, poems, and books; and organized conferences, institutions, and campaigns. They had enough clout, through their writing and organizing, to demand that white feminists pay attention to the situations of black women and other women of color, to demand that the race, gender, class, and often heterosexist discrimination they faced be recognized and rectified. "[I]t is safe to say in 1982 that we have a movement of our own," remarked Combahee River Collective leader Barbara Smith.[2] They challenged white feminists to examine and understand their racism and convert the movement into one in which women of all races and ethnicities were recognized, were affirmed, and could operate fully; they demanded an analysis and a movement that confirmed the importance of race and class as well as gender. At the historic 1977 International Women's Year

Conference in Houston in which 20,000 women participated, 35 percent of the delegates were nonwhite and nearly one in five was low income. The huge conference was inclusive and expansive with a sense of sisterhood evident throughout.[3] One of the important positions the conference adopted in its Plan for Action, in addition to support for ratification of the Equal Rights Amendment, was a plank of minority rights. Women of color took turns reading the minority plank to the entire assembly—"one of the high moments of the conference," according to Bella Abzug.[4] About Houston, Barbara Smith wrote, "At the moment of the passing of the minority women's resolution, there was so much feeling about what it meant. Very different kinds of women, women who had never laid eyes on each other before were all in the same room and they had to deal with each other. They had to. There was no choice. We couldn't get out."[5]

After Bread and Roses disbanded in 1971, committed Boston socialist feminists, often lesbians, continued to work in a variety of projects involving women's health, abortion and reproductive rights, day care, media, violence against women, tenant and labor organizing, and learning about multiracial and multiethnic women's history. Some organized in working-class settings. New and younger women joined all sections and currents of the women's movement, including socialist feminism, some of whose academic and intellectual members debated questions such as how women's unpaid labor, housework, and childcare fit into a Marxist framework. In the belief that such definitions and analyses would shape and inform their practice, a good deal of white socialist feminist activity revolved around defining socialist feminism, particularly the relationship of patriarchy to capitalism. Among the pronounced characteristics of the socialist feminist women's unions that formed around the country in those years were detailed, often abstract, intellectual debates and self-criticism about their white and middle-class membership.

Theorizing competed with bitter moralism as a defining feature of socialist feminist politics as women berated themselves and each other about the demographic narrowness of their membership. Socialist feminist women's unions have been described as "wallowing in self-blame, denial and guilt" because of their white and middle-class base.[6] Sociologist Karen Hansen argued that socialist feminist women's union members chastised themselves to the point of immobilization: "There has to be a middle ground between recognizing the race and class biases of a perspective or an organization and flagellating a membership to the point that it is nonfunctional."[7] In 1975, thousands of women attended a national socialist feminist conference in Yellow Springs, Ohio. The reports of this conference suggest that it was "one more occasion for the politics of division, blame, and guilt. Ideological conflict overrode any wish for organization building or strategic planning." One participant reported that the group had to drop much of what had been planned and "gather on the commons to hear mostly white women denounce the planners as a bunch of racists and then have open mike about that for hours."[8] Nevertheless, in the midst of often fruitless debates about issues of race and class, white socialist feminists did organize, not as immobilized as reports would indicate. Groups were founded, including the Boston Area Socialist Feminist Organization and then the Boston Women's Union, both of which combined theory and activism and whose forerunner was Bread and Roses. The Cambridge Women's Center, the Women's School, and other projects thrived. In spite of sometimes tedious theorizing and acrimonious controversy, socialist feminists helped to organize campaigns, courses, demonstrations, and conferences. White and black feminists— notably the Combahee River Collective—and other feminists of color were very much on the move.

Difference is the word that epitomizes the central political insight of the feminisms of those years. Some would call it *identity politics.* Sisterhood had been the rallying cry of the early radical women's movement of primarily white women as they broke from mixed male and female movement organizations and from male-dominated and male-identified lives. The recognition of male chauvinism and sexism, of patriarchy and misogyny led young white feminists to explore the similarities of their situations as women, to proclaim themselves sisters, to contribute to a powerful social movement for women's equality and liberation. Nevertheless, they wavered between a vision of all women, more alike than different, working together to eradicate power differences between the sexes, and a recognition that differences existed among women as well, central to which was power. Power was deeply implicated in divisions based on skin color, class, and ethnicity.

As black and women of color feminisms developed, white feminists were forced to deal with racism and differences. But all feminists had no choice but to confront differences, primarily sexual preference, ethnic, and class differences within their own movements. Women of color struggled over the terms *women of color* and *third world women:* whether and

Women Decide banner at a reproductive rights rally in Boston, 1979.
© Ellen Shub.

how such an inclusive term effaced their differences, particularly as they often identified in terms of their race or ethnicity. Identity politics were exhilarating for previously marginalized groups, but attempting to carve out bases for cooperation and shared perspectives often was not. The "we" of which black women had never felt a part in the first place was gone. "Whereas in the early seventies white feminists talked about 'women' as a relatively uncomplicated category, by the late seventies feminist journals were filled with criticism and self-recrimination about the 'whiteness' of the movement in response to the increasingly visible presence of feminist groups of women of color," wrote historian Sara Evans.[9] That sisterhood and difference do not necessarily preclude one another had to be learned repeatedly, and in the process, complaints and criticisms of one another were reiterated. Anger and disappointment were common among and between white women and women of color as feminism changed from its earlier ideals to the recognition of the complexities of difference.

In the course of writing this book, it became apparent that many women who did not consider themselves part of the feminist movement had organized on behalf of women during these years. There were thousands of grassroots women, usually working-class women of all races, working in their local communities, including Boston, to set up battered women's shelters, rape crisis centers, programs for women with substance abuse problems, tenants' unions, neighborhood groups, day care and medical programs, afterschool programs, and welfare rights groups. Such activities were evidence of the success of feminist ideas and practice throughout the society, even though community women, particularly community women of color, rarely joined feminist groups and did not self-identify as feminists. They organized in their communities, and if their paths crossed with feminists, they worked together when they could. For example, Kattie Portis, a Boston African-American activist and advocate for poor women, said that she learned from feminism but did what she needed to do guided by her own experience and the community's needs. She sometimes had to stand her ground with feminists who thought they knew better than she, and sometimes she worked with them, but did not define herself as a feminist even if people in her community defined her that way.

Over time there was more overlap and fluidity, at least in some locales, between female grassroots activists and feminists, who were usually more educated, were less encumbered by family and work responsibilities, and had access to more resources. Individuals and groups came together over particular issues, such as children's education or reproductive rights or whatever emergency or issue arose. Anne Valk's study of women's activism during this period in Washington, D.C., entitled "Separatism and Sisterhood," chronicles the fluidity of women's work across organizations and groups and how black and white women were able to work together despite animus and rhetoric that would suggest the impossibility of cooperation. African-American and white women collaborated on various campaigns, including the 1977 National Women's Year conference in Houston. The D.C. women involved in the Houston conference preparation praised it "as a process that united women across racial, sexual, and political lines to address local issues." At a number of conferences that took place in Washington, "the shared impulse to address some of the inequities and violence that D.C. women faced on a daily basis at times superseded the differences based in race, class, sexuality, and ideology." Critically placed women around the country were committed to interracial organizing and facilitated it. Valk suggested that because Washington, D.C.'s population was predominantly black, there was more interracial collaborative political work than in many other locales.[10] In Boston, with a minority black population and a history of racism and segregation, there was less. But in most cities, white and women of color feminists came together at least sporadically.

A number of national events during the 1970s brought radical women activists together across race. Early in the decade, the arrest of leftist African-American activist Angela Davis, who was acquitted in 1972, was one. Many white socialist feminists supported Angela Davis, recognizing her as a political prisoner. Davis was involved in a campaign to free the Soledad Brothers, three black men imprisoned in California. She was accused of aiding the men who had attempted to free George Jackson, one of the Soledad Brothers, at the Marin County courthouse in 1970, during which three people were killed. Davis went underground and was eventually captured and imprisoned. Although they knew that her left-wing allegiances trumped her feminism, white feminists were nevertheless involved in the national interracial campaign to free her. Davis was a high-profile revolutionary woman dedicated to a communist perspective, that is, a mixed movement with a working-class analysis in which gender was not paramount. She was also a persecuted African-American woman devoted to racial justice. And she was an icon, a beautiful, black, female revolutionary with a huge Afro whose image was everywhere. She stood for anticapitalist and antiracist militancy, for Black Power, and her image was used that way by the Left and the Right, the latter to frighten whites about the black revolution under way. The government's vendetta against Davis united leftists, including feminists who, depending upon their politics, were more or less enthusiastic in their support.[11]

Feminists also rallied in support of Joanne (or Joan) Little, a black woman imprisoned and accused of murdering her rapist jailer, whose case became well known in 1974 and 1975. Because she was black and poor, had acted in self-defense, and was threatened with execution in North Carolina, numerous progressive groups mobilized on her behalf. For feminists, her situation raised issues of black women's sexual victimization by white men, of social class, and of the criminal justice system. Violence against women became a major issue for feminists in the 1970s, something that could affect all women and united them across race and class. Campaigns in defense of women, usually poor and sometimes of color, who were victims of sexual violence and who sometimes had killed the perpetrator, brought together diverse women who otherwise would not have found common bonds. Little wrote about her own changing consciousness in the women's liberation newspaper *off our backs*, saying that women's groups like the one that published the newspaper "have given me the strength to go on." Historian Genna Rae McNeil suggested that black and white women from different segments of the population and sections of the country, with varying political perspectives and histories, "came to view Joan Little's plight as an authentic opportunity to consider the possibilities of 'sisterhood' across racial and class lines through the development of an integrated women's alliance." Inevitably, a "self-conscious recognition of *difference* created varying degrees of solidarity among women of diverse racial, socioeconomic, and personal backgrounds." Recently acquitted Angela Davis and Bernice Reagon, long-time SNCC activist and founder of the musical group Sweet Honey in the Rock, were among the well-known African-American women involved in Little's case. Angela Davis wrote an article in feminist *Ms.* magazine urging people to understand the links among rape, race, male supremacy, and exploitation in the case and to struggle to see that justice prevailed. Reagon composed a song, "Joanne Little," which became the anthem of the Free Joanne Little Movement. Public support for Little came from African-American women's, white feminist, and lesbian groups, including the National Organization for Women (NOW). Male Black Power advocates like Amiri Baraka and Maulana Karenga joined the campaign, suggesting the power of feminism to change minds. A multiracial national coalition, informed by the civil rights, Black Power, and feminist movements, worked successfully to free Little. For feminists working across race, this was a political milestone, a moment in the decade when social justice activists came together in an emergency to work for race and gender justice.[12]

One such local case of cross-racial learning and cooperation among feminists was the Coalition for Women's Safety, an interracial group that formed in reaction to the 1979 murders of black women in Boston. Given the racial tensions that plagued the city during the decade, the group's emergence was remarkable. In 1974 and 1975, the citywide busing crisis had developed when whites in South Boston violently taunted and attacked black children who were being bused from their neighborhoods to school there, based on a court order to desegregate the public schools. Police had to escort the buses and children to school. Reminiscent of hateful white southern segregationists defending their white turf, it suggested that virulent racism thrived just under the surface of public life. Boston's busing problem confirmed the city's blatant racism and created serious enmity toward and fear of whites among African Americans, a situation reminiscent of white southern segregationists' attacks on the civil rights movement. Barbara Smith remarked that when she moved to Boston in 1972, "It was absolutely known that as a Black person you did not go to South Boston. You did not go to East Boston. You did not go to Chelsea. . . . It was really frightening, if one got lost in those neighborhoods trying to go from one place to another."[13]

In 1979, twelve black women and one white woman were murdered between January and May in the predominantly black Boston neighborhoods of Roxbury and Dorchester. In late winter, black feminists and female community activists, with white feminist support, mobilized out of fear and rage at the police and the media, which had downplayed the murders. They were especially incensed that the police maintained that most of the women were prostitutes, whose cases were not linked, and at the media's unquestioning acceptance of this story. Activist women called a meeting at Women, Inc., a community-based substance abuse program for women and their children in Roxbury led by Kattie Portis, the community activist. Portis was one of the central organizers of the Coalition for Women's Safety.[14] Her acceptance of a multiracial women's group influenced the coalition, which met often at Women, Inc. Most of the white women involved were from community-based groups, such as Green Light in Dorchester, a safe house program for abused women; feminist Take Back the Night demonstration organizers; and City Life, a racially mixed community organization in Jamaica Plain organized by New Left and feminist activists. The group, based on local grassroots participation and comprising a spectrum of the community, eventually became the Coalition for Women's Safety, a multiracial, multiethnic, almost entirely female activist group. It was designed to publicize the cases, the police inaction, the danger to women, and the racism and sexism of those in power.

Memorial march for murdered black women in Boston, 1979.
© Ellen Shub.

White women positioned themselves as allies, organizing a support group, which women of color deeply appreciated since the white women recognized that the people whose communities were affected should be the leaders. Barbara Smith of the Combahee River Collective and a member of the coalition commented: "When the Boston murders happened, one of the most important things that occurred was the building of coalitions unprecedented in Boston's political history." Among the participants in the coalition was Mel King, a Boston state legislator, who later used it as the basis of his Rainbow Coalition when he unsuccessfully ran for mayor in 1983. About his mayoral campaign, Smith thought, "This is not the beginning of a coalition, not the beginning of the rainbow concept. We did much of that in 1979, when our section of the city was terrorized by these murders." Several other women observed the importance of the coalition's work in laying the basis for the Mel King for Mayor campaign and, although King did not win, he put together an exciting multiracial organization with enormous energy and potential.[15] The multiracial feminist precursor to his campaign is not often acknowledged and suggests one of the coalition's political legacies.

A well-known photograph from a coalition-organized march in Boston shows women of color holding a banner saying, "3rd World Women: We Cannot Live Without Our Lives." The banner is in the hands of Margo Okazawa-Rey, Barbara Smith, and Demita Frazier, all Combahee River Collective members, and Maria Elena Gonzalez. Tia Cross, a white feminist, took the photograph.[16] Women marched to the state house to publicize the unsolved murders, educate the media and the public about violence against women, and protest how little black women's lives seemed to be worth. Snapshots of women at the center of the coalition highlight the diversity of activists that the emergency brought together, as well as the network of groups to which they belonged. Four women—Barbara Smith, Margo Okazawa-Rey, Sondra Stein, and Tia Cross—convey the overlapping backgrounds of radical activists who worked in the coalition on behalf of women of color.

Barbara Smith went to an early march to protest the murders and was outraged both by the male speakers' advice that women should stay home to protect themselves and by the absence of a gender analysis: "The speakers talked about race, but no one said a damn thing about . . . sexual violence."[17] She said that she and her friends were mourning for the women and felt that they themselves were at risk: "So there was that kind

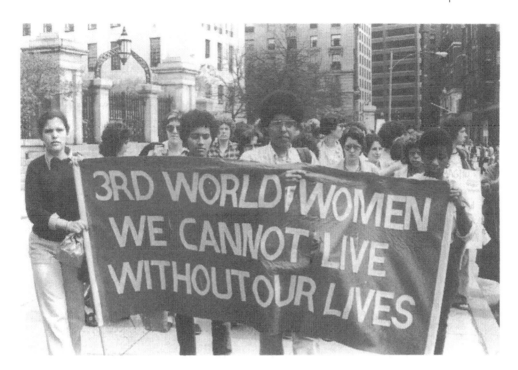

March to protest the murders of black women, Boston, 1979.
Carrying the banner are Maria Elena Gonzalez, Margo Okazawa-Rey,
Barbara Smith, and Demita Frazier. Okazawa-Rey, Smith, and Frazier
were all members of the Combahee River Collective.
By permission of Tia Cross.

of collective shared grieving and then there was this real feeling of fury."
She said, "[W]e knew that it was not a coincidence that everybody who
had been murdered was female."[18] With help from others, Barbara Smith
wrote a pamphlet about the murders signed by the Combahee River Collective, entitled "Six Black Women: Why Did They Die?" As more women
were murdered and they reproduced the pamphlet, they crossed out the
old number and wrote in the new one—which included the point that
"our sisters died because they were women just as surely as they died because they were Black. . . . Both our race and sex lead to violence
against us." Smith wrote, "[A]s Black feminist activists we think it is essential to understand the social and political causes behind these sisters'
deaths. We also want to share information about safety measures every
woman can take and list groups who are working on the issue of violence
against women."[19] Later she noted, "It was the first published, tangible

thing that came out about the murders that people could use." Smith reported that they initially printed 2,000 pamphlets, which disappeared immediately; they eventually printed 30,000 in English and Spanish. People worked together across race and personal difficulties. "I saw people sitting together in rooms who I didn't think would ever have anything to do with each other." Looking back, she stated, "It was a coalition effort that got at a bottom line issue—murder—and dealt with a feminist issue, sexual violence. . . . Those of us who lived through it should always respect ourselves for the work we did, for showing power and resistance instead of lying down and taking it."[20]

Margo Okazawa-Rey had come to Boston to get her master's degree in social work. She was born in Japan to an African-American father and a Japanese mother. She came out as a lesbian in college and in Boston was radicalized, although most of the lesbian feminist women she met were white. Okazawa-Rey was employed as a social worker and organized in black working-class neighborhoods. When a small informal group of black lesbians, who would become known as the Combahee River Collective, began meeting she joined them. Thrilled to meet black, feminist, lesbian, anti-imperialist, and socialist women, she went on early retreats with them where Combahee was formed. Okazawa-Rey had always been less interested in intellectualizing and more inclined toward decentralized community activism. Some of the Combahee women were similarly inclined and had community connections through their paid work, educations, or political activities. She was one of the women who called a community meeting to respond to the murders. Okazawa-Rey became involved with community work and by 1980 had almost no contact with Combahee women although she was still involved with the Coalition for Women's Safety.[21]

Sondra Stein, a white woman, came to Boston in 1976 from Washington University in St. Louis, where she had gone to graduate school and had been active in antiwar activities and the founding of a new women's studies program there. She was originally from Cleveland. Tutoring in a city high school and an interest in radical education led her to urban communities throughout her career. In Boston, she taught on and off campus in traditional and community-based settings, including a women's studies course at Women, Inc., and at the Framingham women's prison. She worked for the Franconia External Degree Program (FRED) based at Franconia College, New Hampshire, which gave classes in the

Demita Frazier protesting the murders of women of color at the mayor's house in Boston, 1979. Margo Okazawa-Rey is sitting behind her, and Beverly Smith is looking through the side of the truck. They were all Combahee River Collective members. © Ellen Shub.

community for nontraditional adult learners, often people who had been community activists and leaders. A large number of students worked and lived in Roxbury, and one of the murdered women was a student of hers. One place that Stein's classes met was at Women, Inc. Eventually she worked there as the director of an educational program she had set up for women coming out of treatment. Being involved in the Coalition for Women's Safety was part of her community and feminist work, particularly as she worked in Roxbury and eventually moved there. With Margo Okazawa-Rey, whom she hired to teach a course at FRED, Stein founded the Campaign for Anti-Racist Education (CARE), which worked with community groups all over the city, including white neighborhoods that wanted to learn how to mobilize against racism. They began to work with the multiracial staffs of women's shelters and other women's organizations that needed help dealing with racial differences. Stein helped to organize and was the main link with the white support group for the Coalition for Women's Safety. The support group, she said, was made up of Cambridge and Somerville women "who worked with us—and were very helpful in organizing fund raising and promotional activities." Everyone in the coalition understood that the black women who lived in Roxbury were the ultimate decision makers but that contributions from all participants were welcome.[22]

Tia Cross was the photographer who captured the image of the Combahee women at the head of the march to protest the murders. Born in Boston, Cross grew up in a prejudiced family and had almost no interaction with black people in the segregated city. She became an activist in food coops, day care, and tenants' organizations in 1971 when she dropped out of college. White, lesbian, and feminist, she lived first in Somerville and then in Cambridge. Especially interested in different cultures and music, she was a member of a group of feminists that organized women's music events. A photographer, Cross eventually made friends with feminists of color and became part of the Bessie Smith Memorial Collective. In October 1979, this multiracial feminist group put on "The Varied Voices of Black Women: An Evening of Words and Music," concerts that featured Linda Tillery, Mary Watkins, Gwen Avery, and Pat Parker and were held at various venues, including the Framingham women's prison. The women were active in the Coalition for Women's Safety. Signed by the collective, a brochure announcing the concerts stated, "It is because of the existence of the Combahee River Collective, a black feminist organization which has been working in Boston since 1974, that the Bessie Smith Memorial Production Collective has been able to produce" the concerts. It explained that the Combahee River Collective has "joined with groups working on sterilization abuse, battered women, abortion rights, and facilitated workshops on racism. Because of this work we have been able to form this coalition of Black, Third World and white women which is the Bessie Smith Memorial Production Collective." They "see Black women's culture as a politically transforming force, long buried under white male rule but now beginning to thrive with the growth of a Black feminist movement and a consciously anti-racist women's movement." They wrote that an important aspect of this music "is its affirmation of women-loving-women and Lesbian identity." The collective was composed of white and black feminists, including Combahee members Beverly Smith and Lorraine Bethel, who wrote a piece on black women's music and Bessie Smith. Over time, Cross developed antiracism workshops for white women to understand and unlearn their own racism.[23]

The intertwined paths of these four Boston feminists, black and white lesbians, led each of them to emergency political work around the murders. With community women at the center of the effort, they built a multiracial coalition. Participants in the Coalition for Women's Safety noted that the political work they had done prior to the emergency prepared them to understand and respond to the murders with a feminist analysis linking gender, race, and class. They repeatedly made the point that these were not simply racist murders and that it was not incidental that the victims were women. The inadequate responses of the authorities and the media reinforced the victims' low status as black, poor, and female. It was a frightening period for women who lived in black neighborhoods, but it was precisely the awful nature of the emergency that made effective activism between black and white women possible.

During the winter of 1978–1979, there were six rapes and two attempted rapes of white women in the white Allston/Brighton section of Boston. In contrast to the Roxbury murders, which began later than the rapes, enormous public pressure was put on the police to solve those cases, interpreted by feminists as a sign that white women's lives were more valuable than were black women's. The media also gave the rape cases a great deal of publicity. Willie Sanders, a black man, whose description did not match the descriptions of the attacker and whom the victims were unable to identify, was arrested for all of the rapes. His arrest, indicating more serious attention to the crimes committed against the white female victims, infuriated and disheartened feminists, particularly black feminists. As the number of Roxbury murders mounted throughout the winter, the race and gender issues emphasized by the Coalition for Women's Safety became even more compelling in the light of the Willie Sanders case. Violence against women and the particular vulnerability of African Americans to violence and state injustice were underscored in their analysis. Due to lack of evidence, in jury trials Sanders was acquitted in two of the cases, and several of the others were dismissed or never went to trial.[24]

Prior to these events, violence against women, an arena in which Boston feminists could forge common ground, united black and white feminists of all perspectives. From early in the decade, they had organized battered women's shelters, rape crisis centers, and Take Back the Night demonstrations in which women symbolically marched to reclaim the night, indicating that they were no longer willing to be afraid. In the August before the rapes and murders, a large Take Back the Night demonstration took place in which nearly 3,000 women marched through Boston to protest male violence. Sidewalks along the march route were filled with a wide mix of supporters. The march concluded in a white section of town, Copley Square, with speakers and musicians. *Sojourner*, the feminist newspaper, reported on the "incredibly successful, effective march" that "transformed fear into a new strength and sense of unity." It emboldened women who were afraid to be out at night.[25] A year later, following the rapes of the white women and the black women's murders in Roxbury, more than 5,000 women marched through Boston neighborhoods in the city's second Take Back the Night event, which culminated in a rally held in the racially mixed South End's Blackstone Park. A flyer publicizing the demonstration, "Women Unite: Take Back the Night," listed resources, mostly service organizations, many in the black section of Boston, including Women, Inc., and the Coalition for Women's Safety, and others such as the Dorchester Green Light program, women's shelters, and Women Against Violence Against Women. The march flyer discussed the daily violence against all women, suggesting that women of color are more susceptible because "violence is . . . a tool of racism." It explained:

We march to empower ourselves to take action. By marching
women say to each other and to our community that we *can* do
and *are* doing something to end violence. . . . Because the
night is the time of our greatest fear, a time when many women
are confined to our homes for fear of attack on the street, we
march at night to say together, we will fight our fear, we will
Take Back the Night.[26]

Women involved in the Coalition for Women's Safety participated in
the Take Back the Night demonstration in 1979 which, in contrast to the
1978 march, had been organized so that different groups of women would
march through various neighborhoods throughout the city and then con-
verge on a common space. Minutes of planning meetings on coalition sta-
tionery reveal that the organizers intended to be more clearly antiracist in
an effort to correct problems from the previous year's march. In 1978, white
women had chanted the slogan "stop rape" as they marched through
neighborhoods of color. Women of color had expressed the opinion that it
was arrogant of white women to march and chant through black neighborhoods because it appeared that they knew better than community residents
what was happening, that rape was more of problem there than in white
neighborhoods. Concerns about racism altered the 1979 march's routes,
slogans, and speakers. Even the service organizations listed on the brochure
were primarily based in communities of color.[27]

At the demonstration in Blackstone Park, rally speakers discussed the
rapes and murders of the past year and how in response women had created their own safety systems: "We should all be inspired by the fact that
we have come together tonight, women from all races, ages, different
communities and different classes, and marched to show our power, our
strength, our unity and our determination to end violence against
women." They continued, "Perhaps the biggest victory this past year has
been the birth of the Coalition for Women's Safety." While violence affects
us all, they said:

the combination of Third World women's efforts over many
years to confront their particular oppression in this society and
the brutal violence directed this year specifically against Black
women has catalyzed an awareness among white women of what
Third World women have known all their lives—that women of
color are singled out as targets of violence both because of their

race and their sex. White women have begun to learn from
Third World women and to organize against the violence
particularly affecting women of color.[28]

The Coalition for Women's Safety was central to the effort to expose the
vulnerabilities of women of color and their need for protection.

Critical to the learning process of white feminists and the structure of
the coalition was the fact that white women organized a support group.
They did not center themselves in the political action. In an information
packet prepared for the coalition by the Support Group for Women's
Safety, they described themselves as "concerned feminists, predominantly
white, who have organized a resource network for use by groups working
against violence against women, with priority to Black and Third World
women." Composed of women from primarily white neighborhoods, the
support group began meeting in April 1979. They saw themselves as literally supporting the coalition: they listed very specific resources and help
they could provide, such as fundraising, babysitting, bulk mailing, typing,
media contacts, and equipment. Their statement of purpose asserted that
no woman is safe in this society: "Horrified by these attacks on our black
sisters, understanding their roots in both the sexism and racism of this society, we felt we could no longer keep silent about this violence against
women." But since most of the members were white and most lived outside
the areas where the murders took place, they felt they could act most effectively as a support group: "As a primarily white group we hold ourselves responsible to raise issues of racism within our communities and neighborhoods in ways that reflect our efforts to deal with our own racism. We
believe that as long as racism and ethnocentrism separate us from our sisters of color, we will never be able to end the violence we all face as women."
At a meeting in June, they agreed that the purpose of the support group,
based in Cambridge and Somerville, was to "provide resources and supportive services to communities working on the issue of violence against
women *in response to specific requests*" (their emphasis). They gave the pro-
ceeds from poetry readings—benefits that featured poets and writers
Audre Lorde and Adrienne Rich—and the Freedom Stride, or Run-a-
Thon, to the coalition. Their goal was support, not leadership.[29]

White feminists had been organizing in the Boston area since the late
1960s, and their concerns about and understanding of racism was deep-
ening. The war in Vietnam, which ended in 1975, had kept imperialism

and the oppression of people of color very much on radicals' minds. Prompted by white lesbians, women of color, and lesbians of color, all feminists explored a politics of difference. The coalition shifted the center of action from the university town, Cambridge, across the Charles River to the black neighborhood of Roxbury, with black women leading the campaign. Participants used their hard-won learning about racism and sexism as the basis of their work together, and when the murders occurred women were able to coalesce in political partnerships that made sense to them all. Reflecting on some of this, in June 1979, Barbara Smith wrote the following in a letter to Coalition for Women's Safety members:

> I think it would be very important to discuss in a supportive and clarifying way what it means for us to be in a coalition in relation to our own specific identities. We need to talk about what it means for Black and other women of color to be working with white women, for white women to be working with women of color, for women who identify themselves as feminists to be working with women who do not identify themselves as feminists and for Lesbians and heterosexual women to be working together. A discussion of class difference[s] might also be productive. I think that all of us have been aware of our differences on some level ever since we began this work, but we've really never had a specific discussion about them and what they mean in relationship to what we're trying to do. Since these differences are definitely there it only makes sense to speak to them. Not for the purpose of divisiveness, but for the purpose of understanding and greater closeness. I feel proud of what we've done so far and how well we have dealt with each other under so much pressure.[30]

Smith clearly articulated a respect for differences among women and acknowledged that the next step entailed political exploration of what differences meant among feminists—critical realizations for a maturing feminism.

In 1980, a year after the formation of the Coalition for Women's Safety, when the murders had stopped and the emergency was over, the *Second Wave*, a Boston feminist magazine, interviewed some of the women from the group in order to "learn how racism was handled within the context of a multi-racial, all-women's group" whose "members come from a wide range of neighborhoods and politically active organizations" and were "working on a common problem." Coalition members recalled, "We came together to really take care of ourselves, because we were afraid." Not until the word went out from Kattie Portis that Women, Inc., would be the central place for providing information and coordination did a group coalesce around the murders. Lili, who like the others was identified only by her first name, stated, "I think that people were organizing already and just came together." The impetus came from the black community and most of the women at the meetings represented black-based organizations. Emphasizing the coalition's origins, Margo said, "In other words, they didn't come and organize us, the white women. We just came together around a cause that we all felt on a real gut level that was literally a life and death matter for all of us." She remarked that some participants were feminists and some weren't, but "I think we're all feminists. We're working on women's issues. . . . A lot of us aren't part of the white feminist community." Corroborating this perspective, Sandi remarked, "A lot of people wouldn't *call* themselves feminists, but their work, their essence, is feminist. . . . The issue isn't the language." People came from all sorts of political positions and perspectives, which occasionally slowed them down but they learned too.

The coalition was still meeting and working on issues of women's safety a year later, providing support for one another despite the fact that a crisis situation no longer existed. Margo believed that it was important that "people are working in their neighborhoods but also going beyond that and working together toward a coalition. People of different color[s] working together, different colors, women." She supported the strategy of not going into other people's neighborhoods to organize but, rather, people coming together and then bringing ideas back to their own groups and neighborhoods so that they could build strong networks there. Respecting each other's turf was central to their politics.[31]

The Coalition for Women's Safety had been able to recognize and work with differences, an achievement that would not have been possible ten years earlier. In an often-cited 1982 essay that began as a talk given at a women's music festival, "Coalition Politics: Turning the Century," African-American activist and singer Bernice Johnson Reagon wrote about the pain and the necessity of coalitions: "Coalition work is not work done in your home. Coalition work has to be done in the streets. And it is some of the most dangerous work you can do. And you shouldn't look for comfort." She argued, "We've pretty much come to the end of a time when you can have a space that is 'yours only'—just for the people who you want to be there. . . . There is nowhere you can go and only be with people who are like you. It's over. Give it up." Recognizing the anger and discomfort of cross-racial alliances, Reagon realistically appraised the situation: "Today wherever women gather together, it is not necessarily nurturing. It is coalition building. And if you feel the strain, you may be doing some good work."[32] Reagon urged women to recognize that even if they continued to identify with their own groups, even if they were uncomfortable, they had to work together.

Coalition for Women's Safety members were uniformly positive about the political experience. Feminists of color, in particular, recalled their work with satisfaction. Barbara Smith wrote at the time, "But this is *new*. Black and white, feminist and non-feminists, women have never come together to work on a woman's issue, an issue of racial-sexual politics, at least not in this era. . . . Women taking leadership from Black women."[33] Years later, Smith spoke of the murders: "for me that was a pivotal time, in some ways the culmination of everything I had done, learned, tried to do until then."[34] Working together with community women, feminists of all races, and, in some cases, men to respond in an exemplary manner felt like progress. Some have mentioned that being out lesbians in the black community was exhilarating. And white feminists took their lead from women of color, supporting them and trying not to direct or crowd. They were not central to this fight, and understood it, although they were important in their provision of resources and support. This recognition was deeply meaningful to black feminists. Written minutes from a summer meeting included an impressive testament to how intensively everyone worked to achieve an effective multiracial campaign and to their respect for one another:

> Everyone comes with a different political orientation and
> experiences but with bottom line commitment to work towards
> ending violence against women in our neighborhoods. There
> was agreement among the members that we should not let our
> differences make us lose sight of our purpose. In fact, the
> differences could make us all grow and perhaps even help focus
> on some of our blind spots.[35]

While the events in Boston were taking place, a number of factors were shaping the national feminist environment. Among those central to the development of feminist racial politics was the boom in writings by feminists of color in the late 1970s and early 1980s. Almost all of the writing presented a bitter and painful picture of the plight of women of color in American society. Several themes were common: the intersection of sex, race, and class as the only adequate way to analyze the situation of women of color; heterosexism; and the racism of the women's movement and the larger society, the predominant motif. Within a year or two of the Combahee River Collective's statement, ntozake shange's *for colored girls who have considered suicide* (1977) and Michele Wallace's *Black Macho and the Myth of the Superwoman* (1978) appeared, both of which focused on heterosexual relationships. In 1979, the *Black Scholar* published a special issue about sexism among African Americans, organized around Wallace's and shange's work, with a very critical piece by sociologist Robert Staples, to which he invited responses for a future issue of the journal. Also in 1979, at the Simone De Beauvoir Conference at Barnard College in New York City, Audre Lorde gave a talk that became famous, "The Master's Tools Will Never Dismantle the Master's House," which among other things was critical of the racism of the conference organizers and white feminism.[36] She criticized the audience for the absence of women of color participants and asked how they dealt with the fact that while they attended conferences on feminist theory, poor women of color were cleaning their houses and taking care of their children. Although socialist feminists had been discussing race and class for years, Lorde's speech was a critical moment when women of color publicly and directly confronted white feminists. White feminist writer Adrienne Rich contributed an important essay, "Disloyal to Civilization: Feminism, Racism, Gynephobia" (1979), in addition to various talks and pieces devoted to race and racism among women. In 1979, *Conditions: Five: The Black Women's Issue* appeared, an issue of the journal devoted mainly to writings by black lesbians edited by Lorraine Bethel and Barbara Smith; and in 1981, Kitchen Table: Women of Color Press was founded. Among the path-breaking books was *This Bridge Called My Back: Writings by Radical Women of Color* (1981), edited by Cherríe Moraga and Gloria Anzaldúa and featuring a foreword by Toni Cade Bambara, the editor of *The Black Woman*.[37] In that same year, feminist writer bell hooks published the first of many influential books, *Ain't I a Woman? Black Women and Feminism*. The year 1982 saw the appearance of *All the Women Are White, All the Blacks Are Men, but Some of Us Are Brave: Black Women's Studies*, edited by Gloria T.

Hull, Patricia Bell Scott, and Barbara Smith, and in 1983 *Home Girls: A Black Feminist Anthology*, edited by Barbara Smith, appeared. This list gives some idea of the burst of political writing by radical feminists of color, many of them lesbians, about race and racism.

This Bridge Called My Back, referred to as "the radical feminist bible," was extremely important for radical women of color and for all leftist feminists.[38] There had been nothing like it before. Filled with primarily short pieces ranging from memoir to poetry to theory to the Combahee River Collective's "A Black Feminist Statement," radical women of color spoke from their hearts. Cherríe Moraga wrote in the preface of spending time in Boston and with Barbara Smith while working on the book, of the segregation of the city and how feminism was "exclusive and reactionary.

A party for *Conditions Five: The Black Women's Issue*, the first widely distributed collection of black feminist writing in the United States, at the New Words bookstore, Cambridge, 1979. *Standing*: Hilary Kay, Barbara Smith, Kate Rushin, Fahamisha Patricia Brown. *Sitting*: Beverly Smith, Brenda L. Haywood. By permission of Susan Fleischmann.

I call my white sisters on this." "Dread" and "terror" are words she used often in descriptions of dealing with the racism of white women and of differences among women of color, especially as a lesbian. She confirmed the "terror and loathing of any difference that lives" deep inside us, of which Audre Lorde speaks in "The Master's Tools Will Never Dismantle the Master's House." Lorde argued that difference must not just be tolerated but experienced as a source of creativity and interdependency. Moraga, by contrast, felt silenced in the face of white women. As a light-skinned Chicana, she had also experienced distance from other women of color, a distance that she felt "most acutely with Black women—Black dykes—who I felt ignored me, wrote me off because I looked white. And yet, the truth was that I didn't know Black women intimately . . . was basically removed from the lives of most Black women. The ignorance, the painful ignorance." Moraga was driven to work on the anthology and to deal with racism "because I couldn't stand to be separated from other women."[39] More positively, in the introduction, she and Anzaldúa wrote, "What began as a reaction to the racism of white feminists soon became a positive affirmation of the commitment of women of color to our *own* feminism."[40]

Each section of *This Bridge Called My Back* is dedicated to a particular aspect of the way the contributors' backgrounds and experiences as women of color inform their lives, theory, and feminist activism. One section, "And When You Leave, Take Your Pictures with You: Racism in the Women's Movement," in the words of Moraga, "attempts to describe in tangible ways how, under the name of feminism, white women of economic and educational privilege have used that privilege at the expense of Third World women." She said that women of color "have had it" with white women's "outreach," their use of women of color as tokens, and their success at the expense of women of color. White women are born with power—the greater the economic privilege, the greater the power: "This is how white middle class women emerge among feminist ranks as the greatest propagators of racism in the movement." Nevertheless, she suggested that the contributors to *This Bridge Called My Back* were challenging white women to be accountable for their racism because they want to believe that white women want all women to be free.[41]

What, at this time, did many feminists of color writing or speaking at meetings and conferences want from white feminists? The central criticism by black feminists of the white feminist movement was its racism,

Reading at the Arlington Street Church in Boston, 1981, to celebrate the publication of *This Bridge Called My Back*. *Standing*: Barbara Smith, Beverly Smith. *Sitting behind them*: Rosario Morales, Aurora Levins Morales, hattie gosset, Cherríe Moraga.
By permission of Susan Fleischmann.

the primary reason they gave for being uninterested or more actively re-pelled. Their experience of racism in feminism was exacerbated by several other factors: the pain, for some, of leaving the mixed male/female move-ments; the failure of the feminist movement to deliver the kind of friend-ship and personal and political transformations for which women hoped; and the continuing racism of the larger society. Over time, one of the more dramatic shifts in the women's movement was that the force of women's anger at men subsided and was redirected toward other women. In the early years of the movement, much of radical women's attention was taken up with understanding sexism and patriarchy and how they op-erated socially and personally, issues that never disappeared. But in the late 1970s, white and black feminists on the Left were self-consciously try-ing to work out political relationships with one another, to create a politics of difference. In order to become feminists, white radical women had broken away from the New Left and white men just as black women had broken away from nationalist movements, black men, and, often, their communities. For white women who had identified with the New Left or the antiwar movement and black women who had identified with the Black Power movement or the black community, this parting was intellectually and personally wrenching. Separation among feminists, differences among feminists, seem to have created, if anything, as deep or even deeper feelings of rage and betrayal than distance from men and, in the case of black women, their communities.

Feminists of all kinds were likely to turn on one another because of the damage they had experienced in the larger society and the disappointment they felt when they discovered that feminism was not going to make their lives as decent or fulfilled as they had hoped. Women, they learned, often could not live up to the high expectations that feminism encouraged.[42] In writings, at conferences and meetings, and in speeches devoted to racism, women unleashed a great deal of anger and disappointment, perhaps simply because the conference topics and the audience provided space and permission for feminists to express their hurt and fury. "While white women in general are treated scornfully in much black women's theoretical writing, white feminists are demonized, treated precisely as we are accused of treating black women," wrote Maureen Reddy, a white woman.[43] Black women wanted white feminists to give up their privileged positions and perspectives, to see things from black women's location, and often whites disappointed them. Looking back on these years, feminists' personal and political hopes and expectations were so high that they could not have satisfied each other. Black women desperately wanted whites to understand their own complicity in racism and to reject it. All feminists wanted a movement that embraced them and changed the world—and quickly. Years later, it is obvious that social change takes time. What Penny Patch wrote about the civil rights movement seems particularly relevant:

> It occurs to me that as the nearest and safest white women, some of us became vessels into which black women, if they chose to, could pour their accumulated anger—anger they had borne for hundreds of years. I am trying to say, I suppose, that if we hurt each other, it was not my fault, nor theirs. It is slavery and

oppression that created the distance between black women and
white women, not the fact that white women slept with black
men during the Civil Rights Movement.[44]

A theme of disappointment and vulnerability is embedded in feminists'
political and racial critiques of other feminists.

In her analysis of feminist organizations, sociologist Verta Taylor
has written, "Given the pain that women bring into the movement, it is
not surprising that . . . feminists turn on one another. Undoubtedly
this contributes to the kind of interpersonal conflict—often dubbed
'trashing'—described by so many feminists and scholars of the women's
movement."[45] The term refers to women wounding each other deeply or a
"vicious form of character assassination," in the words of feminist activist
and theorist Jo Freeman, the effect of which was often to silence the subject.[46] While the rage that women of color turned on white women was
not trashing, it reminds us of how high the emotional and political stakes
were among feminists and how few tools they had to manage and comprehend their own and others' expectations. Years later, bell hooks wrote:

> It saddens me to reflect on the many moments in feminist
> settings where opportunities to grow and learn, to enhance our
> understanding of the politics of difference, were undermined by
> the fact that most of us had no understanding of how to manage
> conflict, reconceptualize power, while simultaneously creating a
> spirit of community that could serve as a basis for building
> solidarity.[47]

Women of color's hurt, articulated in their literature about the ignorance, naiveté, blindness, rudeness, stupidity, and cruelty of white women,
was not solely about what white women had done to them. The fury that
black women turned on white feminists for their racism was also about
their deep feelings about living in a racist society as black women. Centuries of white male and female racism were their histories. bell hooks
wrote that "the insistence that feminism is really 'a white female thing that
has nothing to do with black women' masks black female rage towards
white women, a rage rooted in the historical servant-served relationship where white women have used power to dominate, exploit, and oppress."[48] By the late 1970s, black feminists eloquently and unmistakably
demanded their places in society and in feminism. Reading and listening

to them, white socialist feminists struggled with the legacies of racism, including that of first wave white feminism, recognizing that they might be complicit themselves and wanting to change.

The development of race relations in radical second wave feminism was also furthered at meetings in the nascent academic field of women's studies. The appearance of hundred of articles and books shaped the feminist agenda with a focus on difference. As it was for the Coalition for Women's Safety, this is the context for the regional and national women's studies conferences in 1981, which themselves became part of the literature and lore on race in the women's movement. Barbara Smith explained why: "Racism is being talked about in the context of women's studies because of its being raised in the women's movement generally, but also because women's studies is a context in which white and Third World women actually come together, a context that should be about studying and learning about all of our lives."[49] Women's studies conferences were among the few organizational spaces in the entire society where white women and women of color faced one another and attempted to develop an antiracist and inclusive women's movement.

The National Women's Studies Association (NWSA) had been formed in 1977 at a conference at San Francisco State University. The New England Women's Studies Association (NEWSA), a regional organization affiliated with NWSA, was officially founded in 1977 as well, and both held conferences on racism in 1981. More than 100 women's studies programs existed by 1977; the first one had appeared in 1970 at San Diego State University. At the founding conference in San Francisco, five feminist faculty members from New England circulated a paper stating:

> Women's Studies grew out of the Women's Movement of the late
> 1960s. Through common consciousness-raising, and often
> more specifically through the urgings of our sisters outside the
> university, those of us within traditional academic settings
> began to cast into doubt the old assumptions and teachings
> forged and maintained by patriarchal interests. [W]e propose
> that the principle function of university Women's Studies be to
> serve the Women's Movement.

They emphasized women's studies' relationship to social change and the necessity to "reach out to and serve the wider community, and to nurture and protect feminist teaching and learning through political action."

The constitution adopted in San Francisco supported feminist education at all levels and venues. So did NEWSA, whose founding statement announced:

> Women's Studies, diverse as its components are, at its best
> promotes a vision of a world free not only of sexism, but also
> from racism, class and bias, and heterosexual bias—in fact, a
> world free from *all* the ideologies and institutions by which,
> consciously and unconsciously, one group oppresses and seeks
> to dehumanize another.[50]

Women's studies was part of the women's movement, and the early participants were both academics and activists.

In February 1981, NEWSA held a conference in Boston at Wheelock and Simmons colleges entitled "A Working Conference on Women and Racism in New England." It preceded and was intended to prepare for the national NWSA conference in Storrs, Connecticut, "Women Respond to Racism," to be held three months later. "In that one year . . . both the regional and NWSA confronted political challenges generated by its own commitment to embracing diverse constituencies, and its stated principle of working to end racism as well as sexism," wrote one of the coordinators, Ann Froines.[51] More than 1,000 women (and some men) attended the Boston regional conference, at least a third of whom were women of color. Poet Adrienne Rich was featured, as were attorney Margaret Burnham; Dr. Helen Rodriguez, who spoke about sterilization abuse; and Boston feminist Tia Cross. The agenda, goals, and intensity of both women's studies conferences, where white women and women of color came together to discuss and understand racism, were striking.

The announcement of "A Working Conference on Women and Racism in New England" began:

> Work on racism begins at home, with ourselves, and our
> families, and in the neighborhoods, work places, and schools of
> our regions. While all members of our community must join the
> battle against racism, in the women's movement we have a
> particular need to confront and combat racism, which is a
> barrier to organizing around issues of concern to all women. In
> New England we have an urgent responsibility to work actively
> against white racism.[52]

Feminist academic Marcia Folsom, a NEWSA conference coordinator, wrote:

> An emphasis on racial, class, and cultural diversity among
> conference planners and participants reflected a conscious effort
> . . . to push it beyond representing primarily middle-class,
> white women academics teaching and studying in women's
> studies programs and courses. Without undervaluing the
> importance of academic women's studies programs, we saw that
> the theme and purpose of this conference provided a solid
> opportunity to move toward a multi-cultural vision of feminist
> education.[53]

From the beginning, the coordinators recognized that

> holding a conference on the theme of racism demanded a
> different kind of preparation. . . . Outreach into non-
> academic communities was a priority. In addition, the white
> women working on the conference saw that we would have to do
> serious preliminary work to confront racism in our lives and
> experience before we could presume to offer an open conference
> on the subject.

The coordinators thus held two open meetings in the summer of 1980 in order to plan for the conference the following winter: "Women of color and white women, academic and non-academic women, members of NEWSA and non-members, women with ties to women's studies and women who had no prior connections to women's studies, were among those at the summer meetings." The eclectic mixture often made for difficult and tense interactions.[54] Conference coordinators called for workshop proposals on the topic of racism from everyone who might be interested, asking *Newsletter* readers to share the call with people in their communities. Folsom recalled that they were making it up as they went along; there was an ad hoc sense to it all; and every decision they made had ramifications of which they were often unaware.[55]

From those two early summer meetings, a number of things emerged. In order to move beyond racism in personal terms of guilt and apology, the organizers took concrete steps to understand how racism operated in their own psyches, lives, and society. First, the "white women organizers of the conference committed themselves to participate in training workshops on unlearning racist conditions, and to engage experienced leaders to run these workshops." Second, there would be an emphasis on dealing with the issue of racism personally as well as intellectually. Third, white women would assume responsibility for dealing with racism and not expect women of color to teach them about it. Fourth, conference planners "accepted responsibility for reaching out to women of color to invite their active participation in the conference and committed themselves to supporting the involvement of women of color whether or not they were connected to women's studies, to assure as broadly multiracial and multi-cultural a conference as possible."

The first commitment—to unlearning racism workshops—was a novel departure from the preparation for most academic conferences and proved to be one of its most important: "Twenty-five white women attended five six-hour training sessions while several women of color planned workshops and recruited twelve facilitators to lead groups."[56] If the women were unwilling to attend, they were dropped from the planning committee. At the conference itself, some of the women who had participated in the workshops led consciousness-raising sessions about race. Folsom described the workshops as "uncomfortable" but nonblaming. The planners decided that morning consciousness-raising sessions and training workshops about racism would be compulsory for all white attendees. The subsequent national convention in Storrs made morning workshops on racism compulsory as well.[57]

Explaining the required consciousness-raising sessions for whites, the NEWSA conference program stated:

> After much deliberation, it was decided that a conference on women and racism would be most effective if we worked both separately and together on the issues involved. These morning workshops will provide separate, supportive environments for women of color, white women and men. The afternoon workshops will give us the opportunity to come together and to work together on these issues, to build bridges and networks between us.

In the "Anti-Racism C-R Workshops for White Women," the program continued, white women and white facilitators would meet in

> supportive, non-judgmental atmospheres to deal with our
> racism through an exploration of personal issues around racism.
> We can no longer afford to deal with racism at arm's length, nor
> can we continue to ask women of color to help us with a
> problem which is uniquely our own. All workshop facilitators
> will have participated in similar anti-racism workshops in recent
> months in preparation for these sensitive meetings.

Tia Cross was one of the trainers for and leaders of the morning work-shops. Barbara Smith, Beverly Smith, Demita Frazier, Mercedes Tomp-kins, Margo Okazawa-Rey, and Evelynn Hammonds were among the Combahee-affiliated women involved, as were many white women who had been in Bread and Roses. Women of color used the morning time for the "Women of Color: Barriers and Bridges" workshop to "discuss the barriers that separate us such as: racism, class privilege, educational privi-lege, color, language, culture and sexual preference" and to "bring out the positive links and bridges that exist and can be used to build networks among women of color."[58]

   Boston NEWSA coordinators Professors Laurie Crumpacker, Marcia Folsom, and Ann Froines expected about 500 attendees and were over-whelmed when double that number showed up. Attendees had to impro-vise in terms of process and space, sitting on floors, windowsills, any-where they could find. For the morning session, hundreds of women "who could not fit into the pre-planned groups heard a presentation on the learning of racism by whites, and then formed self-assigned groups for white working class women, Jewish, Catholic, Italian women, women who grew up in the South, or who were raised by black women, or were/are part of multi-racial families." Coordinators, planners, and atten-dees remember the conference as "intense, sometimes fruitful, sometimes frustrating" but "extremely productive." Folsom noted that one measure of the conference's success was the "unexpectedly high level of atten-dance," which was also reflected in the "excitement and intense involve-ment throughout the conference. Sometimes this intensity boiled over into tears or anger, but for the most part the volatile and deeply emotional topic of racism evoked a seriousness of purpose and a sense of ardent lis-tening to each other." People remember their nervousness, anger, interest, and efforts to identify themselves. They recall impassioned talking in packed classrooms and sitting on a floor or standing in a classroom listening to Adrienne Rich. They remember trying, with and without success, to communicate with others.[59] Despite the work, difficulties, and tension, Folsom proudly recalled, "We pulled it off!"[60]

Asian women at the conference used the open microphones to criticize their absence and invisibility. Kathy Gong wrote in the conference *Newsletter*, "The conference on Women and Racism stirred up a lot of anger in me. Anger towards my white sisters, and toward sisters of color, for seeing me as white, not colored enough, or not seeing me at all."[61] In the packed "Jewish Women and Women of Color" panel, women exploded at one another, leaving deep wounds among participants that outlived the conference. Yet, as one black lesbian wrote in "Reflections: A Black Lesbian's Relationship with her Jewish Grandmother-in-Law," "The workshop on Jewish women and women of color was emotionally upsetting, but it deepened my desire to explore the commonalities [*sic*] and the differences between black and Jewish women."[62]

Although conference reactions were mixed, most were positive. Attendees made comments such as "I felt scared and threatened at points but I think a lot of that was my own last ditch efforts to cling to many of my racist beliefs"; "I don't think it is the fault of the conference or that it can be settled in one day, but the problems were brought out and solutions and strategies were barely dealt with"; "This conference was an excellent beginning and continuation of anti-racist work that has been steadily pushed for years by such groups as the Combahee River Collective"; "I liked the attempt at solidarity in spite of and along with the acknowledgement [*sic*] of class and race differences"; "What we've learned this morning is that people have similar experiences of isolation, self-hatred, of alienation from the culture, of feeling that being a woman of color was bad. Everyone had childhood experiences and present day experiences that were very deep and we found strong connections that way"; and simply, "Glad to see so many women interested in racism."[63] The conference both fostered and articulated an excruciating self-consciousness about racism, and the coordinators' and larger committee's extensive planning paid off in the provocative and stimulating two-day NEWSA meeting.

From the vantage point of the twenty-first century, one of the unique characteristics of the conference was how porous the line was between academics and activists, a characteristic that has vanished. In the early years of women's studies, academics were often feminist activists outside and inside the university and had to be in order to make the effort to establish the programs and to have credibility as instructors within them. That the conference was conceptualized as an event that could bring together feminists from outside the academy with those inside indicates how close feminism still was to its movement roots. The theme of racism, too, was chosen in response to the development of women of color feminism. It was no coincidence that NWSA and NEWSA called conferences on racism in the same year; it was high on the feminist agenda at the time. Like the support group for the Coalition for Women's Safety, the consciousness-raising groups were organized so that white women could grapple with racism as whites without burdening women of color. It was a strategy, devised by black and white women, that responded to the objections of women of color that they would no longer educate white women. This recognition was a long way from the "black and white together" of SNCC, of visions of interracial harmony and togetherness, even from the familiar unhappy and guilty responses of whites. The Coalition for Women's Safety and NEWSA represented a stage of feminism in which whites acknowledged and "owned" their racism, and both black and white women interrogated difference and undertook interracial action. The fact that the Combahee River Collective was based in Boston and that white and black socialist feminists had worked together and alongside one another for a number of years was not incidental to the ability of the organizers and participants to organize a successful conference on racism.

Several months later, the third national NWSA conference at Storrs, "Women Respond to Racism," with a similar format to the NEWSA conference, was held. Approximately 1,300 attended the national NWSA conference from around the country. Feminist scholar Chela Sandoval reported, "This conference was the first sponsored by the women's movement to confront the idea of 'racism' and over three hundred feminists of color attended from all over the country, the largest number of third world women to ever assemble under the banner of the women's movement."[64] In Storrs, Adrienne Rich and Audre Lorde both spoke, Sweet Honey in the Rock performed, and poets and writers, including Paule Marshall, Elly Bulkin, Jan Clausen, doris davenport, Joan Larkin, Judith McDaniel, Cherríe Moraga, Minnie Bruce Pratt, and Michele Cliff, read from their work. Authors from *This Bridge Called My Back* gave a collective reading.[65] Unlike Boston, this conference became extremely contentious—although one attendee testified to the significance of women's studies conferences saying that she was "awed that 1,500 women, 'sat there and talked about racism. No other group did that.'"[66] But what had worked in Boston because of the long and careful preparation and common, if conflicted, feminist histories of many participants—women like Margo Okazawa-Rey, Barbara Smith, Sondra Stein, and Tia Cross—backfired in Storrs. White feminist Florence Howe, editor of *Women's Studies Quarterly*, wrote in an issue devoted to the conference that it "opened to swirls of discontent that, even from the beginning . . . sprang into controversy." Setting the tone, she said were keynote addresses by Adrienne Rich on "Disobedience Is What NWSA Is Potentially About" and Audre Lorde on "The Uses of Anger." And Lorde's speech was angry, indeed, at white women and the conference organizers. Deborah Rosenfelt, coordinator of the Women's Studies Program at San Francisco State University and one of the founders of NWSA, remarked that some people were "disheartened" by the keynote addresses, feeling that "anger among women who are essentially allies is a luxury we can little afford."[67] Others felt that the speeches were necessary renderings of the complexity of relations among white women and women of color.

One of the problems was that the campus was too big. So was the program, with too many competing panels and continuous time conflicts over panels and meetings. The more than 200 workshops, panels, and roundtables, as well as keynotes, readings, movies, and musical performances, felt overwhelming and unproductive. But, as Howe analyzed the situation:

> [T]he main controversy focused on the brave attempt to provide
> a daily consciousness-raising experience for more than one
> thousand persons, and on racism. No one thanked the
> conference organizers or the New England regional members
> who worked for months to prepare the fifty facilitators needed
> for the effort. No one thanked the facilitators. Only afterwards
> did some individuals recognize the enormity of the undertaking,
> and some of its successes as well as its failures.[68]

The consciousness-raising sessions, in Rosenfelt's words, "became a focal point of controversy." Based on the NEWSA conference, the session planners had decided to have separate groups for white women and women of color. Rosenfelt explained:

This arrangement was based on the belief that we can work on racism more honestly if we are among peers, and that women of color should not be subjected to the pain of watching white women confront their own racism. Unfortunately, this rationale—a controversial one in itself—was not made sufficiently clear, and many women of color and white women objected to the arrangement.[69]

The following year, Chela Sandoval wrote in "Feminism and Racism: A Report on the 1981 National Women's Studies Association Conference," a scathing attack on the racism of the conference: "[M]any of the women of color felt immediately suspicious of a conference structure which would place them under one, seemingly homogenous category." While white women were offered numerous consciousness-raising groups that related to their class or religious backgrounds, women of color were placed into one undifferentiated group only for third world women. Such segregation, which many considered reminiscent of the larger society's racism, generated doubt and anger. Most of the women of color felt ghettoized and segregated from the conference. The white women believed that dividing women into consciousness-raising groups based on race made sense, as did some women of color, particularly those who had worked on the Boston NEWSA conference. Nevertheless, most of the women of color who came to the conference, according to Sandoval, were not persuaded by the feminist of color organizers' "well-articulated explanations for the structure we confronted." She described how "for two hours we struggled to overcome our anger and disappointment at both the conference and each other."[70]

As secretary of the national Third World Women's Alliance, which was organized out of the 1981 Storrs conference, and as the conference reporter for the third world women, Sandoval pointed out, "The privileging of the binary opposition . . . made invisible important differences. . . . Thus racism was unthinkingly perpetuated in the name of liberation." As they talked, however, they began to fashion a collective perspective on difference. As women of color, they were forced to question the "idea of a united third world women's standpoint." They had difficulties naming their sisterhood since they represented many identities and worried that "women of color" or "third world women" were not accurate representations. They would not erase their own internal differences in the name of unity but realized that they "must develop new definitions of community based on the strength of our diversities." Sandoval wrote, "In spite of, and then *because* of our differences, a solidarity among the group grew slowly."[71]

Sandoval's report discussed the problems with the way the conference was structured. Fragmented and inflexible, it built no community and did not advance participants' comprehension of racism. Unlike the Boston conference, white women and women of color did not come back together in common sessions in the afternoon or evening to discuss their group experiences and conclusions, a crucial absence. By the third day, as the conference was winding down, third world feminists decided to challenge the conference structure. With sympathetic white women, the third world caucus presented resolutions at the NWSA Delegate Assembly which included stinging criticisms of the failures of the conference to deal with racism. "This has been a racist conference in its structure, organization, and individual interaction despite its theme," the women stated. But many delegates were impatient with these resolutions, which were not passed. Accordingly, "by the end of the conference the division between third world and white women had become intensified and cemented with antagonism." Despite the best intentions of the organizers and leaders she concluded, "the grave difficulties which bespeak the condition of racism kept even these, the boldest and the brightest of U.S. women, from overcoming the blocks and barriers intrinsic to self examination and hoped for change."[72]

For third world feminists, according to Sandoval, the conference generated new visions and methods for approaching feminist political change. They had organized themselves into a "National Alliance for American Third World Women." The volatile and time-consuming discussions at Storrs "provided the group the opportunity to hammer out shared standards with which to work together." They discovered unity, ironically, in the process of objecting to being categorized as one unified group, in insisting that the differences among them had to be recognized.[73] Like contributors to *This Bridge Called My Back*, who found themselves developing their own feminism in reaction to white women's racism, women of color articulated positions and perspectives provoked by conflict and anger at the NWSA conference that they did not know were theirs. They simultaneously discovered, invented, and mourned differences as they hammered out a feminist antiracist politics.

In 2002, Sandoval wrote a foreword for a new version of *This Bridge Called My Back* entitled *This Bridge We Call Home*. Two decades later, she recalled how important the earlier book, *This Bridge Called My Back*, was to women of color and the impact it had on the 1981 NWSA conference "when many of the books' radical feminist-of-color contributors read portions of their writings aloud on stage." At the conference academic feminists "became listeners, shocked into stunned silence by what they finally heard, changing them." Sandoval suggested that the book marked and celebrated the unavoidable emergence of the 1970s U.S. third world feminist movement, "a social movement that even today remains unlike any other. Its activists knew they were devising a distinct social movement and peoples who might build and occupy an altered world."[74] Looking back, Sandoval linked the 1981 book, women of color's experiences at the NWSA conference of the same year, white women's changes, and the invention of a new, complex movement as milestones in feminism.

Long-time Boston African-American feminist Evelynn Hammonds concluded years later that conferences had "become one of the most important sites of the articulation and enactment of feminism in the United States." (Recall one of the early locations of this history: the SNCC Waveland conference where anonymous memos about sexism were distributed.) Discussing the role and functions of feminist conferences, she suggested that "one could argue that conferences have accrued a status once awarded to public demonstrations." Among other purposes, "they provide a site of both connection and contestation between . . . so-called academic feminists—and . . . so-called feminist activists." She noted, "Moments of rupture, even explosion, are a common feature of feminist conferences. These moments can be productive, opening up a public space for discussion or resolution of difficult issues, and they can be divisive, making collective discussion almost impossible."[75] Furthermore, Hammonds suggested, "Conferences became sites where Black women repeatedly found themselves demanding accountability from White women on the issue of race in ways that were often perceived as disruptive and divisive by White women." Audre Lorde's talk "The Master's Tools Will Never Dismantle the Master's House" politically disrupted the 1979 De Beauvoir Conference at Barnard College by condemning racism in the women's movement, including the racism of the conference organizers and participants and asking where the women of color were at the conference? Hammonds argued that this was the point "when the nonunity of feminism was recognized by White women." Although socialist feminists had been discussing and struggling about class and race for years, Lorde's speech crystallized a moment when women of color directly confronted white feminists about how to handle difference among women.

Hammonds continued that "the problem of difference was also the problem of Black feminism."[76] At the NWSA conference, the women of color's formation of a conference within a conference forced them to begin to interrogate the very idea of a unified movement of women of color. Years later, at another conference, at MIT, "Black Women in the Academy: Defending Our Name, 1894–1994," of which Hammonds was an organizer, she suggested that fears of undermining black women's collectivity vied with the need to examine their differences, creating productive tensions for black feminism. Black women were reluctant to explore differences among themselves "even though we understood the dangerous ground of sameness upon which it was based."[77]

These are helpful insights into the role of conferences in the development of feminist racial politics. The ritualistic performance aspect of conferences may have encouraged positions to harden and divisions to deepen as women confronted one another. Anger, confusion, guilt, and recriminations populate the reports and memories of many feminist conferences, not only between white women and women of color but among women of similar politics and color. Clearly, however, not all conferences generated rituals of anger; it was not the predominant emotion at the NEWSA conference. Nevertheless, the potential for public misunderstanding and resentment was great when feminists came together; paradoxically, they needed to reinforce their viability as a movement precisely when difference was the leading political theme.

During the 1970s and early 1980s, Audre Lorde led the way in questioning fears of difference. She made this point often: "Only within that interdependency of different strengths, acknowledged and equal, can the power to seek new ways of being in the world" be generated, can new paths be forged for action.[78] Feminists, as women discovered at the women's studies meetings, were in new territory. Not many years before, differences had been unacknowledged by liberals and radicals, a sign of their tolerance. The idea that it was important to interrogate differences not only between racial groups but within them had not been on any agendas. Purposely dividing women by color so that they could come to grips with racism broke new ground. Nevertheless, grouping all women of color into one unified group had insulted them as their own differences based on class, ethnicity, or sexual preference went unrecognized. They were "the other" again. What women of color and all feminists in those years were discovering was that their project was to create a politics that linked them but did not subsume their differences, including their intra-group differences.[79] This was no easy task, to which so many commentaries attest.

The acknowledgment of difference inevitably fostered distress among women. Recognizing difference meant using it to understand oneself and a world in which power inhered in division and separation. I say this not to articulate the standard critique of identity politics—that such a perspective undermines collectivity, solidarity, civil society, and universalism—but to suggest that in this long historical process of understanding the construction of race and racism, feminists were inevitably hard on one another. Their hopes and commitments were as intense as the races, ethnicities, and sexual preferences that divided them. Feelings were deep when radicals, who had often felt like outsiders, believed they had found a home in the movement and then when, in the case of feminism, many discovered they hadn't, they felt betrayed. They struggled to comprehend how and why society so profoundly divided them, politically and personally. Initially, they could not but reproduce racism, suspicion, and anger. Hope was fractured by their divisions, but they determinedly built on them as a way of creating a politics of return and coalition.

A kind of progressive resegregation took place in this process. The goal of racial integration had been dropped along the way. Instead, white women and women of color separated before they were able to reconnect. One of the ironies of this history is that the civil rights movement began with an ideal of integration and by the late 1960s, separation and segregation were reinscribed by members of the black, feminist, ethnic, and gay movements themselves. Their desire to transcend difference had given way to embracing it. Feminists reproduced the identity politics on which American society was built. By the end of the decade, however, they came together in campaigns and conferences, based not on an easy sisterhood but on the difficult recognition of how difference made trouble for them as it simultaneously enriched their movement.

Emergencies, including the trials of Angela Davis and Joanne Little and the murders of black women in Boston, and conferences like NEWSA and NWSA brought black and white socialist feminists together in the

1970s and early 1980s so that they had no choice but to devise ways of working together. Influenced by national feminist literature and working in the same locale over years, theory and practice developed together, enabling Boston activists to inch toward an antiracist feminism.[80] They made choices to work together, to own feminism as a movement supportive of and sensitive to all women. In practice, in theory, at conferences, in personal writings, they were all in the process of recognizing the indivisibility of race, class, and gender. In those years, feminism was characterized by enormous political dedication to eradicating racism and giant learning curves that had begun in the civil rights movement more than twenty years earlier. Black and white feminists worked apart and together, amid guilt and anger, good will and irritation, love and hatred, and passion to rectify the racism they had inherited from and inhabited in their society. Political coalitions, campaigns, and conferences where they labored interracially, not much more than ten or fifteen years after the first stirring of second wave feminism, educated them in the ways of race and racism, on the long path toward women's liberation and social justice for all.

A bout twenty years after the groundbreaking book *This Bridge Called My Back* appeared in 1981, Gloria Anzaldúa, one of the original editors, and Analouise Keating updated and profoundly changed its title, concept, and content. The original book presented the backs of feminists of color as bridges that others walk over, as unwilling links between white women and women of color. Women of color were tired of their bodies being used over and over again, "sick of being the damn bridge for everybody."[1] The new *Bridge, This Bridge We Call Home*, published in 2002, found women of color at home in themselves and actively pursuing new concepts of race. In an affirmation of their complex identities, home is precisely where they are now. And, surprisingly, even amazingly, given the history we have just explored, Gloria Anzaldúa, an editor of both books, wrote that the new book "questions the terms *white* and *women of color* by showing that whiteness may not be applied to all whites, as some possess women-of-color consciousness, just as some women of color bear white consciousness." The book was intended to change notions of identity:

> Today categories of race are more permeable and flexible than
> they were for those of us growing up prior to the 1980s. *This*
> *Bridge We Call Home* invites us to move beyond separate and
> easy identifications, creating bridges that cross race and other
> classifications among different groups via intergenerational
> dialogue. Rather than legislating and restricting racial identities,
> it tries to make them more pliant.

The editors included writings by whites and males in the book, risking the displeasure of women of color. Anzaldúa noted, "Many women of color are possessive of *This Bridge Called My Back* and view it as a safe space, as 'home.' But there are no safe spaces. 'Home' can be unsafe and dangerous."[2] Anzaldúa dramatically articulated the ecumenical move in the new *Bridge*: "Twenty-one years ago we struggled with the recognition of difference within the context of commonality. Today we grapple with the recognition of commonality within the context of difference."[3] The journey from idealistic interracial community to separation and identity politics, to new definitions of identity and home have come full circle here. Anzaldúa's statement reflects tentative, hard-won understandings about racial consciousness and the possibility of solidarity across difference achieved through feminist struggle.[4] The socialist feminist story that began in the civil rights movement and continued through the political activities of the late 1970s and early 1980s was at the heart of such transformations.

One way to consider the changing feminist views about race is to explore the use of the word *home*. Despite endless data and images of dysfunctional, violent, and unnurturing families, "home" still evokes comfort and love, a place where we belong. Activists remarked that they finally felt home in the movements of the 1960s—in contrast to the dominant culture of America, which they found so inhospitable. For white civil rights worker Casey Hayden, the civil rights movement was "home and family, food and work, love and a reason to live."[5] This was especially true for second wave feminists, white and of color, who often felt as if they did not fit in at home or school, that their families were not particularly sympathetic to them, or that they were different.[6] In one of the great feminist pieces by a white woman trying to explore her own racism, Minnie Bruce Pratt poignantly related her conversion to feminism and how being with women was her new home, "to replace the one she had lost," that she "needed desperately to have a place that was mine with other women, where I felt hopeful." She continued, critical of herself, that she had hoped that other women would join her in *her* place, but she learned that it was a limited and narrow place because of her own racism and anti-Semitism.[7] Barbara Smith's decision to call one of her books *Home Girls* emerged from her understanding of extended family in the home in which she grew up. Because many black people believe that being a black feminist means, she wrote, that "you have left the race, are no longer a part of the Black community, in short no longer have a home," she also wanted to underscore the idea that black feminism has its sources at home in the black community, where she had learned her feminism.[8] bell hooks felt home at her grandmother's house where black women created a safe place and a space of resistance to racist domination. She, too, saw black women's daily resistance and their creation of a homeplace as feminist.[9] In a shift in the use of the idea of home, Bernice Johnson Reagon warned that the work of coalition politics could not be accomplished by staying home. She said that such work has to be done in the streets; it's dangerous; you can't always feel good: you're not looking for a coalition if you're looking to feel good, you're looking for home. Here Reagon juxtaposed the comfort of home, any home, with the challenge of coalition politics, of dealing with people who are different from you.[10]

White feminists discovered a home in the women's liberation movement. With sighs of relief, they found sister activists who shared their views and political theories that explained their feelings and experiences. It didn't take Minnie Bruce Pratt long, however, to realize that her new home was more complicated than she had initially realized, even as she wished for comfort and nurturance. As the imperative to attend to differences between women became more insistent, the narrowness of her concept of home became more apparent. Thus, while feminism was home for many women and home could be the source of feminism for black women, it was never uncontested. The necessity of leaving home, in Reagon's terms, of interrogating what seemed to be a place where they finally belonged, compelled feminists to invent a feminist racial politics in which home—and hope—were tentative indeed. None of the feminists who grappled with race, including the editors and contributors to *This Bridge We Call Home*, relax contentedly at home today. Their homes are mutable and fractured, suggesting that racial identities are even more complex than they had believed twenty years before. Home became more contested and fluid, as it is in many homes and families today. By the twenty-first century, feminists were operating with the notion that home is never simple, that race cannot be essentialized, that home girls come in different colors and persuasions.

Younger generations of radical feminists write that the world is their home now, that the concept of a comfortable place in the nation-state doesn't make sense to them. In the years since the flowering of second wave feminism, young feminists, sometimes called the third wave, have embraced the fluidity of racial, sexual, and geographical identities. They define themselves less rigidly than did early second wavers. It is more common now for young people to have contact with those of other races and ethnicities, especially if they have grown up in cities. Black and white are no longer the primary colors. Popular culture directed at young people is filled with images of youth of various races playing together. African-American and Latino styles and music are embraced by whites. While they often do not know each other well, they are more familiar with each other than were whites and blacks in the 1960s and 1970s and better able to imagine working and talking together in ways that earlier feminists accomplished only after years of political work. Young feminists have a stronger basis for a multicultural and integrated movement, although the society is still segregated. One of their strategies, in third wave feminist Rebecca Walker's words, is to cultivate "young women's leadership and activism in order to bring the power of young women to bear on politics as usual"—without necessarily using the term *feminism*. Empowering young women without burdening them with the past is a third wave goal, incorporating both hip-hop feminists and humanist global activists into the feminist movement.[11]

The global economy has linked people worldwide and necessitated an international feminist perspective that takes into account the problems women face globally. In the foreword to *Colonize This! Young Women of Color on Today's Feminism*, Cherríe Moraga wrote admiringly that young feminists have "created an expanded vocabulary to describe an expanded feminism profoundly altered by massive immigration to the United States from North Africa, South and West Asian and Central and South America." The book, according to Moraga, "draws a complex map of feminism, one that fights sexism and colonialism at once and recognizes genocide as a present and daily threat."[12] The editors of *The Fire This Time: Young Activists and the New Feminism* stated:

> If we want to build a feminist world, we must look not only at
> reproductive rights and equal pay for equal work, but also at the
> working conditions of women who labor in sweatshops; we
> must battle sex trafficking as well as the global economic policies
> that have made sex trafficking a thriving industry and a
> normative part of the move toward a borderless economy.[13]

Race, gender, immigration, and globalization are consistently linked in their analyses.

Often, young feminists point out that now there is a diversity of women sitting around the table, but they know that even that is not enough: they are expanding their concerns outward from women of wealth or whiteness to the "poorest and most victimized women in the world." They have announced, "Unlike second wave feminism, which has operated from a monolithic center, multiplicity offers the power of existing insidiously and simultaneously everywhere. 'Woman' as a primary identity category has ceased to be the entry point for much young activist work."[14] Nevertheless, the issue of racism has not disappeared, and debates and insights by second wave feminists are crucial building blocks for younger feminists. One important way that educated feminists learn about race in the second wave is by taking women's studies courses and by reading feminism's literature. They absorb its lessons. Socialist feminists' concerns about racism, experiences across race, and experiments at working together provide models and warnings. Some young feminists of color note that at first they found white feminism liberating but quickly recognized its narrow race and class assumptions. On the other hand, as the editors of *Colonize This!* recognize, they grew up with Audre Lorde, Alice Walker, and Gloria Anzaldúa, and these writings kept them "sane through college." They are, however, less interested in dialogue with white women than in "creating lives on their own terms" as women of color.[15]

The world in which early second wave feminism developed seemed simpler. The framework was racially white and black, and then women of color, but almost always the United States; global capitalism, exploding technology, increased use of third world women's wage labor, forced mobility, and immigration and immigrants were not yet major issues. When in 1964 Mary King and Casey Hayden noted problems in SNCC that were also problems between black and white women, it was a surprise. Young female activists were not prepared for the salience of race among women as race, class, and gender issues followed them from the civil rights movement into the Black Power, women's liberation, and black feminist movements. But by the late 1970s, only a few years after Freedom Summer and the beginning of the second wave women's movement, feminists were confronting race head-on. They worked according to their understandings and skills, attempting to build a radical feminist movement in which all women would feel comfortable and represented. Movement feminists inevitably encountered the sexual, racial, and ethnic divisions within American society. With great effort, they recognized, as Audre Lorde advised, that they could celebrate their differences and create a stronger, if uncomfortable, movement. It took time to absorb ideas that grew out of experience and to practice them, but white and black socialist feminists were impassioned; they pushed on and did not turn away in defeat. "That we were not successful in eradicating racism doesn't change the fact that many of us worked hard to do so," said white movement veteran Chude Pam Allen.[16]

From some young feminists' perspectives, it may appear that the story of white and black socialist feminism in the late 1960s and early 1970s is irrelevant. One of the editors of *The Fire This Time* wrote in 2004,

"Last year I went to feminism and then I left. My perception was that it was a place for a certain kind of professionalized older activist whom I couldn't relate to." Another took a job in an abortion rights organization but "found it impossible to think about abortion rights without thinking about racial and economic justice."[17] The focus on white and black and a single-issue approach to some problems appear old-fashioned to young radical feminists now. This is not to say that they believe that sexism, racism, and heterosexism no longer exist, but that they begin with an understanding that gender, race, class, and sexual preference are deeply interrelated. They take difference for granted as they often do other insights and achievements of the radical feminist activists of the 1960s and 1970s. The uneasy history of white and black women in the second wave has contributed to younger feminists' political vocabulary and perspectives, whether or not they recognize it. Second wave feminists discovered and named difference among themselves, even within their own groups, struggled to understand those differences, and came together to acknowledge rather than hide them, which was white feminists' initial inclination. They did think about racial and economic justice and learned that their new homes had to make space for a diversity of viewpoints and people, that it was never as comfortable as it was in their images, ideals, and yearnings. Younger feminists' recognition of race as a divider even in movements for social justice, of racism in feminism, and of the energetic efforts to create a linked analysis of race, class, and gender owe a great deal to early second wave feminism.[18] White and black socialist feminists were pioneers in a national racial saga in which whites and blacks attempted to work together across the color line, a vanguard in the project of creating multiracial movements and institutions.

Of the histories of the second wave, one theme that continues to resonate today is that the early women's movement was racist and that women of color were excluded and had to create their own movement. Perhaps it still resonates because racism survives, even thrives, today and because this is what young feminists read about the women's liberation movement—which is one reason I wrote this book. But the story is more complicated than white women's racism. While it is true that radical white feminists were abstract in their antiracism and made many mistakes, it is too simple to call them racists or to dismiss their movement because of it. Together, white and black women, and women of color, were active agents in forging feminism. Nevertheless, simpler stories are easier to tell. As long as racism exists, race will enrich and trouble movements for social change. And many will favor transparent interpretations of race relations that omit a great deal. The process that white and black socialist feminists went through alone and together, their painful debates about racism and how to build an inclusive feminist movement have expanded younger women's understanding and strategies. Facing one another across race in a segregated society, even with a global and intersectional perspective, is always fraught with tension. They may not be aware of it, but the racial learning curve that began in the early 1960s continues among younger—and older—feminists in the twenty-first century.

Legacies of racism weighed heavily on activists, and still do. Tradition made it difficult for socialist feminists not to reproduce the history of women's racial division and racism among themselves. It seems obvious now, although it did not then, that it is extremely difficult for a social movement to overcome centuries of slavery, racism, and sexism. This may appear self-evident, but it was not to the young people inspired by idealism. The 1950s contributed as well: a sense of efficacy and optimism characterized the movements, a naiveté perhaps, or even hubris. Young people, especially white, middle-class youth, imbibed a postwar American confidence that included a conviction that even their rejection of the status quo would be successful. But so did young African Americans. Gloria Wade-Gayles wrote, "I grew up believing I was somebody with a special future, in spite of the fact that I lived in a low-income housing project."[19] It dawned on young people startlingly slowly that they were assuming that the movements could be successful in their goals of transforming American society. Young women who came of age in the late 1950s and 1960s attributed too much power to activists, including white and black feminists, and their abilities to reverse American racism in a few short years. They had believed the words of the civil rights anthem "We Shall Overcome" ("black and white together") as had the white civil rights volunteers, that they could build an interracial feminist community quickly and without too much pain. Individual commitment appeared to be enough. They learned that capitalism, racism, and sexism were much more powerful than they were. In that chastening lesson, activists began to understand that racism is not just about confronting a political, economic, and cultural system that has shaped everyone in society. They came face to face with enormous forces that were not only "out there" but were, despite their best intentions, inside of them. Even if young feminists do not know the history or know it only sketchily, the second wave's racial struggles are part of the foundation upon which they build their contemporary politics as they work to create a just world.

Many years later, white and women of color socialist feminists have learned that it is possible to be connected in difference. This claim is not as feeble as it sounds in a conservative society built on tenacious racism. Difference and collectivity have been continually negotiated, and feminists have learned that to "other" themselves and to recognize fluid and multiple locations and split affinities are critical for building multiracial and multiethnic feminist solidarity. There is no clear resolution to the story or the process. The puzzle is still in pieces because of the density of race and racism, the difficulty of overcoming racism, and the land mines that are set off by even talking about it. Minnie Bruce Pratt wrote the following about her pursuit of her own story and of her passion to correct injustice:

> I am speaking my small piece of truth, as best I can. . . . we
> each have only a piece of the truth. So here it is: I'm putting it
> down for you to see if our fragments match anywhere, if our
> pieces, together, make another larger piece of the truth that can
> be part of the map we are making together to show us the way to
> get to the longed-for world.[20]

She wrote this at a time when "the longed-for world" seemed a possibility, which it often does not early in the twenty-first century. She is a woman of a generation whose imagination was inspired by hope for racial and gender justice, who believed that feminists like herself could make it happen.

While nostalgia for integration and for love between the races must be abandoned, many early socialist feminists, white and black, are not yet prepared to relinquish the hope of universality and community, even of integration. Civil rights activist Casey Hayden's words are heartbreaking to many of us: "I think we were the only Americans who will ever experience integration."[21] Why should this be so? we protest, reluctantly understanding why it is. Although acceptable in religion and spirituality, the desire for universal community is no longer popular in progressive or radical politics. Because they have been used to enforce domination and inequality, universality and morality have become suspect categories. Nevertheless, they have their place in liberation movements and civil society. They connect us in a common project and ideals at a time when there is less chance that difference will be submerged in a hegemonic narrative. Interviewed in 1995, Combahee member Demita Frazier said, "One of the things that has always troubled me is that I wanted to be part of a multicultural feminist organization, and I never felt that the feminist movement became fully integrated."[22] Like Frazier, many socialist feminists have been troubled even though they have begun to understand why an integrated women's movement did not develop. Women use words such as love, mourning, hurt, grief, rage, guilt, and loss when they write about civil rights and feminism precisely because of the hopes the movements raised. "In different ways and with different consequences, we all experience the pain and disappointment of failed community," wrote African-American cultural critic Ann DuCille.[23] White and black socialist feminists have experienced the losses differently. But there is no doubt that they have suffered the loss of each other. Hopefully, as young people build movements in the years ahead, they will not suffer that same loss.

Notes

Introduction

1. See, for example, Rivka M. Polatnick, "Poor Black Sisters Decided for Themselves: A Case Study of 1960s Women's Liberation Activism," in *Black Women in America*, ed. Kim Marie Vaz (Thousand Oaks, Calif.: Sage, 1995), 110–130; Benita Roth, *Separate Roads to Feminism: Black, Chicana, and White Feminist Movements in America's Second Wave* (Cambridge: Cambridge University Press, 2004); Rosalyn Baxandall, "Re-visioning the Women's Liberation Movement's Narrative: Early Second Wave African American Feminists," *Feminist Studies* 27(1) (2001): 225–245; Kimberly Springer, *Living for the Revolution: Black Feminist Organizations, 1968–1980* (Durham, N.C.: Duke University Press, 2005), 33–34.
2. Cornel West, "Roundtable: Doubting Thomas," *Tikkun* 6(5) (September–October 1991): 23–30, quotation on 30 (hereafter, the first set of page numbers will indicate the entire article or chapter, while the following page numbers will indicate the source of the quotation in the text).
3. Marilyn Frye, "The Necessity of Differences: Constructing a Positive Category of Women," *Signs: Journal of Women in Culture and Society* 21(4) (1996): 991–1101, 1006.
4. Gayle Greene, "Looking at History," in *Changing Subjects: The Making of Feminist Literary Criticism*, ed. Gayle Greene and Coppelia Kahn (New York: Routledge, 1993), 4–27, 11.
5. Rachel Blau DuPlessis, "Reader, I Married Me: A Polygynous Memoir," in *Changing Subjects*, ed. Greene and Kahn, 97–111, 106.
6. Marianne Hirsch, *Family Frames: Photography, Narrative, and Postmemory* (Cambridge, Mass.: Harvard University Press, 1997), 48.
7. Hirsch, *Family Frames*, 49; also see Eric J. Sandeen, *Picturing an Exhibition: The Family of Man and 1950s America* (Albuquerque: University of New Mexico Press, 1995).
8. Sean Wilentz, "The Last Integrationist," *New Republic* (July 1, 1996): 19–26, 22.
9. Casey Hayden, preface to Mary King, *Freedom Song: A Personal Story of the 1960s Civil Rights Movement* (New York: Morrow, 1987), 7–10, 8–9.
10. Pat Watters, *Down to Now: Reflections on the Southern Civil Rights Movement* (New York: Pantheon, 1971), 57.
11. Lise Vogel, *Woman Questions: Essays for a Materialist Feminism* (New York: Routledge, 1995), 17–18.
12. Vivian Rothstein, "Reunion," *Boston Review* (December–January 1994–1995): 8–11, 11.
13. At times, the South conveyed "a kind of enchantment," wrote volunteer

and subsequent academic Jack Chatfield, foreword to *A Circle of Trust: Remembering SNCC*, ed. Cheryl Lynn Greenberg (New Brunswick, N.J.: Rutgers University Press, 1998), ix–xvi, ix. And Chude Allen commented, "When I was in Mississippi and the South I learned about love in a way I had never known love before." Mississippi Freedom Summer 25th Reunion, West Coast, unpublished, n.d. Copy sent to author by Chude Pam Allen.

14. Elaine DeLott Baker, "They Sent Us This White Girl," in *Deep in Our Hearts: Nine White Women in the Freedom Movement*, ed. Constance Curry et al. (Athens: University of Georgia Press, 2000), 253–287, 280.

15. Barbara Smith, "Breaking the Silence: A Conversation in Black and White, Dialog [*sic*] between Barbara Smith and Laura Sperazi," *Equal Times* (March 26, 1978): 10–12, 12.

16. Eldridge Cleaver, "Requiem for Non-violence," in *Takin' It to the Streets: A Sixties Reader*, 2d ed., ed. Alexander Bloom and Wini Breines (New York: Oxford University Press, 2003), 130–132, 131.

17. Wini Breines, "Sixties Stories' Silences," *NWSA Journal* 8(3) (1996): 101–121.

18. Margo V. Perkins, *Autobiography as Activism: Three Black Women of the Sixties* (Jackson: University Press of Mississippi, 2000): "That the 1960s," xiii; "activists challenging," xiv.

19. For these themes, see essays in Rachel Blau DuPlessis and Ann Snitow, eds., *The Feminist Memoir Project: Voices from Women's Liberation* (New York: Three Rivers, 1998); and Wini Breines, review of *The Feminist Memoir Project*, ed. DuPlessis and Snitow, *Nation* (January 4, 1999): 28–31.

20. See Benita Roth, *Separate Roads to Feminism: Black, Chicana, and White Feminist Movements in America's Second Wave* (Cambridge: Cambridge University Press, 2004), for the idea that feminists self-consciously organized themselves in separate groups based on racial or ethnic identities.

Chapter 1

1. In the late 1950s and early 1960s, Charles Mack Parker, Herbert Lee, Jimmy Travis, Medgar Evers, James Chaney, Andrew Goodman, Mickey Schwerner, Lewis Allen, and others, whose names are less well known, were murdered.

2. Doug McAdam, *Freedom Summer* (New York: Oxford University Press, 1988); Sally Belfrage, *Freedom Summer* (New York: Viking, 1965); Elizabeth Sutherland, ed., *Letters from Mississippi* (New York: McGraw-Hill, 1965); Emily Stoper, *The Student Nonviolent Coordinating Committee: The Growth of Radicalism in a Civil Rights Organization* (New York: Carlson, 1989) (hereafter *SNCC*); Mary Aickin Rothschild, *A Case of Black and White: Northern Volunteers and the Southern Freedom Summers* (Westport, Conn.: Greenwood,1982).

3. See, for example, John Dittmer, *Local People: The Struggle for Civil Rights in Mississippi* (Urbana: University of Illinois Press, 1994), 262–263; Clayborne

Carson, *In Struggle: SNCC and the Black Awakening of the 1960s* (Cambridge, Mass.: Harvard University Press, 1981), 113; Stoper, *SNCC*, 97–103; McAdam, *Freedom Summer*, 103–105; Sutherland, *Letters from Mississippi*, 5, 28, 202–203.

4. Francesca Polletta, *Freedom Is an Endless Meeting: Democracy in American Social Movements* (Chicago: University of Chicago Press, 2002), 107–108. This is from an interview in 1964 with Robert Penn Warren.

5. See, for example, Mary King, *Freedom Song: A Personal Story of the 1960s Civil Rights Movement* (New York: Morrow, 1987); Constance Curry et al., eds., *Deep in Our Hearts: Nine White Women in the Freedom Movement* (Athens: University of Georgia Press, 2000); Belfrage, *Freedom Summer*; Sutherland, *Letters from Mississippi*; Vivian Rothstein, "Reunion," *Boston Review* (December–January 1994–1995): 8–11. All of these authors are white. Blacks don't often write about this, although see the following quotation from Unita Blackwell, in whose home volunteers stayed. She described cooking pinto beans and everyone, including white people, getting around the pot: "We was sitting on the floor and they was talking and we was sitting there laughing, and I guess they became very real and very human, we teach each to one another. It was an experience that will last a lifetime." In Henry Hampton and Steve Fayer (with Sarah Flynn), eds., *Voices of Freedom: An Oral History of the Civil Rights Movement from the 1950s through the 1980s* (New York: Bantam, 1990), 193. Also see letters home from summer volunteers about how attached they felt to their host families and their families to them, e.g., Sutherland, *Letters from Mississippi*, 42ff. On the courage and heroism of the people of the black community, see Gloria Wade-Gayles, *Pushed Back to Strength: A Black Woman's Journey Home* (Boston: Beacon, 1993), 149–156.

6. Penny Patch, "Sweet Tea at Shoney's," in Curry et al., *Deep in Our Hearts*, 133–170, 170.

7. Charles Payne, *I've Got the Light of Freedom: The Organizing Tradition and the Mississippi Freedom Struggle* (Berkeley: University of California Press, 1995), 306. At a West Coast (Berkeley) 25th anniversary reunion of the Mississippi Freedom Summer in 1989, Chude Pam Allen said, "I know that people in Holly Springs, Mississippi, greeted me with love. Yet some part of me keeps denying that, saying that can't be true because I am white and I did at times do things that were arrogant and insensitive." Unpublished, n.p., n.d. Copy given to author by Chude Pam Allen, who attended the reunion.

8. Payne, *I've Got the Light*, 308.

9. See Cynthia Griggs Fleming, *Soon We Will Not Cry: The Liberation of Ruby Doris Smith Robinson* (Lanham, Md.: Rowman and Littlefield, 1998), 170, quoting a SNCC worker who found black deference patterns hurtful: "I was always struck, you know, when I was in the rural areas, in Arkansas, how when it was time to go home . . . how [much] more grateful the

black people were of the white people coming than us." Also see Stoper, *SNCC*, 100–101. In Alice Walker, "Advancing Luna—and Ida B. Wells," in Walker's *You Can't Keep a Good Woman Down* (New York: Harcourt Brace Jovanovich, 1981), 84–104, a fictional story of the civil rights movement, the narrator and Luna, two young SNCC workers, a black and a white woman, are organizing for voter registration in hot, rural Georgia, and the black narrator remarks that she considers "black people superior people." She assumed everyone was superior to white people who would blow up four small black girls and commit other atrocities and was struck by how warm and concerned the black community was about her and Luna. "Even their curiosity about the sudden influx into their midst of rather ignorant white and black Northerners was restrained and courteous. I was treated as a relative, Luna as a much welcomed guest," 88. Also see Randall Kennedy, *Nigger* (New York: Vintage, 2002), 89, for the issue of how black people were addressed in the South before the civil rights movement.

10. Elaine DeLott Baker said that she was also involved in writing the memo. See "They Sent Us This White Girl," in Curry et al., *Deep in Our Hearts*, 253–287, 271. Casey Hayden wrote that she, Mary King, and several other white women were involved in its writing in "Fields of Blue," in Curry et al., *Deep in Our Hearts*, 335–375, 361–366. See Polletta, *Freedom Is an Endless Meeting*, 260, n. 11, where, in addition to King and Hayden, she included Elaine DeLott Baker, Emmie Schrader Adams, and Theresa Del Pozzo, all white women.

11. The memo is reprinted as "SNCC Position Paper," in the appendix to Sara Evans, *Personal Politics: The Roots of Women's Liberation in the Civil Rights Movement and the New Left* (New York: Knopf, 1979), 233–235, 234.

12. Carson, *In Struggle*, 133.

13. Carson, *In Struggle*, 195–206.

14. West Coast (Berkeley), 25th anniversary of the Mississippi Freedom Project, 1989, unpublished, n.d., n.p. Copy given to author by Chude Pam Allen, who attended the reunion.

15. For a useful analysis, see Francesca Polletta, chap. 4, "Letting Which People Decide What? SNCC's Crisis of Democracy, 1964–65," in *Freedom Is an Endless Meeting.* For earlier discussions see, for example, Ella Baker interview in Stoper, *SNCC*, 270–272; Julian Bond interview in Stoper, *SNCC*, 275–277; Stoper, *SNCC*, 81ff.; Carson, *In Struggle*, 133–152; James Forman, *The Making of Black Revolutionaries* (Seattle, Wash.: Open Hand, 1985), 195, 411–447; Dittmer, *Local People*, 331–332; Cleveland Sellers with Robert Terrell, *The River of No Return: Autobiography of a Black Militant and the Life and Death of SNCC* (Jackson: University Press of Mississippi, 1990).

16. Polletta, *Freedom Is an Endless Meeting*, 107; and Polletta, "Strategy and Democracy in the New Left," in *The New Left Revisited*, ed. John McMillian and Paul Buhle (Philadelphia: Temple University Press, 2003), 156–177, 168. Polletta examined issues of democracy in the civil rights, New Left, and

women's movements. See Wini Breines, *The Great Refusal: Community and Organization in the New Left* (New Brunswick, N.J.: Rutgers University Press, 1989), for similar issues in SDS (Students for a Democratic Society). Also see Belinda Robnett, "Women in the Student Non-Violent Coordinating Committee: Ideology, Organizational Structure, and Leadership," in *Gender and the Civil Rights Movement*, ed. Peter J. Ling and Sharon Monteith (New Brunswick, N.J.: Rutgers University Press, 2004), 131–168.

17. Carson, *In Struggle*, 67, 71, 231.

18. Stoper, *SNCC*, 71, 76.

19. Payne, *I've Got the Light*, 381, 368.

20. Polletta, *Freedom Is an Endless Meeting*, chap. 4; Payne, *I've Got the Light*, 365ff., esp. 381–382; Forman, *The Making of Black Revolutionaries*, 411–447; Sellers, *River of No Return*, 94–154; Stoper, *SNCC*, 91–103. For similar problems in the New Left, see Breines, *The Great Refusal*; and Todd Gitlin, *The Sixties: Years of Hope, Days of Rage* (New York: Bantam, 1987).

21. Evans, appendix in *Personal Politics*, 235–238, 235.

22. Evans, *Personal Politics*, 98–101; King, *Freedom Song*, 455–474.

23. King, *Freedom Song*, 452.

24. King, *Freedom Song*, 452.

25. Ruth Rosen, *The World Split Open: How the Modern Women's Movement Changed America* (New York: Viking, 2000), 140.

26. Payne, *I've Got the Light*, 100.

27. See, for example, Belinda Robnett, *How Long? How Long? African-American Women in the Struggle for Civil Rights* (New York: Oxford University Press, 1997); and Fleming, *Soon We Will Not Cry*.

28. Payne, *I've Got the Light*, 424. Also see his "Bibliographic Essay: The Social Construction of History," where he discussed civil rights movement historiography, 413–441.

29. Evans, *Personal Politics*, 88.

30. King, *Freedom Song*, 452–453. King discussed this attribution and said that Robinson, along with most women in SNCC and certainly most black women, repudiated the document—although Robinson did join a women's half-serious sit-in in the SNCC Atlanta office, 452–454; Fleming, *Soon We Will Not Cry*, 151–152. In the introduction to her widely circulated 1970 anthology, *Sisterhood Is Powerful: An Anthology of Writings from the Women's Liberation Movement* (New York: Vintage, 1970), editor Robin Morgan wrote that Ruby Doris Smith Robinson was the author of the memo. As late as 2002, in a history of feminism by white historian Estelle Freedman, Robinson was credited with inspiring King and Hayden to write the memo. Estelle B. Freedman, *No Turning Back: The History of Feminism and the Future of Women* (New York: Ballantine, 2002), 86.

31. Jean Wheeler Smith in Cheryl Lynn Greenberg, ed., *A Circle of Trust: Remembering SNCC* (New Brunswick, N.J.: Rutgers University Press, 1998), 138–139.

32. Reagon in Robnett, *How Long? How Long?* 130–131.

33. Quoted in Polletta, *Freedom Is an Endless Meeting*, 155.

34. Cheryl Lynn Greenberg, introduction to Greenberg, *A Circle of Trust*, 1–17, 13.

35. Patch quoted in Robnett, *How Long? How Long?* 181. Also see Rothschild, *A Case of Black and White*, where she said, "Most women volunteers were too involved in and dedicated to their projects to allow themselves to criticize the movement even to sympathetic outsiders," 142.

36. Debra L. Schultz, *Going South: Jewish Women in the Civil Rights Movement* (New York: New York University Press, 2001), 119–120, 117. See Wini Breines, review of Schultz, *Going South*, in *Signs: Journal of Women in Culture and Society* 30(2) (Winter 2005): 1670–1673.

37. Emmie Schrader Adams, a white civil rights organizer, defended the organization. She remarked on the "distorted" retrospective account of sexism in SNCC: "The real question is: Which organization in the world before 1965 did not manifest male chauvinism? No one ever said SNCC was in any way worse than the world at large. Indeed, it was quite a bit better." In "From Africa to Mississippi," in Curry et al., *Deep in Our Hearts*, 291–331, 325.

38. Michael S. Foley, "'The Point of Ultimate Indignity' or a 'Beloved Community'? The Draft Resistance Movement and New Left Gender Dynamics," in McMillian and Buhle, *The New Left Revisited*, 177–198, 179.

39. A book about the genesis of the women's liberation movement, at least half of it is about the development of that movement out of the New Left.

40. Evans, *Personal Politics*, 83.

41. Evans, *Personal Politics*, 100.

42. King, *Freedom Song*, 462.

43. Patch, "Sweet Tea at Shoney's," in Curry et al., *Deep in Our Hearts*, 133–170, 159; also see Elaine DeLott Baker, "They Sent Us This White Girl," in Curry et al., *Deep in Our Hearts*, 255–287, 277–278.

44. King, *Freedom Song*, 448.

45. Casey Hayden, "Fields of Blue," in Curry et al., *Deep in Our Hearts*, 365. Hayden's use of Alice Walker's term, *womanist*, for black feminism is revealing here. Utilizing it to describe SNCC's early ways and including herself in "womanism," she reaffirmed her integrationist values—and implied that womanist was an integrationist concept that included her, which it was not since Walker was delineating how black feminism differed from white feminism.

46. In Greenberg, *A Circle of Trust*, 144.

47. I want to thank John Dittmer for helping me to see this. See Johnetta Betsch Cole and Beverly Guy-Sheftall, *Gender Talk: The Struggle for Women's Equality in African American Communities* (New York: Ballantine, 2003), for a discussion of the reluctance of African Americans to discuss gender problems in their communities.

48. Cynthia Washington, "We Started from Different Ends of the Spectrum," in Evans, *Personal Politics*, 238–240, 238.

49. Joyce Ladner, "A Sociology of the Civil Rights Movement: An Insider's Perspective," presented at the American Sociological Association meetings, Atlanta, 1988, mimeo, 22ff.

50. Jean Wheeler Smith at the SNCC Trinity Conference, summer 1988, in Greenberg, *A Circle of Trust*, 136; Prathia Hall in Greenberg, *A Circle of Trust*, 145.

51. Fleming, *Soon We Will Not Cry*, 152.

52. Ladner, "A Sociology," 24. Charles Payne's *I've Got the Light of Freedom* is in many ways about the southern organizing tradition in Mississippi as embodied in women and their style of organizing. See also Bernice McNair Barnett, "Invisible Southern Black Women Leaders," *Gender and Society* 7(2) (June 1993): 162–182; Vicki L. Crawford, Anne Rouse, and Barbara Woods, eds., *Women in the Civil Rights Movement: Trailblazers and Torchbearers, 1941–1965* (Brooklyn, N.Y.: Carlson, 1990); and Peter J. Ling and Sharon Monteith, eds., *Gender and the Civil Rights Movement* (New Brunswick, N.J.: Rutgers University Press, 2004).

53. Ladner, "SNCC Women and the Stirrings of Feminism," in Greenberg, *A Circle of Trust*: "We came," 140; "Our mothers," 140; "None of these," 142; "We assumed," 143; "Sure there," 143. Also see Fleming, *Soon We Will Not Cry*, 118–127, for similar points.

54. Recently, feminists have taken Evans to task for not paying more attention to early signs of black feminism in SNCC. For example, E. Frances White, *Dark Continent of Our Bodies: Black Feminism and the Politics of Respectability* (Philadelphia: Temple University Press, 2001), 39. Also see white feminist Becky Thompson's argument against Evans in *A Promise and a Way of Life: White Antiracist Activism* (Minneapolis: University of Minnesota Press, 2001), 72.

55. Greenberg, *A Circle of Trust*: Sarachild, 147; Wheeler Smith, 149; Thelwell and Hayden, 150.

56. Robnett, *How Long? How Long?* 115–116, 117.

57. Robnett, *How Long? How Long?* 137.

58. Ladner in Greenberg, *A Circle of Trust*, 142, 143.

59. Robnett, *How Long? How Long?* 125.

60. Also see Kristin Anderson-Bricker, "'Triple Jeopardy': Black Women and the Growth of Feminist Consciousness in SNCC, 1964–1975," in *Still Lifting, Still Climbing: African American Women's Contemporary Activism*, ed. Kimberly Springer (New York: New York University Press, 1999), 49–69; Benita Roth, *Separate Roads to Feminism: Black, Chicana, and White Feminist Movements in America's Second Wave* (Cambridge: Cambridge University Press, 2004); Becky Thompson, "Multiracial Feminism: Recasting the Chronology of Second Wave Feminism," *Feminist Studies* 28(2) (Summer 2002): 337–360.

61. The untitled, informal power of a woman like Robinson duplicated the gender structure of other civil rights movement organizations like the

Montgomery bus boycott and the Southern Christian Leadership Council, with Ella Baker being the most obvious important female who had no formal leadership position. On Ella Baker, see Barbara Ransby, *Ella Baker and the Black Freedom Movement* (Chapel Hill: University of North Carolina Press, 2003). See Robnett, *How Long, How Long?* for the argument that, despite their lack of formal positions, women were in fact leaders. Also see essays in Ling and Monteith, *Gender and the Civil Rights Movement.*

62. Cleaver joined SNCC late in its history, in 1966. She said:

> One thing I noticed while working in SNCC was that the bulk of the office work, the basic responsibilities of carrying out the day to day work, all the organization were carried out by women and were carried out most efficiently by women. But the first time a woman was elevated to any significant position of power within the organization was in 1966 after the articulation of Black Power when Stokely Carmichael became chairman . . . and Ruby Doris Smith Robinson became the Executive Secretary.

"*Black Scholar* Interviews: Kathleen Cleaver," *Black Scholar* 3(4) (December 1971): 54–59, 55.

63. Zellner quoted in Schultz, *Going South*, 113.

64. Fleming, *Soon We Will Not Cry*, 118–119; also see 39–51. See, too, Marisa Chappell, Jenny Hutchinson, and Brian Ward, "Dress modestly, neatly . . . as if you were going to church": Respectability, Class, and Gender in the Montgomery Bus Boycott and the Early Civil Rights Movement," in *Gender and the Civil Rights Movement*, ed. Ling and Monteith, 69–100.

65. Quoted in Rothschild, *A Case of Black and White*, 148; also see Josephine Carson, *Silent Voices: The Southern Negro Woman Today* (New York: Delacorte, 1969), 254–255, where Robinson is not identified by name. The context for these young black and white activist women's lives were the contradictions in socialization and expectations for young women in late 1950s and early 1960s America, which created confusion and the potential for change. See Fleming, *Soon We Will Not Cry*, 118–124, 166–167. Also see Evans, *Personal Politics*, 78–82; and Wini Breines, *Young, White, and Miserable: Growing Up Female in the Fifties* (Chicago: University of Chicago Press, 2001).

66. Robnett, *How Long? How Long?* 117.

67. Fleming, *Soon We Will Not Cry*, 167. Schultz stated, "For Black women and Black-identified white women, racism was the primary issue in 1964," in *Going South*, 117. In a slightly different argument, to which we will return in a later chapter, Anderson-Bricker wrote, "Black women ignored or reacted negatively to 'A Kind of Memo' because Black activists increasingly defined themselves and SNCC as part of the African American community," in "Triple Jeopardy," in Springer, *Still Lifting*, 49–69, 54.

68. Paula Giddings, *When and Where I Enter: The Impact of Black Women on Race and Sex in America* (New York: Bantam, 1984), 300–302; McAdam,

Freedom Summer, 93–96, 105–111; Rothschild, *A Case of Black and White*, chap. 5; Evans, *Personal Politics*, 78–82; Schultz, *Going South*, 118–119.

69. See the Alice Walker short story "Laurel," an exception to civil rights movement reports and fiction, about a romance between a black woman and a white man. In Walker, *You Can't Keep a Good Woman Down*, 105–117. Also see Alice Walker, "To My Young Husband," in her *The Way Forward Is with a Broken Heart* (New York: Random House, 2000); and a short article about and photo of a white man and a black woman, SNCC organizers who got married in Arkansas, which is reproduced in Danny Lyon, *Memories of the Southern Civil Rights Movement* (Chapel Hill: University of North Carolina Press, 1992), 112–113.

70. Sutherland, *Letters from Mississippi*, 161.

71. Statement by Mississippian Dr. D. L. Dorsey, quoted in Theresa Del Pozzo, "The Feel of a Blue Note," 171–206, in Curry et al., *Deep in Our Hearts*, 190. The statement is from the film *Freedom on My Mind* (1994) by Connie Field and Marilyn Mulford. For additional expressions of how local activists changed, see Endesha Ida Mae Holland and others in the film. Also see Sutherland, *Letters from Mississippi*, where a female volunteer successfully persuaded a local black person to call her by her first name, Ann, instead of Miss Ann, 49, and another in which a volunteer listened to an older man describe "how a Negro must learn to walk through a crowd: weaving, slightly hunched—shuffling helps—in order to be as humbly inconspicuous as possible," 55. Also see Dorothy Dawson Burlage, "Truths of the Heart," in Curry et al., *Deep in Our Hearts*, 105; and William Chafe, *Civilities and Civil Rights* (New York: Oxford University Press, 1980). Historian Drew Gilpin Faust recalled growing up in the privileged white South where no one talked openly about race; it was a prohibited topic and to raise it was a breach of decorum. "Living History," *Harvard Magazine* 105 (5) (May–June 2003): 39–46, 82, 83.

72. Remarking on white women's insensitivity to the southern situation, Cynthia Fleming recounted an interview with black SNCC organizer Chuck McDew, who was in jail and being treated reasonably when that changed abruptly and the guards began beating him. It turned out that a white female SNCC supporter had devised the idea of posing as his wife so that he could receive a visitor in jail, and when the jailers made this "discovery," they cursed and beat him for having a white wife. Fleming, *Soon We Will Not Cry*, 132–133.

73. She continued, "But we has to work for them and many of our womens have a baby with their husbands. They don't seem to see that, though." Belfrage, *Freedom Summer*, 45.

74. Carson, *Silent Voices*, 161.

75. Ladner, "The Emmett Till Generation," *Southern Exposure* 15(2) (Summer 1978): 42. Also see Payne, *I've Got the Light*, 54–55; Ruth Feldstein, "'I Wanted the Whole World to See': Race, Gender, and Constructions of Motherhood in the Death of Emmett Till," in *Not June Cleaver: Women and*

Gender in Postwar America, 1945–1960, ed. Joanne Meyerowitz (Philadelphia: Temple University Press, 1994), 263–303, 289, and Stephen Whitfield, *A Death in the Delta: The Story of Emmett Till* (New York: Free Press, 1988). Clenora Hudson-Weems included reactions from a wide range of artists and ordinary people about the Till case in *Emmett Till: The Sacrificial Lamb of the Civil Rights Movement* (Troy, Mich.: Bedford, 1994).

76. Joel Sinsheimer interview with Sam Block, "Never Turn Back: The Movement in Greenwood, Mississippi," in *Southern Exposure* 15(2) (Summer 1987): 37–50: "What made me," 40; "many of the kids," 41.

77. Sellers, *River of No Return*: "Emmett Till was only," 15; "there was something special," 15; "They showed," 14.

78. Anne Moody, *Coming of Age in Mississippi* (New York: Dell, 1968), 125–126, 128.

79. Ladner, "The Emmett Till Generation," 42. Audre Lorde, Gwendolyn Brooks, Larry Neal, Charlayne Hunter Gault, Endesha Ida Mae Holland, Shelby Steele, John Edgar Wideman, Eldridge Cleaver, and many others have also written about Till. James Baldwin wrote that his play *Blues for Mister Charlie* was based on the Emmett Till case: "I do not know why the case pressed on my mind so hard—but it would not let me go." *Blues for Mr. Charlie* (New York: Dial, 1964), xiv. Echoing Baldwin, Muhammad Ali (whose name was Cassius Clay as a teenager) said:

> Emmett Till and I were about the same age. A week after he was
> murdered in Sunflower County, Mississippi, I stood on the corner
> with a gang of boys, looking at pictures of him in the black
> newspapers and magazines. In one he was laughing and happy. In
> the other, his head was swollen and bashed in, his eyes bulging out
> of his sockets and his mouth twisted and broken. . . . I felt a deep
> kinship to him when I learned he was born the same year and day I
> was. . . . I couldn't get Emmett out of my mind."

Muhammad Ali, with Richard Durham, *The Greatest: My Own Story* (New York: Random House, 1975), 34–35. Also see Feldstein, "I Wanted the Whole World to See," 289 and 303, n. 130, for references to memories of Till.

80. "Can You Be BLACK and Look at This? Reading the Rodney King Video," in *Black Male: Representations of Masculinity in Contemporary American Art*, ed. Thelma Golden (New York: Whitney Museum of American Art, 1994), 91–110, 103. Also see Kendall Thomas's account of his grandfather telling him about the Emmett Till lynching in the context of Thomas's analysis of Supreme Court justice Clarence Thomas's outrageous appropriation, to defend himself against criticism, of the term "high-tech lynching," which "invoked this scandalous history of the ritual torture, mutilation, and murder of thousands of black Americans at the hands of white American mobs." In "Strange Fruit," in *Race-ing, Justice, En-gendering Power: Essays on Anita Hill, Clarence Thomas, and the Construction of Social Reality*, ed. Toni Morrison (New York: Pantheon, 1992), 364–389, 367.

81. In a novel loosely based on the O. J. Simpson murder trial, the white wife narrator reflects on the distance between her black husband and herself. He asks her whether she has heard the Emmett Till story, which he had heard many times at his father's knee, in which a fourteen-year-old boy, "just a child really, had had his terrified face beaten in and his genitalia *cut off* and his eyes *gouged out*, and then, had a cotton gin tied to his neck, and had gotten his body jettisoned into the Tallahatchie River, just because someone said he whistled once, at a white woman?" He said that white girls used to call him up at dinner time, and when he hung up, the specter of Emmett Till would be at the table with him and his family. The narrator reflects, "We Halseys never had a guest like that at our table. What would he have to do with us? We had heard the story, probably, somewhere. Emmett Till, his name was. It was terrible, unspeakable, but what happened to him had nothing to do with us." Kate Manning, *White Girl* (New York: Dial, 2002), 167.

82. Chude Pam Allen, "A Personal Comment: White Women in the Movement," 1989, unpublished, in possession of Wini Breines; e-mail from Allen, October 1, 2003, said that the quotation comes from "Bibliography: The Mississippi Summer Project," unpublished, prepared by her for the 25th West Coast commemoration of the summer project in Berkeley on June 17, 1989. A slightly different version of the bibliography was subsequently published as *Freedom Is a Constant Struggle: An Anthology of the Mississippi Civil Rights Movement*, ed. Susie Erenrich (Montgomery, Ala.: Black Belt, 1999), 511–520. The quote I use is not in the published bibliography, but similar comments and the reference to the book where Allen found the interview are cited in selection no. 28, 518. Also see "Mississippi Mothers: Roots," in *Sturdy Black Bridges: Visions of Black Women in Literature*, ed. Roseann P. Bell, Bettye J. Parker, and Beverly Guy-Sheftall (Garden City, N.Y.: Anchor/Doubleday, 1979), 268–281, 280, where older women report that Emmett Till had been forced to swallow his "privates."

83. Stoper, *SNCC*, 100.

84. Rothschild, *A Case of Black and White*, 134–135.

85. Sellers, *River of No Return*, 95–96. See Patch, "Sweet Tea at Shoney's," in Curry et al., *Deep in Our Hearts*, 153.

86. McAdam, *Freedom Summer*, 93. At the SNCC conference in 1988, Jean Wheeler Smith laughingly remarked, "[T]here was a lot of sex in SNCC. We were twenty years old. What do you expect?" Greenberg, *A Circle of Trust*, 137. It is relevant, too, that this was the beginning of the "sexual revolution" of the 1960s, when young people experimented with sex, a shift from a more chaste 1950s sexual culture.

87. Evans, *Personal Politics*: "the most potent," 78; "there was a sense," 79.

88. McAdam, *Freedom Summer*, 93; Schultz, *Going South*, 118–119.

89. Evans, *Personal Politics*, 78.

90. Rothschild, *A Case of Black and White*: "sexual test," 137; also see 137–142. In

Evans, *Personal Politics*, Staughton Lynd, director of the Freedom Schools, referred to black men who considered it an accomplishment if they slept with white women—and the more the better, 80. Also see McAdam, *Freedom Summer*, 106–107. For an account of a black woman project director, then named Gwen Robinson, who protected female SNCC volunteers from unwanted sexual attention, see Johnetta Betsch Cole and Beverly Guy-Sheftall, *Gender Talk*, 90–91; and Kimberly Springer, *Living for the Revolution: Black Feminist Organizations, 1968–1980* (Durham, N.C.: Duke University Press, 2005), 24.

91. Evans, *Personal Politics*, 80.

92. Rothschild, *A Case of Black and White*: "for the most part," 147; "the hurt," 148.

93. Gloria Wade-Gayles, *Pushed Back to Strength: A Black Woman's Journey Home* (Boston: Beacon, 1993), 180. Also see Rothschild, *A Case of Black and White*, 148; King, *Freedom Song*, 464–465; Evans, *Personal Politics*, 78–82.

94. See Wini Breines, "Sixties Stories' Silences," *NWSA Journal* 8(3) (Fall 1996): 101–121.

95. Belfrage, *Freedom Summer*; Sutherland, *Letters from Mississippi*; Evans, *Personal Politics*; Rothschild, *A Case of Black and White*; McAdam, *Freedom Summer*; Schultz, *Going South*; Evans and Rothschild interviewed black women or drew on interviews with them.

96. Patch, "Sweet Tea at Shoney's," in Curry et al., *Deep in Our Hearts*, 155.

97. Patch, "Sweet Tea at Shoney's," in Curry et al., *Deep in Our Hearts*, 160; Del Pozzo, "The Feel of a Blue Note," in Curry et al., *Deep in Our Hearts*, 197.

98. In Robnett, *How Long? How Long?* 130–131.

99. Schultz, *Going South*, 32.

100. Belfrage, *Freedom Summer*, "Preface to the Virginia Edition" (Charlottesville: University Press of Virginia, 1990), xiii–xx, xvii.

101. Washington, "We Started from Different Ends of the Spectrum," in Evans, *Personal Politics*, appendix, 238–240, 239.

102. Evans, *Personal Politics*, 84.

103. Rothschild, *A Case of Black and White*: "I've seen," 138; "The Movement," 147; "The Negro girls," 147.

104. Wade-Gayles, *Pushed Back to Strength*, 180.

105. King, *Freedom Song*, 465. See Nellie McKay about Alice Walker's story "Advancing Luna—and Ida B. Wells": "The story is about the death of a friendship between two women: the tragedy of women's cross-racial relationships at the intersection of race and sex." In "Acknowledging Differences: Can Women Find Unity through Diversity?" in *Theorizing Black Feminisms: The Visionary Pragmatism of Black Women*, ed. Stanlie M. James and Abena P. A. Busia (New York: Routledge, 1993), 267–282, 278.

106. McAdam, *Freedom Summer*, 124.

107. See Payne, *I've Got the Light*, 382–390.

108. Evans, *Personal Politics*, 239.

109. See Wade-Gayles, *Pushed Back to Strength*: "Many African-Americans who participated in the movement have gone from distancing themselves from white friends, to forgetting that they ever were friends, to adding their friends' names to the lengthening list of white people who can not be trusted. Who deserve our rage," 181. Also see Wade-Gayles's essay "A Change of Heart about Matters of the Heart: An Anger Shift from Interracial Marriages to Real Problems," in her *Rooted against the Wind: Personal Essays* (Boston: Beacon, 1996), 87–131.

110. Fleming, *Soon We Will Not Cry*, 167.

111. Becky Thompson noted

> the tremendous impact the organization had on the education of white antiracist activists. White involvement had the power to explode whole childhoods' worth of racist socialization. In the place of this socialization SNCC encouraged the growth of political consciousness that accompanied many, many white people for the rest of their lives.

Black SNCC organizers and local people can take credit. *A Promise and a Way of Life: White Antiracist Activism* (Minneapolis: University of Minnesota Press, 2001), 71.

Chapter 2

1. Komozi Woodard, *A Nation within a Nation: Amiri Baraka (LeRoi Jones) and Black Power Politics* (Chapel Hill: University of North Carolina Press, 1999): "galvanized," xiv; "self-determination," xiii.

2. See Timothy B. Tyson, *Radio Free Dixie: Robert F. Williams and the Roots of Black Power* (Chapel Hill: University of North Carolina Press, 1999), for a study of armed self-defense in the black South that preceded SNCC and inspired young southern black activists as well as the Black Panther party. He shows that Black Power was not imported from the North but emerged concomitantly in the South.

3. For the influence of Maoism and the Chinese revolution, see Robin D. G. Kelley and Betsy Esch, "Black Like Mao," *Souls* 1 (April 1999): 6–41. Also see Kelley, "Stormy Weather: Reconstructing Black (Inter)Nationalism in the Cold War Era," in *Is It Nation Time? Contemporary Essays on Black Power and Black Nationalism*, ed. Eddie Glaude, Jr. (Chicago: University of Chicago Press, 2002), 67–90; and Kelley, "'Roaring from the East': Third World Dreaming," in his *Freedom Dreams: The Black Radical Imagination* (Boston: Beacon, 2002), chap. 3. Also see Woodard, *A Nation within a Nation*, chap.1, "Groundwork: The Impact of Fidel Castro, Patrice Lumumba, Robert F. Williams, and Malcolm X on Amiri Baraka and the Black Arts Movement."

4. For the influence of the Nation of Islam on black liberation politics, see Melani McAlister, "One Black Allah: The Middle East in the Cultural Poli-

tics of African American Liberation, 1955–1970," *American Quarterly* 51(3) (September 1999): 622–656. There are many books on the Nation of Islam. See, for example, Karl Evanzz, *The Messenger: The Rise and Fall of Elijah Muhammad* (New York: Pantheon, 1999); Claude Andrew Clegg III, *An Original Man: The Life and Times of Elijah Muhammad* (New York: St. Martin's, 1997); and Mattias Gardell, *In the Name of Elijah Muhammad: Louis Farrakhan and the Nation of Islam* (Durham, N.C.: Duke University Press, 1996).

5. For a critique of Malcolm's gender politics and the high regard in which most female black writers held him, see Farah Jasmine Griffin, "'Ironies of the Saint': Malcolm X, Black Women and the Price of Protection," in *Sisters in Struggle: African-American Women in the Civil Rights–Black Power Movement*, ed. Bettye Collier-Thomas and V. P. Franklin (New York: New York University Press, 2001), 214–229. Marlon Riggs made the point that in more contemporary popular appropriations of Malcolm X, it is "the militant, macho, 'by any means necessary' Malcolm" who is idolized and not the more critical after-Mecca, more multicultural Malcolm. "Black Macho Revisited: Reflections of a Snap! Queen," *Black American Literature Forum* 25(2) (Summer 1991): 389–394, 394.

6. See James Smethurst, *The Black Arts Movement: Literary Nationalism in the 1960s and 1970s* (Chapel Hill: University of North Carolina Press, 2005) for an important link between the Popular Front aesthetics of the 1930s and 1940s and cultural nationalism, particularly the Black Arts movement. Also see Smethurst, "Poetry and Sympathy: New York, the Left, and the Rise of Black Arts," in *Left of the Color Line: Race, Radicalism, and Twentieth Century Literature of the United States*, ed. Bill V. Mullen and James Smethurst (Chapel Hill: University of North Carolina Press, 2003), 259–278.

7. For a discussion of intraracial distinctions in Black Arts poetry, see Philip Harper, "Nationalism and Social Division in Black Arts Poetry of the 1960s," in his *Are We Not Men? Masculine Anxiety and the Problem of African-American Identity* (New York: Oxford University Press), chap. 2. For related points, see Nell Ervin Painter, "Malcolm X across the Genres," *American Historical Review* 98(2) (April 1993): 432–439; and Gerald Early, "Their Malcolm, My Problem: On the Abuses of Afrocentrism and Black Anger," *Harper's Magazine* (December 1992): 62–73.

8. Larry Neal, "The Black Arts Movement," in *The Black Aesthetic*, ed. Addison Gayle, Jr. (Garden City, N.Y.: Doubleday, 1972), 257–274, 257.

9. Gayle, introduction to *The Black Aesthetic*, xv–xxiv, xxii.

10. Lester, *Look Out Whitey! Black Power's Gon' Get Your Mama!* (New York: Grove, 1968), 107.

11. Maulana Ron Karenga, "From the Quotable Karenga," in *The Black Power Revolt*, ed. Floyd Barbour (Boston: Porter Sargent, 1968), 162–170, 170.

12. Lee, *Directionscore: Selected and New Poems* (Detroit: Broadside, 1971), 75–76.

13. Quoted in Virginia Fowler, *Nikki Giovanni* (New York: Twayne, 1992), 34; from Nikki Giovanni, *Black Feeling, Black Talk* (1969).

14. See, for example, E. U. Essien-Udom, *Black Nationalism: A Search for Identity in America* (Chicago: University of Chicago Press, 1962); Robert L. Allen, *Black Awakening in Capitalist America* (Garden City, N.Y.: Doubleday, 1969); John. H. Bracey, Jr., August Meier, and Elliot Rudwick, eds., *Black Nationalism in America* (Indianapolis, Ind.: Bobbs-Merrill, 1970); John T. McCartney, *Black Power Ideologies: An Essay on African-American Political Thought* (Philadelphia: Temple University Press, 1992); William L. Van Deburg, *New Day in Babylon: The Black Power Movement and American Culture, 1965–1975* (Chicago: University of Chicago Press, 1992); William L. Van Deburg, *Black Camelot: African American Heroes and Their Times, 1960–1980* (Chicago: University of Chicago Press, 1997), chap. 2; Woodard, *A Nation within a Nation*; Glaude, *Is It Nation Time?*

15. Carmichael, "Power and Racism," in *The Black Power Revolt*, ed. Floyd B. Barbour (Boston: Porter Sargent, 1968), 61–71, 68.

16. For a discussion of the centrality in black liberation poetry of black corporeality as a weapon in the war of liberation, see Michael Bibby, *Hearts and Minds: Bodies, Poetry, and Resistance in the Vietnam Era* (New Brunswick, N.J.: Rutgers University Press, 1966), chap. 2, "'The Transfiguration of Blackness': The Body in Black Liberation Poetry."

17. Glaude, introduction to *Is It Nation Time?* 1–21, 4.

18. SNCC, "The Basis of Black Power," in *Takin' It to the Streets: A Sixties Reader*, 2d ed., ed. Alexander Bloom and Wini Breines (New York: Oxford University Press, 2003), 116–121: "should be," 119; "If we are," 118.

19. See Van Deburg, *New Day in Babylon* and *Black Camelot*.

20. See Jerry Gafio Watts, *Amiri Baraka: The Politics and Art of a Black Intellectual* (New York: New York University Press, 2001), chap. 10, for a discussion of Baraka's antiwhite theme, particularly hostility toward white women. Also see Eldridge Cleaver, *Soul on Ice* (New York: Dell, 1968), 17–29.

21. Karenga, "From the Quotable Karenga": "When the word," 167.

22. Cleaver, *Soul on Ice*, 66.

23. Larry Neal, "New Space/The Growth of Black Consciousness in the Sixties," in *The Black Seventies*, ed. Floyd B. Barbour (Boston: Porter Sargent, 1970), 9–31, 24.

24. See Neal, "New Space," 24, 25. See, for example, the Baraka poem "Black Art," in Gayle, *The Black Aesthetic*, 260–261, and Baraka's antifeminist and anti-Semitic statement in "Black Woman." He wrote, "The Leftists have reintroduced the white woman for the precise purpose of stunting the nation, and changing the young black would be 'revolutionary' into a snarling attachment of jewish [*sic*] political power." In *Raise, Race, Rays, Raze: Essays since 1965: Imamu Amiri Baraka (LeRoi Jones)* (New York: Vintage, 1972), 147–170, 153; also see Fowler, *Nikki Giovanni*, 47; and Giovanni's poem "The True Import of Present Dialogue: Black vs. Negro," in Harper,

Are We Not Men? 194–195. On anti-Semitism, see Bibby, *Hearts and Minds,* 72; Watts, *Amiri Baraka,* 148–152; Van Deburg, *New Day in Babylon,* 171, 173.

25. Glaude, introduction to *Is It Nation Time?* 8. Attributed to Jeffrey Stout.

26. Two examples from many follow. CORE leader Floyd McKissick stated, "The year 1966 shall be remembered as the year we left our imposed status as Negroes and became Black men." Quoted in Belinda Robnett, *How Long? How Long? African-American Women in the Struggle for Civil Rights* (New York: Oxford University Press, 1997), 182. Eldridge Cleaver quoted from Ossie Davis's moving eulogy for Malcolm X, "Malcolm was our manhood, our living, black manhood." *Soul on Ice,* 66.

27. Academic Barbara Christian wrote, "[O]ne of the reasons for the surge of Afro-American women's writing in the 1970s and its emphasis on sexism in the black community is precisely that when the ideologues of the 1960s said *black,* they meant *black male,*" in "The Race for Theory," *Cultural Critique,* no. 6 (Spring 1987): 51–63, 60. In 1970, Pauli Murray wrote that the goal of black males "is to share power with white males in a continuing patriarchal society in which both black and white females are relegated to a secondary status," in "The Liberation of Black Women," in *Voices of New Feminism,* ed. Mary Lou Thompson (Boston: Beacon, 1970), 87–102, 91.

28. Michele Wallace, *Black Macho and the Myth of the Superwoman* (New York: Dial, 1978). For more on black nationalism and the Black Arts movement as sexist see, for example, bell hooks, *Ain't I a Woman? Black Women and Feminism* (Boston: South End, 1981), 106–110; Paula Giddings, *When and Where I Enter: The Impact of Black Women on Race and Sex in America* (New York: Bantam, 1984), 314ff.; Madhu Dubey, *Black Women Novelists and the Nationalist Aesthetic* (Bloomington: Indiana University Press, 1994); Jill Nelson's chapter "The Dickpolitik" in her *Straight, No Chaser: How I Became a Grown-Up Black Woman* (New York: Putnam's, 1997). For critiques during that time, see the essays in Toni Cade, ed., *The Black Woman* (New York: New American Library, 1970).

29. Robyn Weigman, *American Anatomies: Theorizing Race and Gender* (Durham, N.C.: Duke University Press, 1995), 107.

30. Kobena Mercer and Isaac Julien, "True Confessions," in *Black Male: Representations of Masculinity in Contemporary Art,* ed. Thelma Golden (New York: Whitney Museum of American Art, 1994), 191–200, 198; also see Watts, *Amiri Baraka,* 331–336; and Cheryl Clarke, "Queen Sistuh: Black Women Poets and the Circle(s) of Blackness," in *After Mecca: Women Poets and the Black Arts Movement* (New Brunswick, N.J.: Rutgers University Press, 2005), chap. 3.

31. Neal, "New Space," 30.

32. Cleaver, *Soul on Ice,* 188–192: "Across the naked," 189; "heal the wound," 189; "I, the Black Eunuch," 191.

33. Weigman, *American Anatomies,* 107, 108. In "True Confessions," British academics Kobena Mercer and Isaac Julien suggested, "Figures such as El-

dridge Cleaver promoted a heterosexist version of black militance which not only authorized sexism—Stokely Carmichael said the only position of black women was 'prone'—but a hidden agenda of homophobia," 198. See Watts, *Amiri Baraka*, about homophobia in the Black Power movement, particularly about Baraka. For Eldridge Cleaver's attack on James Baldwin, see E. Frances White, *Dark Continent of Our Bodies: Black Feminism and the Politics of Respectability* (Philadelphia: Temple University Press, 2001), 173–176. Also see Kendall Thomas, "Ain't Nothing Like the Real Thing: Black Masculinity, Gay Sexuality, and the Jargon of Authenticity," and Rhonda M. Williams, "Living at the Crossroads: Explorations in Race, Nationality, Sexuality, and Gender," both in *The House That Race Built: Black Americans, U.S. Terrain*, ed. Wahneema Lubiano (New York: Pantheon, 1997), 116–125, and 136–156, respectively; and Harper, *Are We Not Men?* See Alice Walker's critical review of Black Panther David Hilliard's *This Side of Glory*, which analyzed the use of the word *punk* among the Black Panthers in "They Ran on Empty," and "Attack Racism, Not Black Men," Elaine Brown's defense of Panther men, both in the *New York Times*, May 5, 1993, A23.

34. Anne Valk, "Separatism and Sisterhood: Race, Sex, and Women's Activism in Washington, D.C., 1963–1980" (Ph.D. diss., Duke University, 1996), 328.

35. See Harper, *Are We Not Men?* 11.

36. For an important critique of nationalist politics for utilizing romanticized images of Africa, including the notion of complementarity in gender relations, see E. Frances White, "Africa on My Mind: Gender, Counter-Discourse and African-American Nationalism," *Journal of Women's History* 2(1) (Spring 1990): 73–97.

37. Amiri Baraka wrote in "Black Woman":

> [W]e do not believe in the "equality" of women and men. We cannot understand what devils and the devilishly influenced mean when they say equality for women. We could never be equals. . . . nature had not provided thus. The brother says, "Let a woman be a wo-man . . . and let a man be a ma-an. . . ." But this means that we will complement each other, that you, who I call my house because there is no house without a man and his wife, are the single element in the universe that perfectly completes my essence. (148)

38. Nathan Hare, "Will the Real Black Man Please Stand Up?" *Black Scholar* 2(10) (June 1971): 32–35, 32.

39. More recently, Leith Mullings wrote, "Whether 'complementarity' is phrased frankly as superiority and inferiority or in more gender-neutral language, women are associated primarily with the domestic sphere. Their reproductive capacity is essentialized and becomes the primary aspect of their identity." *On Our Own Terms: Race, Class, and Gender in the Lives of African American Women* (New York: Routledge, 1997), 139. She pointed out that "patriarchal gender relationships characterize many nationalist

positions," 138. See her reference to the "prone" comment, 145. Also see Scot Brown, *Fighting for US: Maulana Karenga, the US Organization, and Black Cultural Nationalism* (New York: New York University Press, 2003), for this important organization's "staunchly patriarchal . . . approach to gender roles," 58.

40. Robert Staples, "The Myth of the Impotent Black Male," in *Contemporary Black Thought: The Best from 'The Black Scholar'*, ed. Robert Chrisman and Nathan Hare (Indianapolis, Ind.: Bobbs-Merrill, 1973), 126–137, 134.

41. Recently, critic Margo Perkins noted that radical black women "found themselves in a peculiar situation. In transcending traditional feminine roles and gender expectations in order to participate actively in the struggle, they sometimes encountered rejection from their Black male counterparts precisely because they were no longer seen as feminine." In Margo V. Perkins, *Autobiography as Activism: Three Black Women of the Sixties* (Jackson: University Press of Mississippi, 2000), 103.

42. Elaine Brown, *A Taste of Power: A Black Woman's Story* (New York: Pantheon, 1992), 357.

43. *Angela Davis: An Autobiography* (New York: Bantam, 1974): "man's job," 159; "unfortunate syndrome," 180.

44. See Angela Davis's review of Elaine Brown's *A Taste of Power: A Black Woman's Story* in the *Women's Review of Books* 10(9) (June 1993): 1, 3–4, 3. Also see Giddings, *When and Where I Enter: The Impact of Black Women on Race and Sex in America* (New York: Bantam, 1984), 316–317.

45. Quoted in Giddings, *When and Where*, 316.

46. "*Black Scholar* Interviews: Kathleen Cleaver," *Black Scholar* 3(4) (December 1971): 54–59, 55–56.

47. Giddings, *When and Where*, 322; also see Patricia Morton, *Disfigured Images: The Historical Assault on Afro-American Women* (New York: Praeger, 1991).

48. Alice Walker, "Choosing to Stay at Home: Ten Years after the March on Washington," in Walker, *In Search of Our Mothers' Gardens* (New York: Harcourt Brace Jovanovich, 1984), 158–170, 169.

49. Morton, *Disfigured Images*, 115. Also see Watts, *Amiri Baraka*, 341–342; Wallace, *Black Macho*, 30–31, 118; Inez Smith Reid, *"Together" Black Women* (New York: Emerson Hall, 1972), on black militant women's attitudes toward the Moynihan Report, 55–62, and on attitudes toward black men, 62–78. There is much writing on these topics. See, for example, Jean Carey Bond and Pat Peery, "Is the Black Male Castrated?" in *The Black Woman*, ed. Toni Cade (New York: New American Library, 1970), 113–118. Also see Giddings, *When and Where*, 319–320.

50. Madhu Dubey, *Black Women Novelists and the Nationalist Aesthetic* (Bloomington: Indiana University Press, 1994), 17. See Patricia Morton's indictment of psychiatrists William H. Grier and Price M. Cobb's 1968 book, *Black Rage*: "The primary question that *Black Rage* appeared to be trying to

answer was why the Afro-American woman was continuing to damage her man as [a] man." *Disfigured Images*, 116.

51. Giddings, *When and Where*, 324. Jerry Gafio Watts wrote:

> In black nationalist circles of the late 1960s and early 1970s, black women were frequently less than forceful defenders of gender equality. Trapped in the belief that black male needs were superior to their own, they often participated in subservient activities in order to enhance the black male's image of himself. (Watts, *Amiri Baraka*, 343)

52. Prathia Hall in *A Circle of Trust: Remembering SNCC*, ed. Cheryl Lynn Greenberg (New Brunswick, N.J.: Rutgers University Press, 1998), 146.

53. Valk, "Separatism and Sisterhood": "fertility and nurturing," 305; "removing ourselves," 304; "The white woman seeks," 306.

54. E. Frances White, *Dark Continent of Our Bodies: Black Feminism and the Politics of Respectability* (Philadelphia: Temple University Press, 2001), 27.

55. Reid, *"Together" Black Women*: "I think the woman," 71; "We should," 71; "She should make him," 70; "I'm willing to make," 72; also see section on "Black Men and Black Women," 55–78.

56. Reid, *"Together" Black Women*, 347.

57. "*Black Scholar* Interviews: Kathleen Cleaver," 59.

58. Gwen Patton, "Black People and the Victorian Ethos," in *The Black Woman*, ed. Toni Cade (New York: New American Library, 1970), 143–148, 147.

59. "Who Will Revere the Black Woman?" in Cade, *The Black Woman*: "too many," 82; "Evil?" 83. Also see Jean Carey Bond and Patricia Peery, "Is the Black Man Castrated?" in Cade, *The Black Woman*, where they remarked, "in reality Black women . . . have not had enough power in this male-dominated culture to effect a coup against anyone's manhood," 113–118, 117.

60. Reid, *"Together" Black Women*, 87.

61. Barbara A. Sizemore, "Sexism and the Black Male," *Black Scholar* 4(6–7) (March–April 1973): 2–11, 8.

62. Nikki Giovanni, *Gemini* (New York: Penguin, 1971), 143.

63. Abbey Lincoln, "Who Will Revere the Black Woman?" 83. For invectives against white women by Black Arts poet Sonia Sanchez, see Watts, *Amiri Baraka*, 294. Also see Perkins, *Autobiography as Activism*, 115–118; Reid, *"Together" Black Women*, 79–87.

64. In black liberation historian Peniel E. Joseph's words, "Black Power's tortured relationship with black women has obscured the force and power of black women activists during this era." Peniel E. Joseph, "Black Liberation without Apology: Reconceptualizing the Black Power Movement," *Black Scholar* 31(3–4) (Fall–Winter 2001), 3–19, 12. Joseph suggests about the Black Panther party that local case studies will provide a more clear picture of "the fierce loyalty that many female members held for the organization despite the organization's controversial gender politics," 12.

65. Scholar James Smethurst has argued that the Black Arts movement was diverse and probably no more sexist than any other segment of American so-

ciety and that women were numerous and influential. He proposed that their willingness to struggle in public over male supremacy suggests male receptivity to the issues. Women's gender critiques were constitutive of the movement. James Smethurst, "Coda: Us Each Other's People Now: Woman-Centered Critiques of the Black Arts Movement and Cultural Memory," unpublished manuscript. I want to thank Smethurst and Robin D. G. Kelley for sharing their knowledge and insight into the Black Arts and Black Power movements.

66. Cheryl Clarke, *"After Mecca,"* 168.

67. Beal in Cade, *The Black Woman,* 90–100, 92.

68. Cellestine Ware, *Woman Power* (New York: Tower, 1970), 93. See bell hooks, *Ain't I a Woman? Black Women and Feminism* (Boston: South End, 1981), 182–183.

69. White, "Africa on My Mind," 86. Also see chapter 4 of this book for a discussion of small, explicitly feminist, black women's groups; and Kimberly Springer, *Living for the Revolution: Black Feminist Organizations, 1968–1980* (Durham, N.C.: Duke University Press, 2005).

70. Jill Nelson, *Straight, No Chaser* (New York: Putnam's, 1997), 121–122.

71. Perkins, *Autobiography as Activism,* 17.

72. Karl Knapper, "Women and the Black Panther Party: An Interview with Angela Brown," *Socialist Review* 26(1–2) (1996): 25–67, 46–47; also see Madalynn C. Rucker and JoNina M. Abron, who remarked, "Ex-Panthers are often reluctant to publicly discuss their past BPP affiliation, particularly with people who were not party members," in "'Comrade Sisters': Two Women of the Black Panther Party," in *Unrelated Kin: Race and Gender in Women's Personal Narratives,* ed. Gwendolyn Etter-Lewis and Michele Foster (New York: Routledge, 1996), 139–167, 140.

73. Tracye Ann Matthews, "'No One Ever Asks What a Man's Place in the Revolution Is': Gender and Sexual Politics in the Black Panther Party, 1966–1971" (Ph.D. diss., University of Michigan, 1998), 24.

74. At a 2003 academic conference on the Black Panther party, I raised the issue of sexism and was roundly criticized for emphasizing negative aspects of the party's history for this reason. I could not help but recall the SNCC 1988 conference and even the 1964 and 1965 memos, where white women raised the issue of sexism and were not appreciated and a larger narrative in which white women raised gender concerns that were received by black people as an imposition, a side story to the main issue of racism. I was—and we were—reproducing a familiar pattern, all playing our parts. The Black Panther Party in Historical Perspective, Wheelock College, Boston, Massachusetts, June 11–13, 2003.

75. Rucker and Abron, "Comrade Sisters," 161.

76. Henry Hampton and Steve Fayer, *Voices of Freedom: An Oral History of the Civil Rights Movement from the 1950s through the 1980s* (New York: Bantam, 1990), 434–435.

77. Wade-Gayles, *Pushed Back to Strength: A Black Woman's Journey Home* (Boston: Beacon, 1993), 157.

78. Gloria T. Hull, in "History/My History," in *Changing Subjects: The Making of Feminist Literary Criticism*, ed. Gayle Greene and Coppelia Kahn (New York: Routledge, 1993), 48–63, 50–51.

79. Michele Wallace, "Anger in Isolation: A Black Feminist's Search for Sisterhood," in her *Invisibility Blues: From Pop to Theory* (London: Verso, 1990), 18–25, 19.

80. Assata Shakur/Joanne Chesimard, "Women in Prison: How We Are," *Black Scholar* 9(7) (April 1978): 8–15, 14.

81. Quoted in Springer, *Living for the Revolution*, 25.

82. Nelson, *Straight, No Chaser*, 36.

83. Assata Shakur wrote about Davis, "She was one of the most beautiful women i had ever seen. Not physically but spiritually. I knew who she was, because i had been keeping clippings of her in my file." Assata Shakur, *Assata: An Autobiography* (Chicago: Hill, 1987), 206.

84. Nelson, *Straight, No Chaser*, 37.

85. Nelson, *Straight, No Chaser*, 121.

86. Nelson, *Straight, No Chaser*, 122.

87. Nelson, *Straight, No Chaser*, 138. Black Power historian Komozi Woodard wrote, "Sexism proved a dangerous pitfall to black liberation. To the extent that women seized full political participation, the Black Power movement flourished. However, to the extent that some Black Power advocates stymied the dynamics of women's liberation, they damned the prospects for black liberation." Woodard, "It's Nation Time in NewArk: Amiri Baraka and the Black Power Experiment in Newark, New Jersey," in *Freedom North: Black Freedom Struggles Outside the South, 1940–1980*, ed. Jeanne F. Theoharis and Komozi Woodard (New York: Palgrave Macmillan, 2002), 287–311, 308.

88. Rucker and Abron, "Comrade Sisters," 146. Brenda Presley joined in 1968: "I liked the militancy. I liked the fact that they appeared to be disciplined and they didn't take any mess from anybody. They were really serious." Quoted in Robyn Spencer, "Repression Breeds Resistance: The Rise and Fall of the Black Panther Party in Oakland, California, 1966–1982" (Ph.D. diss., Columbia University, 2001), 113. Tracye Matthews wrote about women's interest in the party in "'No One Ever Asks,'" 118ff. Also see Reid, *"Together" Black Women*, on militant black women's attitudes toward the Panthers, 344–352. Afena Shakur, mother of slain rapper Tupac Shakur, confessed to writer Kevin Powell that "one of the main reasons she joined the Black Panther Party was because that was where an army of brothers were, bringing the noise, quoting Marx and Malcolm and Mao-Tse-Tung, while rocking a uniform of black turtlenecks, black berets, black sunglasses, and black leather jackets." In Powell, *Who's Gonna Take the Weight? Manhood, Race, and Power in America* (New York: Three Rivers, 2003), 88.

89. Rucker and Abron, "Comrade Sisters," 148.

90. Rucker and Abron, "Comrade Sisters," 150.

91. Rucker and Abron, "Comrade Sisters," 154.

92. Rucker and Abron, "Comrade Sisters," 161.

93. Rucker and Abron, "Comrade Sisters," 164.

94. Regina Jennings, "Why I Joined the Party: An Africana Womanist Reflection," in *The Black Panther Party (Reconsidered)*, ed. Charles E. Jones (Baltimore, Md.: Black Classic, 1998), 257–265: "smash racism," 257; "ready to become a Panther," 257; "without race pride," 257; "had finally found," 258.

95. Jennings, "Why I Joined the Party," 261.

96. Jennings, "Why I Joined the Party," 263.

97. Assata Shakur, *Assata* (Chicago: Hill, 1987), 175.

98. Shakur, *Assata*, 223.

99. See Perkins, *Autobiography as Activism*, for a discussion of the activists' relationships to their birth families; and Knapper, "Women and the Black Panther Party," where Angela Brown talked about the Black Panther party as a family, 48. Also see essays by Brown, Burlage, and others in *Deep in Our Hearts: Nine White Women in the Freedom Movement*, ed. Constance Curry et al. (Athens: University of Georgia Press, 2000), for white women whose southern families disowned them for their civil rights politics. For an example of civil rights activists having to stay away from their families because of the harm they might bring them, see Anne Moody, *Coming of Age in Mississippi* (New York: Dell, 1968). Endesha Ida Mae Holland talked about her mother's death in the video *Freedom on My Mind* (1994) by Connie Field and Marilyn Mulford.

100. Knapper, "Women and the Black Panther Party," 47.

101. Rucker and Abron, "Comrade Sisters," 161. Another said, "All of a sudden the organization I had devoted my life to was gone. It was like there was this huge void that I was suddenly existing in." Also in Rucker and Abron, "Comrade Sisters," 161.

102. Historian Peniel Joseph suggested about the Black Panther party that local case studies would provide a more clear picture of "the fierce loyalty that many female members held for the organization despite the organization's controversial gender politics." In "Black Liberation without Apology: Reconceptualizing the Black Power Movement," *Black Scholar* 31(3–4) (Fall–Winter 2001): 3–19, 12.

103. Tracye Matthews, "'No One Ever Asks What a Man's Role in the Revolution Is': Gender and the Politics of the Black Panther Party, 1966–1971," in *The Black Panther Party (Reconsidered)*, ed. Charles E. Jones (Baltimore, Md.: Black Classic, 1998), 267–304, 274. Also see Matthews's Ph.D. dissertation with a similar title.

104. In her study of women's activism in Washington, D.C., "Separatism and Sisterhood," Anne Valk wrote, "After 1968, the increasingly vocal and visible feminist movement in Washington publicly challenged male supremacy

and provided a catalyst for black women to rethink gender relations in their own community, even if they refused to ally themselves with feminism," 346. See 308–338 on the Black Panther party. See Huey P. Newton's progressive 1970 statement, "The Women's Liberation and Gay Liberation Movements," in *To Die for the People: The Writings of Huey P. Newton* (New York: Vintage, 1972), 152–155.

105. Matthews, "No One Ever Asks," in Jones, *Black Panther Party (Reconsidered)*, 288. Also see Spencer, "Repression Breeds Resistance"; Angela D. LeBlanc-Ernest, "'The Most Qualified Person to Handle the Job': Black Panther Party Women, 1966–1982," in Jones, *Black Panther Party (Reconsidered)*, 305–334; and Knapper, "Women and the Black Panther Party."

106. Spencer, "Repression Breeds Resistance," 53.

107. Matthews, "No One Ever Asks," Ph.D. diss., 226.

108. See "Panther Sisters on Women's Liberation," in *Off the Pigs! The History and Literature of the Black Panther Party*, ed. G. Louis Heath (Metuchen, N.J.: Scarecrow, 1976), 339–350.

109. Heidi Steffens, "Panther Rally," *off our backs*, July 10, 1970, 6.

110. Matthews, "No One Ever Asks," in Jones, *Black Panther Party (Reconsidered)*, 275.

111. In "Comrade Sisters," Rucker and Abron attributed the two Panther women's divergent experiences to "differences in actual practices and politics among the BPP chapters and branches," 163.

112. Jon Rice, "The World of the Illinois Panthers," in Theoharis and Woodard, eds., *Freedom North*, 41–64.

113. Matthews, "No One Ever Asks," in Jones, *Black Panther Party (Reconsidered)*, 277. In "The Most Qualified Person to Handle the Job," LeBlanc-Ernest put it this way: "A constellation of intra-organizational factors, such as gender contestation, the dedicated and courageous actions of Panther women, and the ideological maturation of both female and male Party members, fueled the process of establishing a more gender-neutral Black Panther Party," 314.

114. See Huey P. Newton's 1970 statement, "The Women's Liberation and Gay Liberation Movements," in *To Die for the People*.

115. For an extremely insightful essay on the Black Panther party, see Nikhil Pal Singh, "The Black Panthers and the 'Undeveloped Country' of the Left," in Jones, *Black Panther Party (Reconsidered)*, 57–105. Also see Singh's *Black Is a Country: Race and the Unfinished Struggle for Democracy* (Cambridge, Mass.: Harvard University Press, 2004). See Spencer, "Repression Breeds Resistance," for the Panthers' interracialism, 82. Robin D. G. Kelley has suggested that the political ideology of the Black Panther party made it more receptive to gender issues; e-mail correspondence with author, September 6, 2002.

116. LeBlanc-Ernest, "The Most Qualified Person to Handle the Job," 318; Kathleen Neal Cleaver, "Sister Act," *Transition* 60, 3(2) (1993): 84–100, 90;

Spencer, "Repression Breeds Resistance," 360ff. Also see Heath, *Off the Pigs!* 210–214.

117. Ware, *Woman Power*, 93–94.

118. LeBlanc-Ernest, "The Most Qualified Person to Handle the Job," 317. Also see Spencer, "Repression Breeds Resistance," 205; and Matthews, "No One Ever Asks," in Jones, *the Black Panther Party (Reconsidered)*, 290–291.

119. Matthews, "No One Ever Asks," in Jones, *The Black Panther Party (Reconsidered)*, 290–291. See Alice Walker review, "They Ran on Empty," *New York Times*, May 5, 1993, A23.

120. Shakur, *Assata*, 204.

121. Angela Y. Davis, "Black Nationalism: The Sixties and the Nineties," in *Black Popular Culture*, ed. Gina Dent (Seattle, Wash.: Bay, 1992), 317–324, 327.

122. Afeni Shakur explained her attraction to the Panthers: "These were rebels with a cause (Black Power!), righteous ride-em cowboys lining up against FBI don J. Edgar Hoover's G-men and other agents of the oppressive state. . . . Where the brothers were, the sisters were, too." In Powell, *Who's Gonna Take the Weight?* 88.

123. Angela Davis review of Elaine Brown, *A Taste of Power: A Black Women's Story* in the *Women's Review of Books* X(9) (June 1993): 1–4, 3.

124. Robin D. G. Kelley, *Freedom Dreams: The Black Radical Imagination* (Boston: Beacon, 2002), 136.

125. Davis review of Brown, *A Taste of Power*, 3. This sense of the 1960s echoes in Nikki Giovanni's poem, quoted above, "the sixties have been one / long funeral day," in Fowler, *Nikki Giovanni*, 34.

126. See, for example, "Panther Sisters on Women's Liberation," in Heath, *Off the Pigs!*, 342; and Brown, *A Taste of Power*.

127. Valk, "Separatism and Sisterhood," wrote, "Accounts by former members reveal sexual abuse of women by Panther men, at least in selected chapters. In their behavior, the BPP were not unique. But sexual abuse within the BPP has been more widely disclosed and discussed than within other revolutionary groups of the time," 335, n. 78.

128. See *A Lonely Rage: The Autobiography of Bobby Seale* (New York: Times Books, 1978), 187, for a discussion of sex among the Panthers. Also see Bill Ayers, *Fugitive Days: A Memoir* (Boston: Beacon, 2001), for similar white movement practices in the Weatherman faction of Students for a Democratic Society.

129. See Toni Cade, "The Pill: Genocide or Liberation?" in Cade, *The Black Woman*, 162–169; and Black Women's Liberation Group, "Statement on Birth Control," in *Sisterhood Is Powerful: An Anthology of Writings from the Women's Liberation Movement*, ed. Robin Morgan (New York: Vintage, 1970), 360–361.

130. Margo V. Perkins, "'Inside Our Dangerous Ranks': The Autobiography of Elaine Brown and the Black Panther Party," in *Still Lifting, Still Climbing:*

African American Women's Contemporary Activism, ed. Kimberly Springer (New York: Oxford University Press, 1999), 95.

131. Barbara Omolade, *The Rising of African American Women* (New York: Routledge, 1994), 166.

132. Wallace, "Twenty Years Later," in *Invisibility Blues*, 170–171. For a similar evaluation in 1970, see Kay Lindsay, "The Black Woman as Woman," in Cade, *The Black Woman*:

> [T]he Black movement is primarily concerned with the liberation of Blacks as a class and does not promote women's liberation as a priority. Indeed, the movement is for the most part spearheaded by males. The feminist movement, on the other hand, is concerned with the oppression of women as a class, but is almost totally composed of white females. Thus the Black woman finds herself on the outside of both political entities, in spite of the fact that she is the object of both forms of oppression. (85–89, 85)

Chapter 3

1. Allen continued, "It may not be for a long time, if ever, that most of us will see ourselves as allies of poor black women and be willing to risk all we would risk in joining them in their demands towards the system." In "Conversations," Pam Allen interviewed by Julius Lester, May 5, 1968, WBAI radio program, mimeograph, 6, in author's possession.

2. Jo Freeman, "On the Origins of the Women's Liberation Movement from a Strictly Personal Perspective," in *The Feminist Memoir Project: Voices from Women's Liberation*, ed. Rachel Blau DuPlessis and Ann Snitow (New York: Three Rivers, 1998), 171–196, 183.

3. Sara M. Evans, *Tidal Wave: How Women Changed America at Century's End* (New York: Free Press, 2003), 13.

4. Mary King, *Freedom Song: A Personal Story of the 1960s Civil Rights Movement* (New York: Morrow, 1987), 456–457; Sara Evans, *Personal Politics: The Roots of Women's Liberation in the Civil Rights Movement and the New Left* (New York: Knopf, 1979), 155.

5. Evans, *Personal Politics*, 157.

6. Evans, *Personal Politics*, 193ff.; on ERAP see Jennifer Frost, *"An Interracial Movement of the Poor": Community Organizing and the New Left in the 1960s* (New York: New York University Press, 2001), 153–155, 163–168; Kirkpatrick Sale, *SDS* (New York: Vintage, 1973), 95–115, 131–150.

7. Evans, *Personal Politics*, 197ff.; Alice Echols, *Daring to Be Bad: Radical Feminism in America, 1967–1975* (Minneapolis: University of Minnesota Press, 1989), 45–49.

8. Vivian Rothstein, "Our Gang of Four: Friendship and Women's Liberation," in DuPlessis and Snitow, *The Feminist Memoir Project*, 35.

9. Echols, *Daring to Be Bad*, 49. This was reprinted in SDS's newspaper *New Left Notes*, November 13, 1967.

10. Evans, *Personal Politics*, 201. See chaps. 4 and 5 and 158ff. for the development of socialist feminism in Evans, *Tidal Wave*.

11. Quoted in Evans, *Personal Politics*, 205.

12. Jo Freeman, *The Politics of Women's Liberation* (New York: McKay, 1975), 103–104.

13. Heather Booth quoted in Evans, *Personal Politics*, 211.

14. Ann Hunter Popkin, "Bread and Roses: An Early Moment in the Development of Socialist Feminism" (Ph.D. diss., Brandeis University, 1978), 61.

15. Leslie Cagan, "Something New Emerges: The Growth of a Socialist Feminist," in *They Should Have Served That Cup of Coffee: Seven Radicals Remember the Sixties*, ed. Dick Cluster (Boston: South End, 1979), 225–258, 241.

16. Benita Roth, *Separate Roads to Feminism: Black, Chicana, and White Feminist Movements in America's Second Wave* (New York: Cambridge University Press, 2004). See especially chap. 2, "The 'Fourth World' Is Born: Intra-Movement Experience, Oppositional Political Communities, and the Emergence of the White Women's Liberation Movement," which is about women's relation to the New Left.

17. See Marge Piercy, "The Grand Coolie Damn," in *Sisterhood Is Powerful: An Anthology of Writings from the Women's Liberation Movement*, ed. Robin Morgan (New York: Vintage, 1970), 421–438; Echols, *Daring to Be Bad*, 51–137; Leslie Rabine, "Stormy Weather: A Memoir of the Second Wave," in *Changing Subjects: The Making of Feminist Literary Criticism*, ed. Gayle Greene and Coppelia Kahn (New York: Routledge, 1993), 211–225; Anne Valk, "Separatism and Sisterhood: Race, Sex, and Women's Activism in Washington, D.C., 1963–1980" (Ph.D. diss., Duke University, 1996), 207–208; Roth, *Separate Roads to Feminism*, 57–62; Robin Morgan, "Goodbye to All That," in *Takin' It to the Streets: A Sixties Reader*, 2d ed., ed. Alexander Bloom and Wini Breines (New York: Oxford University Press, 2003), 418–421; and Ruth Rosen, *The World Split Open: How the Modern Women's Movement Changed America* (New York: Viking, 2000), 94–140.

18. Linda Gordon and Ann Popkin, "Women's Liberation: Let Us All Now Emulate Each Other," in *Seasons of Rebellion: Protest and Radicalism in Recent America*, ed. Joseph Boskin and Robert Rosenstone (New York: Holt, Rinehart, and Winston), 286–312: "We have tried," 307; "We were usually," 287.

19. Amy Kesselman with Heather Booth, Vivian Rothstein, and Naomi Weisstein, "Our Gang of Four: Friendship and Women's Liberation," in DuPlessis and Snitow, *The Feminist Memoir Project*: Kesselman, "So after years," 39; Weisstein, "heterosexual chill," 38.

20. Morgan, "Goodbye to All That": "the friends," 418; "Women are," 421.

21. Piercy, "The Grand Coolie Damn," 422.

22. Piercy, "The Grand Coolie Damn," 430.

23. Ellen Willis, "Letter to the Left," in *Dear Sisters: Dispatches from the Women's Liberation Movement,* ed. Rosalyn Baxandall and Linda Gordon (New York: Basic, 2000), 51.

24. Kathy McAfee and Myrna Wood, "Bread and Roses," in *Voices from Women's Liberation,* ed. Leslie B. Tanner (New York: New American Library, 1970), 415–433, 425.

25. See chaps. 1 and 2 in this volume for this theme. Also see Leslie Cagan, "Something New Emerges," in Cluster, *They Should Have Served That Cup of Coffee,* 232; Bettina Aptheker, "Memories of FSM," in *Takin' It to the Streets: A Sixties Reader,* 1st ed., ed. Alexander Bloom and Wini Breines (New York: Oxford University Press, 1995), 121–125; and Margot Adler, *Heretic's Heart: A Journey through Spirit and Revolution* (Boston: Beacon, 1997), 102ff.

26. Piercy, "The Grand Coolie Damn," 438.

27. Betty Friedan, *The Feminine Mystique* (New York: Norton, 1963).

28. Meredith Tax, mimeo, n.d., in author's possession. Also see Tax, "Woman and Her Mind: The Story of Daily Life," a Bread and Roses publication, New England Free Press pamphlet, n.d., in author's possession.

29. See Wini Breines, *Young, White, and Miserable: Growing Up Female in the Fifties* (Chicago: University of Chicago Press, 2001).

30. Popkin, "Bread and Roses": "vehement," 77; "catch-all source," 78.

31. Willis, "Letter to the Left," 51.

32. Ginger Goldner, Meredith Tax, and Ruth Balser, "A Proclamation of the Rights of Women," mimeo, n.d., in author's possession.

33. Linda Gordon, "Functions of the Family," in Tanner, *Voices from Women's Liberation,* 181–188: "harnessed men," 182; "harnessing women," 182; "people into small," 183; "training them," 183; "chained women," 184; "only model," 185; "it is absolutely clear," 187. See Popkin, "Bread and Roses," 77–79 and 231, n. 22, on the importance of Gordon's piece, which was first a mimeographed handout, an article, and then printed as a pamphlet.

34. "Draft of Political Program for Bread and Roses, November 1970," mimeo, 4, 5, in author's possession. For a sampling of early influences on socialist feminist thinking about the family, see Juliet Mitchell, "Women: The Longest Revolution," in *Women, Class, and the Feminist Imagination: A Socialist-Feminist Reader,* ed. Karen V. Hansen and Ilene J. Philipson, (Philadelphia: Temple University Press, 1990); Margaret Benston, "The Political Economy of Women's Liberation," and Mariarosa Dalla Costa and Selma James, "Women and the Subversion of the Community," both in *Materialist Feminism: A Reader in Class, Difference, and Women's Lives,* ed. Rosemary Hennessy and Chrys Ingraham (New York: Routledge, 1997); and Pat Mainardi, "The Politics of Housework," in Morgan, *Sisterhood Is Powerful.*

35. See Lauri Umansky, *Motherhood Reconceived: Feminism and the Legacies of*

the Sixties (New York: New York University Press, 1996), for the argument that motherhood comprised a critical positive component of second wave cultural feminism of the 1970s, in part influenced by black women's pronatalism and the counterculture.

36. Vivian Rothstein, "The Magnolia Street Commune," *Boston Review* (February–March 1998): 30–32, 30.

37. See, for example, Kathie Sarachild, "Consciousness-Raising: A Radical Weapon," 144–150, and Anne Forer, "Thoughts on Consciousness-Raising," 151, both in Redstockings, *Feminist Revolution* (New York: Random House, 1978); Kathie Sarachild, "A Program for Feminist Consciousness-Raising," 273–276; Pamela Allen, "The Small Group Process," 277–281; and Vivian Gornick, "Consciousness," 287–300, all in *Radical Feminism: A Documentary Reader*, ed. Barbara A. Crow (New York: New York University Press, 2000); Barbara Susan, "About My Consciousness Raising," in Tanner, *Voices from Women's Liberation*, 238–243; Evans, *Personal Politics*, 214–215; Popkin, "Bread and Roses," 98–122; Popkin, "The Personal Is Political: The Women's Liberation Movement," in Cluster, *They Should Have Served That Cup of Coffee*, 181–222; Myra Marx Ferree and Beth B. Hess, *Controversy and Coalition: The New Feminist Movement across Three Decades of Change*, rev. ed. (New York: Twayne, 1994), 71–72. See Linda Gordon on consciousness-raising groups with a focus on Bread and Roses, "Social Movements, Leadership, and Democracy," *Journal of Women's History* 14(2) (Summer 2002): 102–117.

38. Freeman, *The Politics of Women's Liberation*, 103.

39. Anita Shreve, *Women Together, Women Alone: The Legacy of the Consciousness-Raising Movement* (New York: Viking, 1989), 6.

40. Gornick, "Consciousness," in *Radical Feminism*, 287–300, 288.

41. Popkin, "The Personal Is Political," 192.

42. Popkin "The Personal Is Political," 222.

43. Adler, *Heretic's Heart*: "But it wasn't," 160; "I realized," 160–161.

44. Popkin, "The Personal Is Political," 193.

45. Gornick, "Consciousness," in *Radical Feminism*, 289.

46. See Ferree and Hess, *Controversy and Coalition*, 72.

47. Shirley Goek-lin Lim, "'Ain't I a Feminist?' Reforming the Circle," in DuPlessis and Snitow, *The Feminist Memoir Project*, 450–466, 452.

48. Shreve, *Women Together, Women Alone*, 180.

49. Evans, *Tidal Wave*, 116, from D.C. Women's Liberation, "Herstory and Development of D.C. Women's Liberation Movement," c. 1971.

50. Jo Freeman discussed the homogeneity in the small groups and noted that informal elites developed whose members possessed particular characteristics linked to, for example, class, marital status, and access to networks. See chap. 4, "The Small Groups," in *The Politics of Women's Liberation*.

51. Jane Gerhard, *Desiring Revolution: Second-Wave Feminism and the Rewriting of American Sexual Thought, 1920–1982* (New York: Columbia University Press, 2001), 103.

52. Freeman, *The Politics of Women's Liberation*, 106–107.

53. Springer, *Living for the Revolution*: "riddled with," 34; "refused to recognize," 36. In *Separate Roads to Feminism*, Benita Roth argued, "The idea that 'radical black women don't want to work with radical white women' . . . led to an acceptance by white women's liberationists that a separation between feminists of different colors was necessary." Roth is quoting radical women in Chicago. Unsigned, "Meeting of Radical Women, Chicago, March 24–25, 1968," 206. Roth's book argued that an ethos of organizing one's own infused white and racial/ethnic feminisms, leading to a conclusion by all that it was impossible to organize across racial lines.

54. Roxanne Dunbar, "Outlaw Woman: Chapters from a Feminist Memoir-in-Progress," in DuPlessis and Snitow, *The Feminist Memoir Project*, 90–114, 101–102.

55. Echols, *Daring to Be Bad*, 106.

56. Echols, *Daring to Be Bad*, 107. See also Umansky, *Motherhood Reconceived*, 93–94; and Valk, "Separatism and Sisterhood," 218–219.

57. Popkin, "Bread and Roses," 45; "Bread and Roses: Interview with Chris [*sic*] Rosenthal, Wini Breines, Beth Rimanoczy, and Eleanor Stephens," special supplement on women's groups, *Hysteria: A Paper by and for Women* 1(4) (February 5, 1971): S-3, S-4, in author's possession.

58. Echols, *Daring to Be Bad*, 103ff.

59. Freeman, *The Politics of Women's Liberation*, 107.

60. Echols, *Daring to Be Bad*, 330, n. 172.

61. See Dana Densmore, "A Year of Living Dangerously: 1968," 71–89; and Roxanne Dunbar, "Outlaw Woman," both in DuPlessis and Snitow, *The Feminist Memoir Project*.

62. According to Popkin, "Bread and Roses," the average age in 1969 was 24.3 years old; median age was 25 years. Her study was based on a sample of 71 women. Kristine Rosenthal said the majority of the women were between 25 and 29 years and that 77 percent who answered her questionnaire came from large East Coast urban areas. Her study was based on a random sample of 150 members of Bread and Roses. Rosenthal, "Women in Transition: An Ethnography of a Women's Liberation Organization as a Case Study of Personal and Cultural Challenge" (Ph.D. diss., Harvard Graduate School of Education, 1972), 21–22.

63. According to Rosenthal, "Women in Transition," 54.7 percent never married, 27.6 percent were currently married, 10.6 percent were separated, 7.0 percent were divorced; and 60 percent of the women who had been married had children, usually one child under the age of 5, which made child care a significant concern, 23–24.

64. Popkin, "Bread and Roses," 58.

65. Rosenthal, "Women in Transition," 58. The short-lived nature of the group is not unusual for socialist feminist organizations. See Karen V. Hansen, "Women's Unions and the Search for Political Identity," in *Women, Class*

and the Feminist Imagination, ed. Hansen and Philipson, 213–238. The two longest, the Chicago Women's Liberation Women's Union and Baltimore Women's Union, lasted seven and a half and ten years, respectively, but most lasted only two or three years—and after 1975 most of them disappeared. Also see Popkin, "Bread and Roses," 226.

66. Rosenthal, "Women in Transition," 59.

67. Umansky, *Motherhood Reconceived*, 107. See the section in her book titled "A White Feminist Lament: How to Draw Black Women into the Movement," 93–102.

68. Meredith Tax, "Caste and Class," mimeo handout, n.d., in author's possession.

69. Gordon and Popkin, "Women's Liberation: Let Us All Now Emulate Each Other," 304–305. This statement also contained the implicit assumption that all women are white. See *All the Women Are White, All the Blacks Are Men, but Some of Us Are Brave: Black Feminist Studies*, ed. Gloria T. Hull, Patricia Bell Scott, and Barbara Smith (Old Westbury, N.Y.: Feminist Press, 1982).

70. Margaret Strobel, "Consciousness and Action: Historical Agency in the Chicago Women's Liberation Union," in *Provoking Agents: Theorizing Gender and Agency*, ed. Judith Kegan Gardiner (Urbana: University of Illinois Press, 1995), 53.

71. *Women's Liberation Newsletter* 1(2) (n.d.), in author's possession.

72. *Women's Liberation Newsletter* 1(3) (October 1969), in author's possession.

73. *Women's Liberation Newsletter* 1(4) (November 18, 1969), in author's possession.

74. Abortion flyer, n.d., in author's possession. The text was taken from an article by Washington, D.C., Women's Liberation.

75. Priscilla Long, "We Called Ourselves Sisters," in DuPlessis and Snitow, *The Feminist Memoir Project*, 324–337, 328.

76. Women's School Papers, M23, 1971–1992, Box 1, Folders 39 and 40, University Libraries and Special Collections, Northeastern University; Cambridge Women's Center Herstory, 1996, taped discussion with Sue Lyons, Judy Norris, Mary Rowe, and Rochelle Ruthchild of 888 Memorial Drive building takeover for a women's center, in Ruthchild's possession; interview with Laura Whitehorn, 1976, David Holmstrom Collection, Archives and Manuscripts Collections, University of Massachusetts, Boston; Carol McEldowney Papers, in which there are letters to and from her about the building takeover, Archives and Manuscripts Collections, University of Massachusetts, Boston. Thanks to Suzanne McCormick for bringing some of these to my attention. Ruthchild and Elizabeth Bouvier are making a video of recollections about this event. Also see Amy Brodkey Papers, Box 1, clippings about 888 Memorial Drive takeover, Schlesinger Library Archives, Radcliffe Institute for Advanced Study; and the underground newspaper *Old Mole* (April 1971): 3, 4, 19, Lamont Library, Harvard Univer-

sity, microfilm. Thanks to Jane Mansbridge for her notes on the building takeover.

77. Flyers for the Women's School, March 5, 1972, and fall term, 1972, Women's Center School, in author's possession. In the words of Susan Brownmiller, "*Our Bodies, Ourselves* sold more than a million copies and earned more than a half a million dollars in royalties during its first five years of commercial distribution, and became the premier source book for a generation of sexually active young women, crossing all lines of race and class." *In Our Time: A Memoir of a Revolution* (New York: Dial, 1999), 185.

78. Women's School, M23, Box 1, Folder 41, mimeo, University Libraries, Archives and Special Collections, Northeastern University, Boston.

79. This is signed by Ginger Ryan, Melanie Berson, Kathy McAfee, Marla Erlien, Laura Whitehorn, Tess Ewing, Jackie Pine, Laura Tillem, Marsha Steinberg, Susie Waysdorf, and Debby Knight. Mimeo, Women's School, M23, Box 1, Folder 40, Northeastern Archives.

80. Women's School, M23, Box 1, Folder 40, Northeastern Archives.

81. Women's School, M23, Box 1, Folder 40, Northeastern Archives.

82. Evans, *Tidal Wave*, 102.

83. Lise Vogel, *Woman Questions: Essays for a Materialist Feminism* (New York: Routledge, 1995), 100–101. In a testament to the early women's liberation movement, Bonnie Zimmerman wrote:

> No body of literature will ever have as strong an impact on my ideas as that produced in the first few years (roughly 1968 through 1972) of the women's liberation movement. Everything we have written since has been a refinement, development, refutation or reconfiguration of the concepts developed in that pioneering literature. Even the important work on difference that characterizes the feminist theory of the 1980s is not totally new, for the early women's liberation movement had a substantial sensitivity toward class and race oppression that seems to have been muted by later theoretical emphases on "women's nature" and "women's culture."

In "In Academia and Out: The Experience of a Lesbian Feminist Literary Critic," in *Changing Subjects: The Making of Feminist Literary Criticism*, ed. Gayle Greene and Coppelia Kahn (New York: Routledge, 1993), 112–120, 115.

84. Marilyn Frye, "The Necessity of Differences: Constructing a Positive Category of Women," *Signs: Journal of Women and Culture in Society* 21(4) (Summer 1996): 991–1010, 1006 n. 17. Also see Susan Bordo, "Feminism, Postmodernism and Gender-Scepticism," in *Feminism/Postmodernism*, ed. Linda Nicholson (New York: Routledge, 1990), 133–156, 141; and DuPlessis and Snitow, *The Feminist Memoir Project*.

85. Echols, *Daring to Be Bad*, 217.

86. Echols, *Daring to Be Bad*, 204; see 210–241 on lesbianism. Also see Valk, "Separatism and Sisterhood," on the Furies, chap. 6; and Valk's "Living a Feminist Lifestyle: The Intersection of Theory and Action in a Lesbian

Feminist Collective," *Feminist Studies* 28(2) (Summer 2002): 303–332; Karla Jay, *Tales of the Lavender Menace: A Memoir of Liberation* (New York: Basic, 1999); Freeman, *The Politics of Women's Liberation*, 134–142; Popkin, "Bread and Roses," 181–184; and Popkin, "The Personal Is Political," 212.

87. Popkin, "Bread and Roses," 183.

88. See, for example, Echols, *Daring to Be Bad*, 204–210; Freeman, *The Politics of Women's Liberation*, 122–123; Debby D'Amico, "To My White Working Class Sisters," in *Liberation Now! Writings from the Women's Liberation Movement*, ed. Deborah Babcox and Madeline Belkin (New York: Dell, 1971), 177–181; and Priscilla Long, a Bread and Roses member, who wrote of her self-consciousness and confusion at being from a working-class background, in "We Called Ourselves Sisters," in DuPlessis and Snitow, *The Feminist Memoir Project*, 324–337.

89. Popkin, "Bread and Roses," 84; Echols, *Daring to Be Bad*, 10.

90. Bay Area Women's Union, mimeo, Nancy Osterud Papers, Folder 13, Bread and Roses Collection, Schlesinger Library, Radcliffe Institute for Advanced Study.

91. Colletta Reid and Charlotte Bunch, "Revolution Begins at Home," in *Class and Feminism: A Collection of Essays from the Furies*, ed. Charlotte Bunch and Nancy Myron (Baltimore, Md.: Diana, 1974), 70–81: "Women's Liberation," 70; "much of my," 71; "Bringing down," 81.

92. Documents in author's possession.

93. Although white women also worked in schools and community organizations in black communities. In early 1971, groups of men and women organized around the country to support black radical Angela Davis, who was accused of abetting murders in conjunction with her support of the Soledad Brothers. On the Panthers in Washington, D.C., see Valk, "Separatism and Sisterhood," 308–338ff. and chap. 5, "'Building a People's Army': Women and Black Liberation." Also see Echols, *Daring to Be Bad*, 222–224.

94. Valk, "Separatism and Sisterhood," 325 and 315–338; also see Cagan, "Something New Emerges," 245; Echols, *Daring to Be Bad*, 222–223; and *off our backs: a women's liberation bi-weekly* (September 30, 1970): 4–5, in which white lesbian movement women who attended the Revolutionary People's Constitutional Convention in Philadelphia expressed anger and bitterness at the Panthers' dismissal, manipulation, and hostility toward them and their issues. In author's possession.

95. Letter to Bread and Roses members from Linda Gordon, Susie Orchard, and Jean Tepperman, mimeo, n.d., Bread and Roses Collection, Wini Breines Papers, Schlesinger Library, Radcliffe Institute for Advanced Study.

96. *Old Mole*, no. 36 (April 3–April 16, 1970), Lamont Library, Harvard University, microfilm, 7. See the pamphlet "So What Are We Complaining About? A Collection of Women's Articles from *The Old Mole*," articles originally published in the newspaper and prepared by the paper's women's caucus,

which was a Bread and Roses collective, Schlesinger Library, Radcliffe Institute for Advanced Study.

97. "Our Autonomous Women's Movement," a "collective speech by B. U. women's lib groups," mimeo, n.d., in author's possession.

98. Barbara Smith, *The Truth That Never Hurts: Writings on Race, Gender, and Freedom* (New Brunswick, N.J.: Rutgers University Press, 1998), 159.

99. In a scathing critique of white radicals' relationships to blacks, particularly Weatherman, Howard Machtinger noted their "pathetic need to be accepted by black radicals," their efforts to "legitimize themselves through a relationship with Third World radicals rather than to legitimize themselves through their own base or their own political trajectory." He referred to the New Left's unquestioning and uncritical support for black initiatives as "public toadyism" and "unabashed hero worship." Howard Machtinger, "Clearing Away the Debris: New Left Radicalism in 1960s America" (M.A. thesis, San Francisco State University, 1995), 231–232.

100. "Conversations," Pam Allen interviewed by Julius Lester, 6.

101. Piercy, "The Grand Coolie Damn," 421–438: "Such a man," 434; "When I am told," 437.

102. Rabine, "Stormy Weather," 211–225, 216.

103. Rabine, "Stormy Weather," 216–217.

104. Meredith Tax, "For the People Hear Us Singing, 'Bread and Roses, Bread and Roses!'" in DuPlessis and Snitow, *The Feminist Memoir Project*, 311–323, 318.

105. Naomi Weisstein quoted in Miriam Schneir, *Feminism in Our Time: The Essential Writings, World War II to the Present* (New York: Vintage, 1994), 108. In *Separate Roads to Feminism*, Benita Roth noted, "To counter claims that feminist interests were somehow narrower than those of the working class (or of Third World peoples), white women's liberationists claimed that gender oppression was as fundamental and widespread as racism and class domination," 188.

106. Ellen Willis, "Sisters under the Skin? Confronting Race and Sex," *Voice Literary Supplement* (June 1, 1982): 10–12, 12. This is an important review of several books on black and white feminism and is reprinted in her book *No More Nice Girls: Countercultural Essays* (Hanover, N.H.: Wesleyan University Press, 1992), 101–116.

107. "SDS Statement on the Liberation of Women," in Schneir, *Feminism in Our Time*, 104–107: "As we analyze," 106; "the importance of the analogy," 107.

108. See, for example, Naomi Weisstein, "Woman as Nigger," which is about psychology's erroneous picture of the nature of women and has nothing to do with African Americans, in Tanner, *Voices from Women's Liberation*, 296–303. Nevertheless, the title was chosen to make a point. And in Piercy's "The Grand Coolie Damn," in Morgan, *Sisterhood Is Powerful*, she referred to herself as a "house nigger in the Movement," 436.

109. See Roth, *Separate Roads to Feminism*, 188–195, on the race/sex analogy.

110. "SDS Statement on the Liberation of Women," in Schneir, *Feminism in Our Time*, 110–124, 113.

111. "Conversations," Pam Allen interviewed by Julius Lester, 6.

112. See Jean Wyatt, *Risking Difference: Identification, Race and Community in Contemporary Fiction and Feminism* (Albany: State University of New York Press, 2004), esp. chap. 7, "Toward a Cross-Race Dialogue: Cherrié Moraga, Gloria Anzaldúa, and the Psychoanalytic Politics of Community," for a fascinating psychoanalytic analysis of white women's unconscious identification and idealization of women of color, which derive from a drive toward imaginary unity that often obstructs a perception of the other as a subject. Wyatt argued that women need to participate in an ongoing multicultural community if they are really going to know each other.

113. Kobena Mercer, "'1968': Periodizing Postmodern Politics and Identity," in *Cultural Studies*, ed. Lawrence Grossberg, Cary Nelson, and Paula A. Treichler (New York: Routledge, 1992), 424–449, 433.

114. Gordon and Popkin, "Women's Liberation: Let Us All Now Emulate Each Other," 307.

115. Popkin, "The Social Experience of Bread and Roses," in Hansen and Philipson, *Women, Class and the Feminist Imagination*, 209, n. 9. Chicago socialist feminist and Chicago Women's Liberation Union member Vivian Rothstein recalled that white women in the early women's movement had virtually no contact with politically active black women. E-mail to author, January 23, 1998.

116. Umansky, *Motherhood Reconceived*, 98. Also see Evelynn Hammonds, who in 1980 criticized the use of special issues of women's journals, for example, *Heresies*, that focused on third world women. She decried the idea that racism in the women's movement "can be addressed *merely* by the publication of a 'special issue' of a journal devoted to third world women." In "Invisible Sisters," *Sojourner* (May 1980): 10–11, 10.

117. Strobel, "Consciousness and Action," 58.

118. Benita Roth wrote that "white women's liberation groups desperately wanted women of color to join *them*" and that "gender universalism did lead to the neglect of issues raised by racial/ethnic feminist[s] regarding racist domination," in *Separate Roads to Feminism*, 195; see 188–200 for discussion of these issues.

Chapter 4

1. Alice Walker's term for black feminists, *womanist*, suggested that black feminism was different from white feminism and raised the question of black feminism's different historical legacies. Walker, *In Search of Our Mothers' Gardens* (New York: Harcourt Brace Jovanovich, 1984), xi–xii.

2. Beverly Guy-Sheftall, ed., *Words of Fire: An Anthology of American-American Feminist Thought* (New York: New Press, 1995), 14–15; see "Introduc-

tion: The Evolution of Feminist Consciousness among African American Women," for a concise history of and tribute to black feminism. Also see Farah Jasmine Griffin, "Conflict and Chorus: Reconsidering Toni Cade's *The Black Woman: An Anthology*," in *Is It Nation Time? Contemporary Essays on Black Power and Black Nationalism*, ed. Eddie S. Glaude, Jr. (Chicago: University of Chicago Press, 2002), 113–129.

3. Kimberly Springer, *Living for the Revolution: Black Feminist Organizations, 1968–1980* (Durham, N.C.: Duke University Press, 2005), indicated the importance of Beal's "Double Jeopardy" and also mentioned the essays by Pauli Murray, Mary Ann Weathers, and Linda La Rue as critical; see 116–117 and 209 n. 8. Beal, La Rue, Weathers, Murray, Haden, Middleton, and Robinson are all reprinted in Guy-Sheftall, *Words of Fire*. The Weathers and the Haden, Middleton, and Robinson essays were published in an early women's liberation anthology edited by Leslie B. Tanner, *Voices from Women's Liberation* (New York: New American Library, 1970), as was Beal's, which was commissioned for *Sisterhood Is Powerful: An Anthology of Writings from the Women's Liberation Movement*, ed. Robin Morgan (New York: Vintage, 1970). In her study of black feminism, Springer considered five groups: the Third World Women's Alliance (TWWA), the National Black Feminist Organization (NBFO), the National Alliance of Black Feminists (NABF), the Combahee River Collective, and Black Women Organized for Action, arguing that independent black feminist organizations developed early and with different analyses than white feminism.

4. For the Third World Women's Alliance, see Springer, *Living for the Revolution*, 45–50 and throughout the book; Benita Roth, *Separate Roads to Feminism: Black, Chicana, and White Feminist Movements in America's Second Wave* (Cambridge: Cambridge University Press, 2004), 89–93; Kristin Anderson-Bricker, "'Triple Jeopardy': Black Women and the Growth of Feminist Consciousness in SNCC, 1964–1975," in *Still Lifting, Still Climbing: African American Women's Contemporary Activism*, ed. Kimberly Springer (New York: New York University Press, 1999), 49–69.

5. See Anderson-Bricker, "Triple Jeopardy," on SNCC and black feminism. In her provocative interpretation of the development of the TWWA out of SNCC, she said: "Most Black women were openly hostile toward white women following Freedom Summer, and their anger, in combination with Black nationalist ideas, led them to support separatism and, along with males, to help to purge whites from SNCC," 55–56. Anderson-Bricker argued that rifts that emerged out of Freedom Summer prevented black women from supporting white feminism. The focus of black SNCC women was on "developing a Black identity to fight racism," 56.

6. Anderson-Bricker, "Triple Jeopardy," 62–63. SNCC had basically disintegrated by this time so that the actual link to SNCC as an organization was tenuous. See "Third World Women's Alliance," in *Radical Feminism: A Documentary Reader*, ed. Barbara Crow (New York: New York University

Press, 2000), 460–465. Also see Robin D. G. Kelley, *Freedom Dreams: The Black Radical Imagination* (Boston: Beacon, 2002), 143–144.

7. Springer, *Living for the Revolution,* 91–93; Roth, *Separate Roads to Feminism,* 93; Anderson-Bricker, "Triple Jeopardy," 61–62.

8. The black female activists of the 1970s were unique in calling themselves feminists. For discussion about whether to define poor, working-class, and third world women's activism on behalf of their communities and families, which included almost all of black women's activism until then, as feminist, see, for example, Patricia Hill Collins, *Black Feminist Thought: Knowledge, Consciousness, and the Politics of Empowerment* (Boston: Unwin Hyman, 1990), 139–161; Barbara Omolade, *The Rising Song of African American Women* (New York: Routledge, 1994), 117–128, 161–177; Mary Pardo, "Doing It for the Kids: Mexican American Community Activists, Border Feminists?" in *Feminist Organizations: Harvest of the New Women's Movement,* ed. Myra Marx Ferree and Patricia Yancy Martin (Philadelphia: Temple University Press, 1995), 356–371; Sherna Berger Gluck et al., "Whose Feminism? Whose History?" in *Community Activism and Feminist Politics: Organizing across Race, Class and Gender,* ed. Nancy Naples (New York: Routledge, 1998), 31–56; Nancy Gabin, "Revising the History of Twentieth Century Feminism," *Journal of Women's History* 12(3) (Autumn 2000): 227–234; Kimberly Springer, "Third World Black Feminism?" *Signs* 27(4) (Summer 2002): 1059–1082.

9. Deborah Gray White, *Too Heavy a Load: Black Women in Defense of Themselves, 1894–1994* (New York: Norton, 1999), 242–253: "more than any organization," 247; "a frontal assault," 242. Feminist authors Gloria Joseph and Jill Lewis view the NBFO as "one of the most influential organizations of the early 1970s. It introduced large numbers of Black women to the concept of Black feminism and raised many essential questions and problems that Black women are still trying to answer and solve." Gloria I. Joseph and Jill Lewis, *Common Differences: Conflicts in Black and White* (Garden City, N.Y.: Anchor, 1981), 34. Also see "Brenda Verner Examines 'Liberated' Sisters," *Encore* 3(4) (April 1974): 22–24; Margo Jefferson and Margaret Sloan, "In Defense of Black Feminism," *Encore* 3(7) (July 1974): 46–47; Paula Giddings, *When and Where I Enter: The Impact of Black Women on Race and Sex in America* (New York: Bantam, 1984), 344; Alice Walker, "A Letter to the Editor of *Ms.*," in her *In Search of Our Mothers' Gardens*; Beverly Davis, "To Seize the Moment: A Retrospective on the National Black Feminist Organization," *Sage* 5(2) (Fall 1988): 43–47; Michele Wallace, "Anger in Isolation: A Black Feminist's Search for Sisterhood," in Wallace, *Invisibility Blues: From Pop to Theory* (London, Verso, 1990), 18–25, esp. 24–25; Guy-Sheftell, *Words of Fire,* 15–16; Tamara Roberts, "Lost to History: The Rise and Fall of the National Black Feminist Organization," unpublished paper, 1996, Northwestern University.

10. Polls showed that black women were more supportive of the women's movement and women's equality than were white women. See, for example, Anne Valk, "Separatism and Sisterhood: Race, Sex, and Women's Ac-

tivism in Washington, D.C., 1963–1980" (Ph.D. diss., Duke University, 1996), 347–348; Miriam Lynell Harris, "From Kennedy to Combahee: Black Feminist Activism from 1960 to 1980" (Ph.D. diss., University of Minnesota, 1997), 90; Jane J. Mansbridge, "'You're Too Independent!' How Gender, Race, and Class Make Many Feminisms," in *The Cultural Territories of Race*, ed. Michele Lamont (Chicago: University of Chicago Press, 1999), 291–317, 297–299; Jane Mansbridge and Barbara Smith, "How Did Feminism Get to Be All White?" *American Prospect* (March 13, 2000): 30–36, 31. For a later period when support for feminist ideology was strong among both African-American men and women, see Andrea Hunter and Sherrill Sellers, "Feminist Attitudes among African American Women and Men," *Gender and Society* 12(1) (February 1998): 81–99.

11. Quoted in Davis, "To Seize the Moment," 43–44.

12. In *Too Heavy a Load*, historian Deborah Gray White wrote, "The responses the NBFO prompted suggest that all over the country black women were, and had been, searching for something" and made "clear that the silence imposed on them by black liberation movements and black misogyny had been broken," 247.

13. Roth, *Separate Roads to Feminism*, 108–109.

14. On the NABF, see Springer, *Living for the Revolution*, 53–56 and throughout the book; and Roth, *Separate Roads to Feminism*, 118–121.

15. Margaret Sloan, "Black Feminism: A New Mandate," *Ms.* (May 1974): 97–100, 100.

16. See Michele Wallace, "On the National Black Feminist Organization," in *Feminist Revolution*, ed. Redstockings of the Women's Liberation Movement (New York: Random House, 1978), 174, for an analysis of its failures and the lack of a black women's movement at the time and in the foreseeable future.

17. Demita Frazier, "Interview by Karen Kahn: Rethinking Identity Politics," *Sojourner* (September 1995): 12–13, 23, 12. Also see Barbara Smith, ed., *Home Girls: A Black Feminist Anthology* (New York: Kitchen Table: Women of Color Press, 1983), 295–296; Barbara Smith, *The Truth That Never Hurts: Writings on Race, Gender, and Freedom* (New Brunswick, N.J.: Rutgers University Press, 1998); Margo Okazawa-Rey, taped interview, December 26, 1999, by Nancy Richard, University Libraries, Archives and Special Collections, Northeastern University, Boston.

18. Barbara Smith, "Black Writers Illuminate Hidden Lives," *Sojourner* (August 1978): 7 and 23, 7. A historian of women's movement activism in Washington, D.C., Anne Valk, wrote, "After 1968, the increasingly vocal and visible feminist movement in Washington publicly challenged male supremacy and provided a catalyst for black women to rethink gender relations in their own community, even if they refused to ally themselves with feminism." Valk, "Separatism and Sisterhood," 346.

19. It is notable that both Bread and Roses and the Combahee River Collective

named themselves, as did the Boston feminist newspaper *Sojourner*, after militant historical events that featured working-class women and women of color.

20. Harris, "From Kennedy to Combahee," 102.

21. Springer, *Living for the Revolution*, 56.

22. Frazier interview, 12.

23. See J. Anthony Lukas, *Common Ground: A Turbulent Decade in the Lives of Three American Families* (New York: Knopf, 1985).

24. Frazier interview, 13.

25. Roth *Separate Roads to Feminism*, 123; Combahee River Collective, "A Black Feminist Statement," in *All the Women Are White, All the Blacks Are Men, but Some of Us Are Brave: Black Women's Studies*, ed. Gloria T. Hull, Patricia Bell Scott, and Barbara Smith (Old Westbury, N.Y.: Feminist Press, 1982), 13–22, 20–21.

26. Combahee River Collective, "A Black Feminist Statement," 20; see also Springer, *Living for the Revolution*, 56–61; and Harris, "From Kennedy to Combahee," where she wrote that the women who defected from the NBFO and formed the Combahee River Collective wanted to discuss lesbianism and critique capitalism, 99.

27. Springer, *Living for the Revolution*, 146; see also Roth, *Separate Roads to Feminism*, 123.

28. Smith, *The Truth That Never Hurts*, 171–172.

29. Barbara Smith quoted in Harris, "From Kennedy to Combahee," 131.

30. Okazawa-Rey interview.

31. Quoted in Harris, "From Kennedy to Combahee," 125.

32. Kimberly Springer, "'Our Politics Was Black Women': Black Feminist Organizations, 1968–1980" (Ph.D. diss., Emory University, 1999), 196.

33. Springer, "Our Politics Was Black Women," 226.

34. Smith quoted in Harris, "From Kennedy to Combahee," 113, 114. See Springer, *Living for the Revolution*, on the retreats, 106–111.

35. Harris, "From Kennedy to Combahee," 121.

36. Harris, "From Kennedy to Combahee," 113. In a letter to her sister Beverly Smith, Barbara Smith wrote, "I think we are also extremely threatening to Black men as well as to certain white people. Lorraine Hansberry said in one of her recorded interviews that Beneathea in *Raisin* is a totally unfamiliar character on the American stage (and also in American life!!) because she is a Black woman with intellectual aspirations." In Barbara Smith and Beverly Smith, "'I Am Not Meant to Be Alone and without You Who Understand': Letters from Black Feminists, 1972–1978," *Conditions: Four* 2(1) (Winter 1979): 62–77, 66–67.

37. Harris, "From Kennedy to Combahee," 120.

38. Gloria T. Hull, "History/My History," in *Changing Subjects: The Making of Feminist Literary Criticism*, ed. Gayle Greene and Coppelia Kahn (New York: Routledge, 1993), 48–63, 60–61.

39. Harris, "From Kennedy to Combahee," 113.

40. Smith and Smith, "I Am Not Meant to Be Alone."

41. Harris, "From Kennedy to Combahee," 128. See Springer, *Living for the Revolution*, 130–138, on sexual orientation in black feminist organizations. She stated that the NBFO "was one of the few Black feminist organizations besides Combahee to have a committee dedicated to connecting the concerns of Black lesbians to the organization's agenda," 137. Springer also noted that the Combahee River Collective was the first organization in her sample of black feminist organizations to publicly mention heterosexual oppression, 130. The TWWA experienced homophobia in its midst and the NABF struggled with the issue. Cheryl Clarke recalled that she was motivated to come out as a lesbian at an NBFO meeting where Margaret Sloan and Jane Galvin Lewis spoke. In Harris, "From Kennedy to Combahee," 91–92. Also see White, *Too Heavy a Load*, 247; "Third World Women's Alliance," in *Radical Feminism*, 460–465; and Anderson-Bricker, "Triple Jeopardy," 49–69.

42. Mansbridge and Smith, "How Did Feminism Get to Be All White?" 32.

43. Audre Lorde, "Scratching the Surface: Some Notes on Barriers to Women and Loving," *Black Scholar* 9(7) (April 1978): 31–35, 34.

44. In her anthology of African-American feminist writing, Beverly Guy-Sheftall wrote, "Black lesbians have indeed been critical to the development of black feminism as ideology and praxis. . . . They have been denied their rightful place in African American cultural, intellectual, and political history." In *Words of Fire*, 231. And in a 1979 review of Michele Wallace's *Black Macho and the Myth of the Superwoman*, Susan McHenry noted the foundations upon which young black feminists were building, among them "the brilliant and particularly embattled voices of black lesbian feminist writers like Audre Lorde, Barbara Smith, Chirlane McCray." In "Notes of a Native Daughter," *Sojourner* (November 1979): 30. See also Patricia Hill Collins, *Black Feminist Thought: Knowledge, Consciousness, and the Politics of Empowerment* (Boston: Unwin Hyman, 1990), 192–196; Cheryl Clarke, "The Failure to Transform Homophobia in the Black Community," in *Home Girls: A Black Feminist Anthology*, ed. Barbara Smith (New York: Kitchen Table: Women of Color Press, 1983), 197–208; E. Frances White, *Dark Continents of Our Bodies: Black Feminism and the Politics of Respectability* (Philadelphia: Temple University Press, 2001), 72–80, 151–183; Frazier interview, 12; Harris, "From Kennedy to Combahee," 128; author conversation with Barbara Smith, Boston, June 6, 1997.

45. White, *Dark Continent of Our Bodies*, 25.

46. Gloria T. Hull, "History/My History," in *Changing Subjects*, 48–63, 52.

47. Combahee River Collective, "A Black Feminist Statement," 13.

48. Combahee River Collective, "A Black Feminist Statement," 14.

49. Combahee River Collective, "A Black Feminist Statement," 16.

50. Harris, "From Kennedy to Combahee," 130.

51. Kelley, *Freedom Dreams*, 150. See Kelley's chapter "'This Battlefield Called Life': Black Feminist Dreams," on black feminism.

52. Frazier interview, 13; also see Elizabeth Higginbotham, *Too Much to Ask: Black Women in the Era of Integration* (Chapel Hill: University of North Carolina Press, 2001), which is about black women's college attendance in the 1960s and considers issues of class, gender, and family.

53. Anita Shreve, *Women Together, Women Alone: The Legacy of the Consciousness-Raising Movement* (New York: Viking, 1989), 180.

54. White, *Dark Continent of Our Bodies*, 61; on class, see 61–66. Also see bell hooks, "Keeping Close to Home: Class and Education," in *Talking Back: Thinking Feminist, Thinking Black* (Boston: South End, 1989), 73–83; bell hooks, "Revolutionary Black Women," about differences and rage between black women, in *Black Looks: Race and Representation* (Boston: South End, 1992), 41–60; Springer, *Living for the Revolution*, on class in black feminist organizations, 122–130.

55. Springer, *Living for the Revolution*, 129.

56. Springer, *Living for the Revolution*, 129.

57. Okazawa-Rey interview; Tompkins quoted in Springer, *Living for the Revolution*, 128. Black feminists Margaret Sloan (NBFO) and Brenda Eichelberger (NABF) have pointed out that black male organizations were not maligned for being too middle class. Dr. Martin Luther King, Stokely Carmichael, and Panther Fred Hampton were not criticized nor undercut for their educational achievements or middle-class backgrounds while radical black women and their groups were. Springer, *Living for the Revolution*, 125.

58. Smith continued, "I found it ironic in later years that some of those who gave me a hard time about pursuing that level of education themselves went on and got their degrees." In Springer, *Living for the Revolution*, 129.

59. Smith and Smith, "I Am Not Meant to Be Alone," 66.

60. Frazier interview: "[S]traight women" and "But I never," 12; "I am" and "in our history," 13. Also see Paula Giddings, "The Last Taboo," in *Race-ing Justice, Engendering Power: Essays on Anita Hill, Clarence Thomas, and the Construction of Social Reality*, ed. Toni Morrison (New York: Pantheon, 1992), 441–463, on the taboo on black sexuality and gender in black public discourse, which ultimately hurts black women.

61. Cellestine Ware, *Woman Power: The Movement for Women's Liberation* (New York: Tower, 1970): "It is not unlikely," 95; "unable," 78.

62. Barbara Smith, "Letter," *Sojourner* (September 1979): 2.

63. Michele Wallace, "Anger in Isolation: A Black Feminist's Search for Sisterhood," in her *Invisibility Blues: From Pop to Theory* (London: Verso:1990), 18–25, 23.

64. Ware, *Woman Power*, 78; Joseph and Lewis, *Common Differences*, 7.

65. Smith and Smith, "I Am Not Meant to Be Alone"; first letter is dated April 2, 1975, 75; second letter is dated March 27, 1978, 76.

66. hooks, *Talking Back*, 180.

67. White, *Dark Continent of Our Bodies*: "authoritative," 27; "In contrast," 28; "early rumblings," 38–39; "Clearly," 41.

68. Springer, *Living for the Revolution*, 33. Gloria Hull and Barbara Smith said, "Black women were a part of that early women's movement, as were working class women of all races," in "Introduction: The Politics of Black Women's Studies," in *All the Women Are White, All the Blacks Are Men, but Some of Us Are Brave*, ed. Gloria T. Hull, Patricia Bell Scott, and Barbara Smith (Old Westbury, N.Y.: Feminist Press, 1982), xvii–xxxi, xx.

69. Roth, *Separate Roads to Feminism*, 98–99.

70. Roth, "The Making of the Vanguard Center: Black Feminist Emergence in the 1960s and 1970s," in Springer, *Still Lifting, Still Climbing*, 70–90, 75.

71. In addition to Springer and Roth, see Rivka Polatnick, "Poor Sisters Decided for Themselves: A Case Study of 1960s Women's Liberation Activism," in *Black Women America*, ed. Kim Marie Vaz (Thousand Oaks, Calif.: Sage, 1995), 110–130; Rosalyn Baxandall, "Revisioning the Women's Liberation Movement's Narrative: Early Second Wave African American Feminists," *Feminist Studies* 27(1) (spring 2001): 225–245; Jane Mansbridge, "'You're Too Independent!' How Gender, Race, and Class Make Many Feminisms," in *The Cultural Territories of Race: Black and White Boundaries*, ed. Michele Lamont (Chicago: University of Chicago Press, 1999), 291–317.

72. Becky Thompson more drastically rewrote the history of second wave feminism by suggesting that white feminists centered themselves as the main protagonists, which she contentiously called "hegemonic feminism," when there was always a "multiracial feminism" consisting of women of color and white antiracists who, in fact, spearheaded second wave feminism. Her revisionist history is wrong, in my opinion, in that it underestimated white feminism and overcompensated for "white feminist" chronology and narratives in the opposite direction, overcorrecting by deeming early signs of feminism of color to be as strong as or equal to early second wave radical feminism. She has compiled separate chronologies for white feminism and multiracial feminism. In addition, many of her white antiracist heroines were not feminists. It is a misleading depiction of second wave feminism. "Multiracial Feminism: Recasting the Chronology of Second Wave Feminism," *Feminist Studies* 28(2) (Summer 2002): 337–355. Also see Springer, *Living for the Revolution*, about periodization of the women's movement, 7–10.

73. Roth, *Separate Roads to Feminism*, 44.

74. E. Frances White, "Listening to the Voices of Black Feminism," *Radical America* 18(2–3) (1984): 7–25, 10.

75. bell hooks, *Feminist Theory: From Margin to Center* (Boston: South End, 1984), 3. See also hooks, *Ain't I a Woman? Black Women and Feminism* (Boston: South End, 1981), 119–58; and many of her other books and essays that reiterate this point of view.

76. Omolade, "Sisterhood in Black and White," in DuPlessis and Snitow, *The Feminist Memoir Project*, 377–401, 388. Omolade continued: "The fear of Black women's power and abilities and denial about the significance of race caused many white women scholars to place French feminism at the center of their politics and intellectual work," 388.

77. doris davenport, "The Pathology of Racism: A Conversation with Third World Wimmin," in *This Bridge Called My Back: Writings by Radical Women of Color*, ed. Cherríe Moraga and Gloria Anzaldúa (New York: Women of Color Press, 1983), 85–90, 86.

78. Lorraine Bethel, "What Chou Mean *We*, White Girl?" in Lorraine Bethel and Barbara Smith, eds., "The Black Women's Issue," *Conditions: Five* 2(2) (1979): 86–92, 86; see also Springer, *Living for the Revolution*, 36.

79. Sheila Radford-Hill, introduction to *Further to Fly: Black Women and the Politics of Empowerment* (Minneapolis: University of Minnesota Press, 2000), xv–xxiv, x.

80. Barbara Omolade, "Black Women and Feminism," in *The Future of Difference*, ed. Hester Eisenstein and Alice Jardine (New Brunswick, N.J.: Rutgers University Press, 1980), 247–257, 255.

81. Leith Mullings, *On Our Own Terms: Race, Class and Gender in the Lives of African American Women* (New York: Routledge, 1997), xix.

82. Deborah K. King, "Multiple Jeopardy, Multiple Consciousness: The Context of Black Feminist Ideology," *Signs* 14(2) (Autumn 1988): 42–72, 57, 63.

83. White, *Too Heavy a Load*, 249.

84. Quoted in Giddings, *When and Where*, 305; also see Springer, *Living for the Revolution*, 88–89.

85. White, *Too Heavy a Load*, 222.

86. Springer, *Living for the Revolution*, 57.

87. Assata Shakur/Joanne Chesimard, "Women in Prison: How We Are," *Black Scholar* 9(7) (April 1978): 8–14, 14.

88. Davis's review of Elaine Brown's *A Taste of Power: A Black Woman's Story* in the *Women's Review of Books* 10(9) (June 1993): 1–4, 3.

89. Barbara Smith, "Black Writers Illuminate Hidden Lives," *Sojourner* (August 1978): 7, 23, 7 ([*sic*] is in original quote).

90. Michele Wallace, *Black Macho and the Myth of the Superwoman* (New York: Dial, 1978), 169.

91. Reid, *"Together" Black Women*, 53–54. See Valk on Reid's study in "Separatism and Sisterhood," 347.

92. Kimberly Springer, "Third Wave Black Feminism?" *Signs* 27(4) (Summer 2002): 1059–1082, 1074.

93. Springer, "'Our Politics Was Black Women': Black Feminist Organizations, 1968–1980" (Ph.D. diss., Emory University, 1999), 58.

94. Barbara Smith, "Black Lesbian/Feminist Organizing: A Conversation," in Smith, *Home Girls*, 296.

95. Beal, "Double Jeopardy: To Be Black and Female," in Cade, *The Black Woman*, 90–100, 92. Echoing SNCC's Stokely Carmichael remark, Bernette Golden wrote, "But Black women, regardless of their attitudes toward the women's movement, are largely disregarding male rhetoric about 'stepping back' and the benefits of the 'prone position.'" In "Black Women's Liberation," *Essence* (February 1974): 36–37, 75–76, 86, 36.

96. White, *Dark Continent of Our Bodies*, 27.

97. Margo V. Perkins, *Autobiography as Activism: Three Black Women of the Sixties* (Jackson: University Press of Mississippi, 2000), 114.

98. White, *Too Heavy A Load*, 243–244.

99. Wallace, *Black Macho*, 10.

100. Reid, *"Together" Black Women*, 79.

101. Reid, *"Together" Black Women*, 84.

102. Reid, *"Together" Black Women*, 85. See "Black Men and White Women," 79–87.

103. Toni Morrison, "What the Black Woman Thinks about Women's Lib," *New York Times Magazine* (August 22, 1971): 14, 15, 63–66, 64.

104. Norton continued, "But we can't let that fear blind us to the fact that white women are our natural allies." This was in an article interviewing founders of the NBFO by Bernette Golden, "Black Women's Liberation," *Essence* (February 1974): 36–47, 75–76, 86, 86. Also see Nathan and Julian Hare on black women's anger toward white women who, among other things, said one interviewee, "are using everything in the book to catch our men." In "Black Women 1970," *Transaction* (November–December 1970): 65–68, 90, 67; and Gloria Wade-Gayles, chap. 4, "A Change of Heart about Matters of the Heart: An Anger Shift from Interracial Marriages to Real Problems," in her book *Rooted against the Wind: Personal Essays* (Boston: Beacon, 1996).

105. Staples, "The Myth of Black Macho: A Response to Angry Black Feminists," *Black Scholar* 10(6–7) (March–April 1979): 24–38, 30. Springer wrote, "[T]he mainstream black press vilified black women writers, in particular Wallace and shange," in *Living for the Revolution*, 5.

106. Writing in 2003, Johnetta Betsch Cole and Beverly Guy-Sheftall stated, "There is perhaps no intracommunity topic about which there has been more contentious debate than the issue of gender relations in Black America." They also remarked, "Black feminists are often targeted for particular public scorn because of their public pronouncements and writings about the problems of sexism within Black communities," *Gender Talk: The Struggle for Women's Equality in African American Communities* (New York: Ballantine, 2003): "There is perhaps," xxiv; "Black feminists," xxxiii. A recent introduction to the Cole and Guy-Sheftall book in *Essence* magazine remarked that the ways in which black men hurt and oppress black women is "the dirty little secret we don't want to talk about": (July 2003): 161–162, 161.

107. Alice Echols, *Daring to Be Bad: Radical Feminism in America, 1967–1975* (Minneapolis: University of Minnesota Press, 1989), 49.

108. Echols, *Daring to Be Bad*, 106.

109. Giddings, *When and Where*, 308.

110. Linda La Rue, "The Black Movement and Women's Liberation," in *Contemporary Black Thought: The Best from "The Black Scholar*," ed. Robert Chrisman and Nathan Hare (Indianapolis, Ind.: Bobbs-Merrill, 1973), 116–125, 118; and Giddings, *When and Where*, 308. Also see hooks, *Ain't I a Woman?* 141–142; Reid, *"Together" Black Women*, 53; and for an especially vituperative attack on the white women's movement and its theft of the black liberation movement, see Nathan Hare, "Revolution without a Revolution: The Psychology of Sex and Race," *Black Scholar* 9(7) (April 1978): 2–7.

111. Morrison, "What the Black Woman Thinks about Women's Lib," 15.

112. Barbara Omolade, "Black Women and Feminism," in *The Future of Difference*, ed. Hester Eisenstein and Alice Jardine (New Brunswick, N.J.: Rutgers University Press, 1985), 247–257, 255.

113. White, *Too Heavy a Load*, 222.

114. bell hooks, *Killing Rage, Ending Racism* (New York: Holt, 1995), 100. Johnetta B. Cole wrote that "the term 'feminism' is one that large numbers of African American women believe will hurt them," that there is a "dread" of being called feminist. Cole, "Epilogue," in Guy-Sheftall, *Words of Fire*, 549–551, 550.

115. See White, *Dark Continent of Our Bodies*, 44–48, for a critique of black feminist identity politics, including Patricia Hill Collins's work. Also see bell hooks's criticisms in "feminist politicization: a comment," in *Talking Back: Thinking Feminist, Thinking Black* (Boston: South End, 1989), 105–111; and "Revolutionary Black Women," in *Black Looks: Race and Representation* (Boston: South End, 1992), 41–60, where she argued against essentializing black women's experiences, against "constructing a homogenous black female subject," 46. Also see the last chapter of Nancie Caraway's *Segregated Sisterhood* (Knoxville: University of Tennessee Press, 1991), "Crossover Dreams: Toward a Multicultural Feminist Politics of Solidarity"; and L. A. Kauffman, "The Anti-Politics of Identity," in *Identity Politics in the Women's Movement*, ed. Barbara Ryan (New York: New York University Press, 2001). For a more politically enthusiastic interpretation of late 1960s racialized identity politics, see Kobena Mercer, "1968: Periodizing Politics and Identity," in *Cultural Studies*, ed. Lawrence Grossberg, Cary Nelson, and Paula Treichler (New York: Routledge, 1992), 424–449.

116. Combahee River Collective, "A Black Feminist Statement," 16.

117. *Equal Times* (March 26, 1978): 12, in author's possession.

118. Roth, *Separate Roads to Feminism*, 206–207. The title of her book suggested this central point about the significance of identity politics in shaping

separate white, black, and Chicana women's movements based on racial and ethnic identities.

119. Frazier interview, 23.

Chapter 5

1. "Tidal wave" and "crest" are Sara M. Evans's formulations in *Tidal Wave: How Women Changed America at Century's End* (New York: Free Press, 2003).

2. "Introduction," *Home Girls: A Black Feminist Anthology*, ed. Barbara Smith (New York: Kitchen Table: Women of Color Press, 1983), xix–lvi, xxxi.

3. See Ruth Rosen, *The World Split Open: How the Modern Women's Movement Changed America* (New York: Viking, 2000), 292. On the inclusiveness of the conference, see Marjorie Spruill, "Women's Rights and Family Values: The 1977 International Women's Year Conferences and the Polarization of American Women," presentation at Radcliffe Institute for Advanced Study conference "Feminism on the Record: ReViewing the 1960s and 1970s," March 19, 2005, sponsored by the Schlesinger Library on the History of Women in America.

4. Quoted in Evans, *Tidal Wave*, 141.

5. "Breaking the Silence: A Conversation in Black and White, Dialog [*sic*] between Barbara Smith and Laura Sperazi," *Equal Times* (March 26, 1978): 10–12, 12, in author's possession.

6. Karen V. Hansen, "Women's Unions and the Search for a Political Identity," in *Women, Class, and the Feminist Imagination: A Socialist-Feminist Reader*, ed. Karen V. Hansen and Ilene J. Philipson (Philadelphia: Temple University Press, 1990), 213–238, 235.

7. Hansen, "Women's Unions," 235.

8. Evans, *Tidal Wave*: "one more occasion," 163; "gather on the commons," 164.

9. Evans, *Tidal Wave*, 175. Evans also noted, "Anger and guilt played out a familiar duet in organizations, conferences, and the feminist media with increasing intensity throughout the late seventies and into the eighties," 166.

10. Anne Valk, epilogue to "Separatism and Sisterhood: Race, Sex, and Women's Activism in Washington, D.C., 1963–1980 (Ph.D. diss., Duke University, 1996), 487; for interracial coalitions, also see Kimberly Springer, *Living for the Revolution: Black Feminist Organizations, 1968–1980* (Durham, N.C.: Duke University Press, 2005), 153–155.

11. Angela Davis provoked a range of positions. Among black women, recall Third World Women's Alliance founder Frances Beal's outraged response at a New York City feminist demonstration where she carried a poster in favor of the jailed Angela Davis and was chastised by a white feminist who said that the Angela Davis case had nothing to do with feminism. Beal was indignant that the National Organization for Women's member did not

recognize that the liberation of Angela Davis, a black radical woman, was central to all women's freedom. In Paula Giddings, *When and Where I Enter: The Impact of Black Women on Race and Sex in America* (New York: Bantam, 1984), 305. See bell hooks for a critique of the admiration for Davis as a beautiful and good woman who was devoted to black men; she quoted Michele Wallace making a similar point in *Ain't I a Woman? Black Women and Feminism* (Boston: South End, 1981), 183; and E. Frances White, "Listening to the Voices of Black Feminism," *Radical America* 18(2–3) (March–June 1984): 7–25, where she criticized Wallace's and hooks's position on Davis:

> However much we rejected and continue to reject Davis's
> Communist Party positions, we cried for her because she challenged
> this racist and capitalist system. To reduce, as hooks and Wallace
> effectively have, our anti-racist struggles to an attempt by black men
> to recapture their patriarchal rule over black women is unfair not
> only to black men but also to all black people. (15)

For a white radical feminist critique of Davis's orthodox Marxist politics, which relegated sexism to uninformed attitudes with no material basis, see Ellen Willis's 1982 "Sisters under the Skin." Willis referred to Davis's book *Women, Race and Class* as an example of "left antifeminism" in Willis, *No More Nice Girls: Countercultural Essays* (Hanover, N.H.: University Press of New England, 1992), 103. Also see a white feminist's report on Angela Davis at the University of Maryland, where she spoke as a member of the executive committee of the Communist party. When she was asked whether she supported women's liberation, she said that sexism and racism exploit working-class women and that relating to the economic exploitation of women of color and white working-class women was paramount. The author said she was disturbed by Davis's denial of the struggle against sexism as a "priority in and of itself." She wrote, "As a feminist sitting in the audience, I admired her courage and intelligence, but I was disappointed in her apparent writing-off of feminism." Fran Moira, "Angela Skirts Feminism," *off our backs* (April–May 1975): 15. Despite the range of opinions, the common position among leftist feminists was support.

12. Genna Rae McNeil, "'Joanne Is You and Joanne Is Me': A Consideration of African American Women and the 'Free Joan Little' Movement, 1974–75," in *Sisters in Struggle: African American Women in the Civil Rights–Black Power Movement*, ed. Bettye Collier-Thomas and V. P. Franklin (New York: New York University Press, 2001), 259–279: "have given me the strength," 265; "came to view," 267; "self-conscious recognition," 267. See *off our backs*, November 1974, January 1975, and September–October 1975, for more on Joanne Little.

13. Miriam Lynell Harris, "From Kennedy to Combahee: Black Feminist Activism from 1960 to 1980" (Ph.D. diss., University of Minnesota, 1997), 129.

14. See Benita Roth, *Separate Roads to Feminism: Black, Chicana, and White*

Feminist Movements in America's Second Wave (New York: Cambridge University Press, 2004), on the Coalition for Women's Safety, 221–222; and Harris, "From Kennedy to Combahee," 131–137.

15. Barbara Smith, "Black Feminism: A Movement of Our Own," in *Front Line Feminism: Essays from Sojourner's First 25 Years*, ed. Karen Kahn (San Francisco: Aunt Lute, 1995), 22–27, 25; and Kattie Portis, interview with author, Boston, June 30, 2003. Margo Okazawa-Rey also remarked that the coalition was the basis for Mel King's Rainbow Coalition and run for mayor. Okazawa-Rey, oral taped interview by Nancy Richard, University Libraries, Archives and Special Collections, Northeastern University.

16. In addition to appearing in this book, it appears as the frontispiece of *All the Women Are White, All the Blacks Are Men, but Some of Us Are Brave: Black Feminist Studies*, ed. Gloria T. Hull, Patricia Bell Scott, and Barbara Smith (Old Westbury, N.Y.: Feminist Press, 1982). Hull had also been a Combahee member.

17. Smith, "Black Feminism," 25.

18. Harris, "From Kennedy to Combahee," 135.

19. Pamphlet in author's possession; also in the Sondra Stein Papers, Archives and Special Collections, Northeastern University.

20. Smith, "Black Feminism": "It was the first," 25; "I saw people," 26; "It was a coalition effort," 26.

21. Margo Okazawa-Rey information based on oral taped interview by Nancy Richard, University Libraries, Archives and Special Collections, Northeastern University; Okazawa-Rey conversation with author, San Francisco, March 20, 2003; Harris, "From Kennedy to Combahee," 108–109; Roth, *Separate Roads to Feminism*, 121–123.

22. Stein, e-mail to author, July 3, 2003; Stein, telephone conversation with author, July 22, 2003.

23. See, for example, Tia Cross, Freada Klein, Barbara Smith, and Beverly Smith, "Face-to-Face, Day-to Day—Racism CR," *Sojourner* (May 1979): 11. This essay is reprinted in Hull, Scott, and Smith, *All the Women Are White*, 52–56; Tia Cross information, interview with author, Boston, July 14, 2003; brochure in Stein papers, Archives, Northeastern University.

24. See Aimee Sands, "Rape and Racism in Boston: An Open Letter to White Feminists," *off our backs* (January 1981): 16–17.

25. "Women March, Reclaim Night," *Sojourner* (September 1978): 19.

26. Flyer and minutes from May 28, 1980, meeting, Coalition for Women's Safety, Stein papers, Archives, Northeastern University.

27. Flyer and minutes from May 28, 1980, meeting, Coalition for Women's Safety, Stein papers, Archives, Northeastern University.

28. "5000 Women March to Take Back the Night," *Sojourner* (September 1979), reprinted in Karen Kahn, ed., *Front Line Feminism: Essays from Sojourner's First 20 Years* (San Francisco: Aunt Lute, 1995), 378–381: "We should all," 379; "Perhaps the biggest," 380; "the combination," 380.

29. Support Group Papers, Stein papers, Archives and Special Collections, Northeastern University.

30. Letter from Barbara Smith, June 26, 1979, Stein papers, Archives and Special Collections, Northeastern University.

31. Interview with the Coalition for Women's Safety by Deborah Rose Gallagher, Miriam Kenner, and Linda Stein, *Second Wave* 5(4) (1980): 8–11, in Archives and Special Collections, Northeastern University: "learn how racism," "we came together," "I think that people," 8; "In other words" and "I think we're all feminists," 9; "A lot of people" and "people are working," 11.

32. Bernice Johnson Reagon, "Coalition Politics: Turning the Century," in *Home Girls: A Black Feminist Anthology*, ed. Barbara Smith (New York: Kitchen Table: Women of Color Press, 1983), 356–368: "Coalition work," 359; "We've pretty much," 357; "Today wherever," 362.

33. Smith, "The Boston Murders," in *Life Notes: Personal Writings by Contemporary Black Women*, ed. Patricia Bell Scott (New York: Norton, 1994), 315–320, 318–319.

34. Smith, "Black Feminism," 25.

35. Minutes, Coalition for Women's Safety, August 15, 1979, Stein papers, Archives, Northeastern University.

36. See Barbara Omolade on the conference in "Sisterhood in Black and White," in *The Feminist Memoir Project: Voices from Women's Liberation*, ed. Rachel Blau DuPlessis and Ann Snitow (New York: Three Rivers, 1998), 377–401, 387–388.

37. For an interesting interpretation of the use of *This Bridge Called My Back* by white feminists who, the author noted, cited but did not engage it, see Rebecca Aanerud, "Thinking Again: *This Bridge Called My Back* and the Challenge to Whiteness," in *This Bridge We Call Home: Radical Visions for Transformation*, ed. Gloria Anzaldúa and Analouise Keating (New York: Routledge, 2002), 69–77, esp. 71.

38. Alicia Gaspar de Alba, "Crop Circles in the Cornfield: Remembering Gloria E. Anzaldúa (1942–2004)," *American Quarterly* 56(3) (September 2004): iv–vii, vi. See Cynthia G. Franklin, *Writing Women's Communities: The Politics and Poetics of Contemporary Multi-Genre Anthologies* (Madison: University of Wisconsin Press, 1997), for a discussion of the significance of women's anthologies, including *This Bridge Called My Back*.

39. Cherríe Moraga, preface to *This Bridge Called My Back*, xiii–xi: "exclusive and reactionary," xiv; "terror and loathing" xvi; "most acutely" and "because I couldn't stand," xvii; "what began," xxiii. For testimonies about the importance of the book, see Analouise Keating, "Charting Pathways, Marking Thresholds . . . A Warning, an Introduction," 6–20, and section 1, both in *This Bridge We Call Home: Radical Visions for Transformation*, ed. Gloria E. Anzaldúa and Analouise Keating (New York: Routledge, 2002).

40. Moraga and Anzaldúa, introduction to *This Bridge Called My Back*, xxiii–xxvi, xxiii.

41. Moraga, *This Bridge Called My Back*: "attempts to describe," 61; other quotations from 62.

42. For more on this, see Wini Breines, review of Rachel Blau DuPlessis and Ann Snitow, eds., *The Feminist Memoir Project: Voices from Women's Liberation*, in *Nation* (January 4, 1999): 28–32.

43. Maureen T. Reddy, *Crossing the Color Line: Race, Parenting, and Culture* (New Brunswick, N.J.: Rutgers University Press, 1994), 151.

44. Patch, "Sweet Tea at Shoney's," in *Deep in Our Hearts: Nine White Women in the Freedom Movement*, ed. Constance Curry et al. (Athens: University of Georgia Press, 2000), 131–170, 155.

45. Verta Taylor, "Watching for Vibes: Bringing Emotions into the Study of Feminist Organizations," in *Feminist Organizations: Harvest of the New Women's Movement*, ed. Myra Marx Ferree and Patricia Yancy Martin (Philadelphia: Temple University Press, 1995), 223–233, 232.

46. Freeman quoted in Ruth Rosen, *The World Split Open: How the Modern Women's Movement Changed America* (New York: Viking, 2000), 228. See Rosen, 227–239, for a discussion of "trashing."

47. hooks, "Feminism in Black and White," in *Skin Deep: Black Women and White Women Write about Race*, ed. Marita Golden and Susan Richards (New York: Anchor/Doubleday, 1995), 273.

48. hooks, "Black Women and Feminism," in her *Talking Back: Thinking Feminist, Thinking Black* (Boston: South End, 1989), 177–182, 179. Also see hooks, "Where Is the Love: Political Bonding between Black and White Women," in her *Killing Rage, Ending Racism* (New York: Holt, 1995), 215–225. African-American writer Marita Golden commented on black women's writing on race: "[W]hat throbs within the arteries of the text is a bitterness, a feeling that they have received too often a much smaller bounty in return, from discourse (attempted and achieved) as well as relations public, private, and political with white women." "Introduction," *Skin Deep*, 1–5, 4.

49. Barbara Smith, "Racism and Women's Studies," in Hull, Scott, and Smith, *All the Women Are White*, 48–51, 49. See Hull and Smith, "Introduction: The Politics of Black Women's Studies," in *All the Women Are White*, for a discussion of the development of black women's studies, xvii–xxxiv.

50. Joan Rothschild, "NEWSA25: In the Beginning," *NWSA Journal* 14(1) (Spring 2002): 22–28: "Women's Studies grew," 26; "reach out to," 26; "Women's Studies, diverse," 27. Schlesinger Library, Radcliffe Institute for Advanced Study.

51. Ann Froines, "1981: Women's Studies Confronts Racism," in *Re-membering the National Women's Studies Association, 1977–1987*, comp. Kathryn Towns (College Park, Md.: National Women's Studies Association, Schlesinger Library, Radcliffe), 88–89, 88.

52. New England Women's Studies Association, *Newsletter* (Fall–Winter 1980): 5, Schlesinger Library, Radcliffe.

53. Marcia Folsom, "Report from the Planning Coordinators: An Overview of

'A Working Conference on Women and Racism in New England' February 1981," in "A Working Conference on Women and Racism," New England Women's Studies Association *Newsletter* (May 1981): 1–2, 1. This is a post-conference newsprint *Newsletter* about the conference. Hereafter referred to as *Newsletter*.

54. Folsom, "Report from the Planning Coordinators": "holding a conference," 1; "Women of color and white women," 1; Folsom interview with author, Boston, July 2, 2003.

55. Folsom interview.

56. Folsom, "Report from the Planning Coordinators": "white women organizers," 2; "accepted responsibility," 2; "Twenty-five white women," 2.

57. Rothschild, "NEWSA25: In the Beginning"; and Folsom interview.

58. Program, "A Working Conference on Women and Racism in New England," NEWSA, Fifth Annual Conference, February 6–7, 1981, 1, in author's possession

59. Folsom, "Report from the Planning Coordinators": "who could not fit," 2; Rothschild, "NEWSA25," quoting Ann Froines, "intense, sometimes fruitful," 25; Folsom, "Report from the Planning Coordinators": "unexpectedly high level" and "excitement and intense," 2; author's interviews with Laurie Crumpacker, Boston, July 23, 2003; Marcia Folsom, July 2, 2003, Boston; and Evelynn Hammonds, July 25, 2003, Cambridge, Massachusetts.

60. Folsom interview.

61. Kathy Gong, "It's Just Not Right," *Newsletter* (May 1981): 7–8, 7; see Andra J. Fischgrund, "Feminists Continue to Confront Racism about the lack of an Asian presence," *Sojourner* (March 1981): 22.

62. Author's interview with Evelynn Hammonds; Yaniya, "Reflections: A Black Lesbian's Relationship with Her Jewish Grandmother-in-Law," *Newsletter*, 6–7, 6; also see Rosario Morales, "Double Allegiance: Jewish Women and Women of Color," and Tova Green, "Rediscovering My Jewishness," who experienced "a mixture of comfort, nervousness, and excitement" when she entered the room, both in *Newsletter*, 6. See Barbara Smith, introduction to *Home Girls*, xix–lvi, for a reference to this conference workshop, xliii–xliv.

63. *Newsletter* quotations: "I felt scared," 7; "I don't think," 7; "This conference," 2; "I liked," 5; "What we've learned," 4; "Glad to see," 4, all from the retrospective *Newsletter* (May 1981). Predictably, several critical letters appeared in the Boston feminist newspaper *Sojourner*. One criticized the "predominance of white thinking which permeated the conference," charging that "white, middle class, college-educated women" were in the majority, indicating the failure of the conference planners' outreach to communities of color. In addition, the writers pointed out that the evening's entertainment was dominated by white women. Stacey Gurion and Robin Carton, "Letters," *Sojourner* (April 1981): 2. Marcia Folsom recalled that the coordinators and other academics often felt defensive. During the planning and at the conference, women without college or graduate educations were some-

times critical of academic organizers and participants, evaluating them as privileged and arrogant, distant from and uninterested in the "real world." A certain amount of anti-intellectualism was always characteristic of the movements of the 1960s, including feminism. Action was seen as preferable to theorizing, and the two were often considered to be mutually exclusive. Folsom noted that the conference planners and others in the university were vulnerable to attacks as academics and whites, and "we felt painfully eager to overcome that." Folsom interview.

64. Sandoval, "Feminism and Racism: A Report on the 1981 National Women's Studies Association Conference," in *Making Face, Making Soul: Creative and Critical Perspectives by Women of Color*, ed. Gloria Anzaldúa (San Francisco: Aunt Lute Foundation, 1990), 55–71, 59.

65. Information about the NWSA conference from Deborah S. Rosenfelt, "A Time for Confrontation," *Women's Studies Quarterly* 9(3) (Fall 1981): 10–12.

66. Quoted in Evans, *Tidal Wave*, 171.

67. Florence Howe, "Editorial," *Women's Studies Quarterly* 9(3) (Fall 1981), "opened to swirls," 2; Rosenfelt, "A Time for Confrontation," 11.

68. Howe, "Editorial," 2.

69. Rosenfelt, "A Time for Confrontation," 11. From Rosenfelt's perspective, the heart of the confrontations was about the future of NWSA. Some women, whom she calls the "pragmatists," were concerned above all with the survival of NWSA. Others, the "ideologues," believed that it was not worth preserving unless it became "very quickly, more representative of racial minorities and community women" and unless it made "financial arrangements to ensure the participation of low-income women as members and Convention-goers." One of the most heated debates was over the site of the next conference at Humboldt State University in northern California. The Third World Caucus, seeing this campus as inaccessible, was furious. Rosenfelt said that the polarization between the two, when "the ideologues were at their angriest and most rhetorical and the pragmatists at their most defensive and frustrated," took place over the location. She suggested that, despite their differences, they were all trying to find a common ground ultimately, to legitimize each others' stances. She argued that the Third World Caucus was asking, "*Does* NWSA care about us? . . . *Is* NWSA really committed to a definition of feminism that includes combating racism? If so, prove it to us." They did reach a compromise in which, among other things, they committed themselves to support the participation and attendance of low-income women, especially women of color. Rosenfelt, "A Time for Confrontation": "very quickly," 11; "the ideologues were," 11; "Does NWSA care," 12.

70. Sandoval, "Feminism and Racism": "[M]any of the women," 60; "well-articulated," 60; "for two hours," 60–61.

71. Sandoval, "Feminism and Racism": "The privileging," 65; "idea of a united third world," 61; "must develop," 67; "In spite of," 63.

72. Sandoval, "Feminism and Racism": "This has been a racist conference," 69; "by the end of the conference," 70; "the grave difficulties," 57.

73. Sandoval, "Feminism and Racism," "provided the group," 61. The National Alliance for American Third World Women did not last long, and the NWSA continued to be confronted with accusations of racism.

74. Sandoval, "Foreword: AfterBridge: Technologies of Crossing," in *This Bridge We Call Home: Radical Visions for Transformation*, ed. Gloria E. Anzaldúa and Analouise Keating (New York: Routledge, 2002), 21–26, 22.

75. Evelynn Hammonds, "When the Margin Is the Center: African-American Feminism(s) and 'Difference,'" in *Transitions, Environments, Translations: Feminism in International Politics*, ed. Joan Scott, Cora Kaplan, and Debra Keates (New York: Routledge, 1997), 295–309: "become one," 296; "one could argue," 296; "they provide," 296; "Moments of rupture," 297.

76. Hammonds, "When the Margin Is the Center": "Conferences became," 301; "when the nonunity," 299; "the problem of difference," 300.

77. Hammonds, "When the Margin Is the Center," 305. Hammonds queried the accountability that black women demanded of white women at conferences:

> In what ways was Black feminism shaped by Black feminists making this demand at conferences where they were in the minority? How often did the public nature of the scene lure people into using the occasion to posture, to take advantage of the movement in ways that sometimes opened up discussion of racial difference but also foreclosed discussion of difference within Black communities? . . . Did Black women, in performing the role of Other to White women in such settings, lose sight (as well as voice) of the need to interrogate their own theorizing and practices with respect to difference? (301)

78. Audre Lorde, "The Master's Tools Will Never Dismantle the Master's House," in her *Sister Outsider: Essays and Speeches of Audre Lorde* (Berkeley, Calif.: Crossing Press, 1984), 110–113, 111.

79. See Diane L. Fowlkes, "A Writing Spider Tries Again: From Separatist to Coalitional Identity Politics," in *Identity Politics in the Women's Movement*, ed. Barbara Ryan (New York: New York University Press, 2001), 277–290, for an interesting discussion of working through identity politics toward coalitions, including a description of the shame and guilt that a conference on race provoked in her as a white woman.

80. See Valk, epilogue to "Separatism and Sisterhood," for a similar point about feminism at the local level in Washington, D.C., 489.

Epilogue

1. Donna Kate Rushin, "The Bridge Poem," in *This Bridge Called My Back: Writings by Radical Women of Color*, ed. Cherríe Moraga and Gloria Anzaldúa (New York: Kitchen Table: Women of Color Press, 1983), xxi–xxii, xxi.

2. Anzaldúa, "Preface: (Un)natural Bridges, (Un)safe Spaces," in *This Bridge We Call Home: Radical Visions for Transformation*, ed. Gloria E. Anzaldúa and Analouise Keating (New York: Routledge, 2002), 1–5: "questions the terms," 2; "Today categories," 2; "Many women," 3. Also see Paula Stewart Brush, "Problematizing Race Consciousness of Women of Color," *Signs* 27(1) (2001): 171–198, where she argued that race consciousness among women of color cannot be assumed.

3. Anzaldúa, preface to *This Bridge We Call Home*, 2.

4. See Cheryl Clarke, *"After Mecca": Women Poets and the Black Arts Movement* (New Brunswick, N.J.: Rutgers University Press, 2005), for an interesting account of radical black poets, mostly lesbians, who forged a feminist literary place for themselves by first struggling with the homophobia in the Black Arts movement. She suggested that, by the late 1970s, lesbian poets of color and white lesbian poets created spaces for more diverse participation in feminist organizations. Widening their lenses beyond the racial, despite their longing for black racial solidarity, black women poets "have adopted diasporic, feminist/womanist, international perspectives," and in the process black and white lesbians found a measure of solidarity, 168.

5. Hayden, preface to Mary King, *Freedom Song: A Personal Story of the 1960s Civil Rights Movement* (New York: Morrow, 1987), 7–10, 7.

6. See Wini Breines, *Young, White, and Miserable: Growing Up Female in the Fifties* (Chicago: University of Chicago Press, 2001); and bell hooks, "Introduction: Some Opening Remarks," in her *Talking Back: Thinking Feminist, Thinking Black* (Boston: South End, 1989), 1–4.

7. Pratt, "Identity: Skin Blood Heart," in Ellie Bulkin, Minnie Bruce Pratt, and Barbara Smith, *Yours in Struggle: Three Feminist Perspectives on Anti-Semitism and Racism* (Ithaca, N.Y.: Firebrand, 1984), 11–63, 30.

8. Smith, introduction to *Home Girls: A Black Feminist Anthology*, ed. Barbara Smith (New York: Kitchen Table: Women of Color Press, 1983), xix–lvi, xxii.

9. bell hooks, "Homeplace: A Site of Resistance," in her *Yearning: Race, Gender, and Cultural Politics* (Boston: South End, 1990), 41–49. Also see hooks, "Choosing the Margin as a Space of Radical Openness," in *Yearning*, 147–148.

10. Reagon, "Coalition Politics: Turning the Century," in Smith, *Home Girls*, 356–368, 359. Also see Chilla Bulbeck about the ambiguity of feminism as "home" in *Re-Orienting Western Feminism: Women's Diversity in a Postcolonial World* (Cambridge: Cambridge University Press, 1998), 219.

11. Rebecca Walker, foreword to *The Fire This Time: Young Activists and the New Feminism*, ed. Vivien Labaton and Dawn Lundy Martin (Garden City, N.Y.: Anchor, 2004), xi–xx, xvi.

12. Cherríe Moraga, foreword to *Colonize This! Young Women of Color on Today's Feminism*, ed. Bushra Rehman and Daisy Hernandez (New

York: Seal, 2002), xi–xv: "created an expanded," xii-xiii; "draws a complex map," xiii.

13. Labaton and Martin, introduction to *The Fire This Time*, xxi–xxxvii, xxvi–xxvii.

14. Labaton and Martin, introduction to *The Fire This Time*: "poorest and most victimized," xxix; "Unlike second wave feminism," xxxi.

15. Rehman and Hernandez, introduction to *Colonize This!* xvii–xxviii, xxiv.

16. Chude Pam Allen, e-mail to author, November 6, 1998.

17. Martin, introduction to *The Fire This Time*: "Last year," xxii; Labaton: "found it impossible," xxiii.

18. See Kimberly Springer, *Living for the Revolution: Black Feminist Organizations, 1968–1980* (Durham, N.C.: Duke University Press, 2005), 7–10, where she noted that the wave analogy is deficient from the perspective of multiracial and class-based women's movement scholars.

19. Gloria Wade-Gayles, *Pushed Back to Strength: A Black Women's Journey Home* (Boston: Beacon, 1993), 9. For more on this point, see Wini Breines, *Young, White, and Miserable*.

20. Pratt, "Identity: Skin Blood Heart," 16.

21. Hayden, preface to King, *Freedom Song*, 8.

22. Frazier, "Interview by Karen Kahn: Rethinking Identity Politics," *Sojourner* (September 1995): 12, 13, 23, 13.

23. Ann DuCille, *Skin Trade* (Cambridge, Mass.: Harvard University Press, 1996), 119. Jill Nelson said of the silence about the 1960s and 1970s, "I think we are silent because we are heartbroken, have not figured out how to tell young people what happened without transferring onto them our own feeling of hopelessness and despair." *Straight, No Chaser: How I Became a Grown-Up Black Woman* (New York: Putnam's, 1997), 124.

Index

Italicized page numbers refer to illustrations and captions.